One morning, as she was pushing a broom over pine planks moistened with sawdust, Susan looked up to see a thin young cowboy hurrying toward her with a worried look on his face.

"Ma'am, ma'am, Dave . . ." She was afraid he was going to cry as he waved his hat back toward the door. "Dave got cut up in barbed wire and he's butchered pretty bad. Ma'am, they say you're a doctor and I need help real bad."

"My bag is at my house, just across the tracks." She whistled for her dog, leaned her broom behind the counter, untied her canvas apron and hung it on a peg. People stopped their shopping and stared.

"Where is your friend?"

"Down at the corral."

She stopped. "Can't he be moved from there?"

"No ma'am."

She stopped and looked him in the eye. "Is Dave your partner?"

"No ma'am, he's my horse."

DOC SUSIE

The True Story of a Country Physician in the Colorado Rockies

Virginia Cornell

IVY BOOKS • NEW YORK

Ivy Books
Published by Ballantine Books
Copyright © 1991 by Virginia Cornell

ISBN 0-8041-0956-7

This edition published by arrangement with Manifest Publications

Manufactured in the United States of America

First Ballantine Books Edition: August 1992

Acknowledgments

I am indebted to many informants. Susan Anderson's heir and nephew, Roger Brady of Marine City, Michigan, provided a cache of valuable material: family geneology, pictures and letters. Without Brady's cooperation, I would have had grave difficulty understanding Doc Susie's early years. Minnie Cole and Hazel Briggs, sisters who lived next door to Doc Susie's log cabin for many years, trusted her so totally that on one occasion when their dog had a hurt paw he limped right over to see Doc Susie. "See, he knows just where to get help," laughed Doc. They spent patient hours answering my questions.

In her memoir, *I Remember Fraser*, Gertrude Arkell Hollingsworth afforded pertinent glimpses of everyday life in Fraser. I visited her in Southern California where she gave me insights made doubly valuable because she had not returned to Fraser since the time when the Moffat Tunnel opened. Hazel Benson Howell offered sharp insights into community attitudes toward Doc Susie. From Ralph and Ruth Phillips I obtained a vivid picture of working conditions in the Moffat Tunnel, where Susie's duties as Grand County coroner took her, and of a typical house call. Glenn Wilson illuminated the sterling character of the

Swedish immigrants who worked in the lumber camps. From Rudy and Clarbelle Just came recollections of ranch life.

Without the memories of the following people, this book would have been difficult indeed: Edna Leonard Tucker, Jim Leonard, Fern Smith Conklin, Violet Smith Frye, Lucille Peterson Morrow, Mildred Peterson Thompson, Estelle Willhite Smith, Alta Gesellman, Jean and Junior O'Neill, Louise Record Van Buskirk, Edith Johnson Henson, Fay Johnson Baber, Ruby Johnson Zahn, Morris Long, Jim Daxton, Dick Mulligan, Elsie Clayton, Frank Carlson, Helen (Mrs. Iver) Florquist and Bob Florquist.

In Cripple Creek I owe an appreciative word to Ray Drake, Katherine Shaler and Museum Curator Leland Feitz.

Among my most helpful book sources were *Rails that Climb* and *The Moffat Road* by my late friend Rev. Edward Bollinger and Edgar Carlisle McMechan's *The Moffat Tunnel of Colorado: An Epic of Empire. Rocky Mountain Medicine: Doctors, Drugs and Disease in Early Colorado* by Robert H. Shikes, M.D. documents the history of health in Colorado. Dr. Robert Black's *Island in the Rockies* is the standard reference to Grand County. The *Grand County Historical Association Journals* provided detailed source material. Dr. Henry Swain, Assistant Dean for faculty affairs at the University of Michigan Medical School, supplied me with a copy of Horace W. Davenport's invaluable *Fifty Years of Medicine at the University of Michigan 1891–1941*.

Much material, including newspapers from Cripple Creek and Denver, is preserved in the excellent Western Collection of the Denver Public Library whose director, Mrs. Eleanor Gehres, and her staff extended themselves on my behalf as did Jim Parker at the Colorado History Museum.

Articles written during her lifetime include: "Doc Susie" by Margery Frank, *Pic*, May 11, 1943; "81-year-old Doc Susie is Fraser's Only Physician," by Leo Zuckerman,

Rocky Mountain News, Dec. 14, 1951; an article syndicated by Associated Press in August of 1952 written by Eugene Foster; "Dr. Anderson Makes Her Calls" in *Friends* magazine, December, 1952. Posthumous articles include: "Pioneer Personalities" by Idealia D. Baumgarten, Jan. 5, 1950; "Dr. Susan Anderson" by Cale Kenney, *Alpenglow*, Vol. 51; "Little—and Mighty" by Ruth G. McLain, *Colorado Crosscut,* 1975.

I want also to acknowledge the helpful suggestions of Jean Miller, Ida Sheriff, Dr. Jim Wier, Reggie Black and Jan Catlow of the Grand County Historical Association; the research into Grand County archives by Andy Miller of Fraser for records of Doc Susie's real estate, plus her service as coroner; the aid of Barbara Taylor, R.N. of Carpinteria, CA, who edited my copy for medical accuracy.

Patient proofreaders included Hiroko Akima, Steve and Lisa Berta and Tisha Roth. I would also like to thank Stephen Stone for outsmarting my computer programs from time to time. Medill Barnes at Straight Creek Company in Denver caused this story to become a book.

Without the editorial assistance of Ted Berkman it is unlikely that this book would ever have stayed on the track. His constant encouragement, assistance and patience kept it chugging along the mainline, on schedule, with a firm destination in mind.

Author's Note

In the early years of the Twentieth Century Susan Anderson, M.D. trudged through the towering snow-covered Rockies. She braved dangers that ranged from mountain lions to avalanches in her determination to reach critically ill patients. Dainty and frail, a former tuberculosis patient, she defied conditions that would have taxed the stamina of a healthy section hand, stubbornly bringing the healing arts to a region where men, women and children had formerly been consigned to early graves.

Hers is a story without self-importance or grandiose pretensions, yet vibrant enough to have intrigued the late Ethel Barrymore who, having seen a photo-spread about the then 73-year-old Doc Susie in the May, 1943 *Pic* magazine, phoned long distance, wrote importuning letters and sent bunches of roses in her vain attempt to obtain dramatic rights to Doc Susie's life story.

I met Doc Susie just once, when I was thirteen years old. My father, always in search of unusual entertainment for the paying guests who visited our mountain lodge, announced one evening that he had invited Dr. Susan Anderson to dinner. Everyone reacted with interest because in the late 1940s women physicians were as rare as palm trees above timberline. Personally, I considered the invitation risky. I had heard that Doc Susie was an elderly eccentric who walked the streets of Fraser in shabby garb, gathering up discarded bottles and bits of wire. When she arrived I was relieved to see her neatly attired in an elegant, if out-of-fashion, black silk dress. To the disappointment of my father, the wizened old woman showed no disposition to spin tall tales at the dinner table; when a fellow diner asked her to relate something about the "olden days," she dismissed the inquirer rather curtly, "I don't know what I could tell you." She did, however, seem enormously appreciative of our cook's delicious meal. After dinner the tiny doctor sat awkwardly on one of our big couches, a pillow propped behind her back because her legs were not long enough for her feet to reach the floor. Summoning up my courage, I ventured to ask if she knew anything about a small white marble gravestone I had stumbled across one day in the forest. When I told her the name on the stone, Doc Susie's piercing blue eyes scrutinized me thoroughly. Then, in matter-of-fact tones, she recalled the sad fate of the infant Agnes Knutson and her immigrant parents. I have always been sorry that I did not ask additional *specific* questions that night, because she seemed prepared to answer sensible questions.

A dozen years later, busy with the miscellany of getting an education, I barely noted the death in a Denver nursing home of Susan Anderson, M.D. at the age of 90.

The stimulus for writing this book came two years ago from Jean Miller of the Grand County Historical Association. She asked if I would be interested in chronicling Doc Susie's life. I was immediately intrigued and began to investigate what sources might still be available. Her story is particularly important to me because I have always considered my real home to be along the forest trails of the Fraser Valley.

I began a year of research by informing myself about the history of medicine. I needed to know what an aspiring physician studied at the University of Michigan in the

1890s, how a rural doctor would have gone about her practice at the turn of the century, what remedies were — or were not — at her disposal. I was gratified to discover that members of her family had preserved letters and photos from before the turn of the century.

In the Grand County Seat, Hot Sulphur Springs, I scoured holdings in the Historical Association Museum. To understand events that affected her life, I wound my way through what seemed like miles of filmed copies of the *Denver Post* and *Rocky Mountain News*. I read books about Wichita, Cripple Creek, the lumber industry, pioneer women and/or pioneer doctors. Then I refreshed myself on railroad lore, particularly the incredible period when the Moffat Road went over Rollins Pass. But the best help came from interviews made during my several trips to Colorado and Southern California, where I located and chatted with old-timers who remembered Doc Susie from their own childhoods. Several claimed they owed their lives to her excellent treatment. Because I wanted readers to step directly into Doc Susie's world, one that was both marvelous and cruel, I determined to present her story in narrative style. Modern readers, particularly women, will have no difficulty understanding her frustrating desire for the traditional blessings of husband and family, while remaining a dedicated professional. I have used dialogue freely, always on the basis of documented research. Although no events of consequence have been deliberately omitted, where facts were sketchy or sources disagreed, gaps have sometimes been bridged by informed speculation. The chronology of many events in her life was a matter of some dispute among informants; in some cases I have compressed time in order to present a coherent picture. I have also ventured occasionally inside Susie's mind. There is something to be gained in the way of intimacy from fleshing out the bare bones of history — so long as the bones have been left intact.

No episodes have been introduced that did not happen, and no characters appear who did not figure in Susie's life.

Particularly elusive, but confirmed by many sources including her own hand, were the events surrounding the interruption of Susan's matrimonial arrangements in Cripple Creek; I was forced to hint at who the gentleman might have been and what might have occurred. In a handful of cases I have attached a name to a character whose existence was fully established but whose precise identity had, for reasons of incomplete records and fading memories, been lost in the mists.

A thin line frequently separates readable biography from the biographical novel which uses a life as a springboard for free invention of characters and events. I have tried scrupulously to stay on the legitimate biography side of that line, to confine myself to harmless embroidery of atmosphere and setting, and to present Doc Susie as she always presented herself: with unflinching honesty.

CHAPTER 1

Across the Great Divide

The locomotive of Train Number One on the Denver, Northwestern and Pacific Railway steamed, hissed and clanked impatiently alongside the Moffat Station platform. Conductor George Barnes, fresh-faced and almost rakish with his bow tie and brass-buttons, stood beside the train's sole passenger car stamping his feet for warmth against the frigid Denver morning. Barnes pulled his pocket watch from his vest to the length of its thick chain: 8:05, five minutes until departure—right on schedule. Although the December sunshine was bright he glanced nervously to the west, toward the Rocky Mountains less than 30 miles in the distance. There, the Great Plains jammed to an abrupt halt against an impenetrable wall; white peaks jutted more than twice the height of mile-high Denver. Tall clouds behind the peaks could signal trouble, the possible build-up of a blizzard on the western side of the Continental Divide; the pristine picture of sunshine on alpine crests

1

could be wiped out within the two hours it would take for his train to climb to 11,660 feet, where the roadbed crossed the mountains over the highest rail line ever built in North America. Barnes didn't relish the idea of spending Christmas of 1907 marooned by avalanches, far above timberline at Corona, the "Top of the World."

"All aboard . . ." he bawled, consulting his watch again.

"Hold yer horses, Mr. Barnes." A baggage handler bolted from the station waiting room. "There's another passenger."

"Who is he?"

"Ain't a he! There's a lady in the station, feelin' poorly, so the agent is loadin' her on a trolley."

Barnes' booted foot stamped an extra beat. As if he didn't have enough problems getting his outdated rolling stock over the Divide, now he had a woman to look out for—and if she was being hauled out on a baggage cart it figured that she was a lunger. In summer the Moffat Road—dubbed for its owner, David Moffat—hauled scores of tubercular "invalids" west in search of a cold, dry climate. Some found health in the lush meadows and virgin forests. The poorer ones got off the train and asked around until they found an agreeable rancher's wife who would feed hearty pot roast and venison for a small fee. Richer ones rode the train to mineral baths located at the Grand County Seat, Hot Sulphur Springs. Others got off the train in Granby and headed fifteen miles up the Colorado River to the shores of Grand Lake. The bracing mountain air seemed to make the victims feel better, but most departed when the weather started getting cold in September. According to rumor, when they returned to Eastern cities many died.

A colored porter was approaching on the platform, straining to pull a cart piled high with trunks, barrels and cartons. Perched on one side sat a delicately attractive little woman ramrod straight as though mounted sidesaddle, a small white dog cradled in her lap. Intrigued despite his annoyance, as the cart rolled to a halt Barnes hastened to assist the lady down. Lifting her by the waist he found his suspicion of fragility confirmed; beneath her voluminous petticoats she weighed very little.

Her bags were tagged for a lumber camp named Fraser, in Grand County about 85 miles across the Continental Divide from Denver. From October until June the railroad was the only means of getting there. Berthoud Pass, the wagon road between Denver and the area called Middle Park, was blockaded during the long winters by deep snows. Until tracks had been laid over the front range three years previously, there had been no winter route to pierce the area's splendid isolation. Although less than 50 miles from Denver "as the crow flies," people joked that no sensible crow would ever attempt to wing it over 13,000-foot peaks, even in summer.

"Ma'am, are you sure you want to go to Fraser? Nothin' there but a sawmill and a few shacks. And it's so cold they say you've got to get out of town to get warm."

"I know Fraser," the woman replied. Her voice was low and pleasant. "I've been there."

"This is a dangerous trip in winter even for men. Avalanches can leave you stranded for weeks. Why don't you wait until July or August. Can't beat summertime in the high country."

"Because the Continental Divide won't go away, no matter when I travel. And you're going there with or without me, so it may as well be with me."

"What's the hitch?" A short stocky man with a bushy beard was leaning out from the vestibule of the passenger car. His eyes met Barnes's and rolled in dismay as the two watched the diminutive stranger dictate to the baggage handlers exactly how they should stack her belongings alongside mail bags. To an offer to tie her dog next to her luggage she said, "Of course not," and that was that.

Covertly, Barnes studied the woman. High cheekbones gave her face distinction. Her delicate nostrils were set over full lips that drooped in a perpetual pout. Dark eyebrows arched perfectly over piercing blue eyes fringed with long lashes. Only the deep, lavender circles showing through the transparent skin beneath her eyes contradicted the suggestion of buoyant youth. Barnes took her for thirty-odd; actually she was thirty-seven.

Her clothing was well-cut, from fur hat and woolen coat to expensive, but sensible, boots. She certainly didn't look like one of the homely mail order brides who showed up from time to time. And she definitely was too refined to be a soiled dove headed for a logging camp like Arrow or Fraser to open her own crib to service lumberjacks. If somebody had expected a relative from the East, he probably would have heard about it. Whoever she was, he heartily wished she would stay in Denver and wrap Christmas presents.

As he assisted the woman aboard, her dog growled and pawed at him. "Careful," she said matter-of-factly. "He will bite."

She made her way down the aisle, a small proud figure balancing white dog and a black bag. A contingent of plaid-shirted Swedish lumberjacks scrambled to their feet and, trained to Old World respect for a lady, doffed their black knitted caps.

Members of the train crew tugged at their overall straps, trying not to stare; ranchers peered sideways from beneath their Stetsons. When she paused at the center of the car, clearly reluctant to ride farther back over the wheels, two lumberjacks quickly offered her their seat.

Barnes tossed the foot stool onto the platform, leapt up after it, leaned out and signaled to the engineer. A thin man with a very large nose waved his canvas glove in reply and blew the whistle. Engine Number 300 hauled in a deep breath and set about the deliberate process of alternating its pistons, pushing west out of Denver.

The woman collapsed next to the window; her dog settled between her and the aisle. She deliberately turned her pebbled black leather bag 90 degrees, as though trying to hide the lettering on its side.

"Tickets, please."

As Barnes came up the aisle behind her, he saw the woman pull a white handkerchief from her bag. She swiped ineffectively at the frosty window. When the hanky came back from the glass smudged with coal soot she looked at the grime distastefully. A moment later she broke into a cough, hastily pressing the handkerchief to her lips. As the spasm increased her narrow shoulders heaved; her dog crept into her lap and looked up at her face. Stroking his soft fur, she seemed to relax; the hacking eased.

Barnes located a cushion and found a blanket, reached over and tucked it between her legs and the drafty wooden wall of the car. He pointed to her black bag. "You a lady Doc?"

"I'm a very tired lady. From nursing children through a diphtheria epidemic." She lifted her elbows and pulled the long pins from her hat; her hair was wrapped firmly into a bun on the nape of her neck but a few defiant wisps escaped to frame her face.

"Sorry if I frightened you, ma'am; we've lost quite a few railroaders up there on Corona, but,"—he rapped his knuckles on the wooden ceiling—"never a passenger yet."

He raised his voice, "Arvada, next stop Arvada."

A couple of cowboys boarded and the train was under way again. Arvada was the last town before the railbed began its climb through the foothills. The woman watched as the vestiges of the Great Plains, stiff sagebrush and frozen buffalo grass, gave way to the ponderosa pines of the lower reaches of the Rocky Mountains. She looked eastward, back toward where the empty prairie stretched toward Kansas, a faint smile flickering across her face. Her father and stepmother didn't know that their prodigal daughter had suddenly quit her job in Greeley, packed up everything, and was at this very moment on a train making a dangerous journey to a rough new logging camp at the edge of the world.

She closed her eyelids, remembering the previous August, haying season, when she was the only person in Fraser who was not busy. Each day she had walked alone into the forest to pick wildflowers and search for berries. Afternoons, it rained a little. When clouds rolled over toward the divide and the sun came out, intense double rainbows spread their bands of blue, purple, yellow and green across the sky. What luxury it had been to pull the dry, thin mountain air into her fragile lungs and to exhale a full, deep breath. Haunted by that memory, for the last few weeks she could think of nowhere else where she wanted to die—or live if God willed it—than the little lumber camp of Fraser, Colorado, beneath the double rainbows.

Her ears popped, a clear signal they were gaining altitude; she opened her eyes. The bushy-bearded man who had sized her up from the vestibule in Denver was evidently in charge of the Swedes, who were just about as tall sitting down as he was standing up. He held their tickets in his stubby fingers and shifted them in the car, in the special way that small men love to affect when bossing bigger ones around. Now he came up the aisle, a .38 strapped to each hip; her little dog snarled. The woman looked up calmly. In Colorado, almost everybody kept, and could use, a gun. "We don't wait for introductions west of Denver city limits, ma'am. I'm takin' these fellows up to camp in Arrow. Name's Woods, Billy Woods."

She hesitated for a moment, then lifted her finger in recognition, "And you own a sawmill—quite appropriately. My name is Susan Anderson." Woods seemed pleased that his reputation had preceded him.

"I see you brought snowshoes," she said, pointing to the rack above his seat. "Are you planning to get off the train before we reach Arrow?"

"Hope I don't have to get off no sooner, ma'am, but I never take the train over Corona in winter without carrying snowshoes and grub. Been caught on the wrong side of an avalanche once too much. You could sit there a week waiting to be rescued, or you can showshoe across the slide after it settles."

"But the sun is shining, surely we won't have any trouble today."

"Hard to tell," said Woods. "The weather on the west side of the divide can be as different as Chicago from Shanghai. Don't see many ladies on the train in winter. Don't nobody ride the train unless they got to. Me, I gotta go to Denver to recruit loggers. Ever payday I lose a few, hire a few."

She reached again into the black bag, pulled out a small vial of salts and sniffed. When she looked up again Barnes was back. He offered the handle of a water dipper, the communal cup that hung over the stone crock at the end of the car. Instead of drinking from it she fished into her bag and pulled out a collapsible metal cup, into which Barnes poured the water. Woods and the conductor were amused at this fastidious gesture, and more so when, after taking a few sips she held the cup down at her waist so her dog could lap water from it. His eager tongue splashed everything within three feet.

They were in tunnel terrain now, plunging into the first of thirty-odd. Barnes turned on the lights. A small potbelly stove at the end of the car was beginning to put out heat, so lumberjacks removed their big outer mackinaws. Susan Anderson eyed the men, drifting into what she called her "Gray's Anatomy Game." She looked each man up and down, imagining the musculature beneath flannel shirts and long underwear. She knew men did it to women, why couldn't she turn the tables? A strapping young Swede of about twenty-five, his hair blonde as a shock of wheat, flushed faintly crimson at her gaze.

He needn't be embarrassed, she thought. She had no designs on him. Lumberjacks were like miners she had known in Cripple Creek—strong in sinew and thick of skull. Aside from the conformation of his pectorals, he didn't interest her. This natty Barnes fellow, now he was more her sort. Alas, she had already spotted a gleam of gold on his wedding finger.

With a tired sigh, she closed her eyes to the steady

rhythmic clack-clack of train wheels, her head nodding to her chest.

She awoke with a start to a blinding flash of light, dimly aware of receding heavy timbers. The train was emerging into bright sunshine from the blackness of a long tunnel. For a moment disoriented, she leaned closer to her dog and squeezed the scruff of his neck. Below in South Boulder Canyon a creek bubbled into and out of little ice patches, then hurled itself rambunctiously over boulders into cascades.

Noting her alarm, Bill Woods presented himself again. "Never did see a creek in such a hurry to get to Nebraska. Can't think why. I never cared for it much, myself."

Susan Anderson managed a smile.

"Nothin' to worry about," Woods continued, "Not yet anyhow. Barnes told me the engineer just snagged a message from that downhill freight sided at Crescent. Said the wind was blowin' somethin' terrible at the top—driftin' the snow that fell yesterday. But I figgur we ought to get to the top okay."

She said, "I'll feel safer under the snowsheds."

"Naw. Them sheds keep the snow from drifting across the tracks all right, but they're stinkin' terrible when smoke and gas builds up inside. Smoke stacks can't clear it when there's several locomotives underneath, belchin' smoke and gas. Gandy dancers—that's what they call the odd-job fellers on the road—pass out in there all the time. Couple of 'em even died. Poisoned by the air."

She shuddered. "I've known miners to take caged canaries underground. If the birds die, they know to get out."

Woods chuckled, "Canary'd freeze his tail before he'd die of gas. Moffat Road uses gandy dancers instead. One of 'em keels over, we know to get outa there." He tugged at his whiskers. "What I worry about is them avalanches. Even if they don't hit your train, they cut you off. Plows can't cut through all of the boulders and trees packed in with the snow. Coupla years ago a fella by the name of

Sterling Way was stranded by avalanches at both ends of his train. Got hungry waitin' to be rescued and decided to ride the fireman's shovel down from Needle's Eye Tunnel to Yankee Doodle Lake. He was goin' so fast that ever' time he hit a rock it spun him round and round." Woods' hand gestured an energetic spiral. "Shovel got so hot from friction that first it burnt the pants right offa him and then he got frostbite on his rear."

Susan paused, as though evaluating the truth of his tale, "Well, the Moffat Tunnel ought to fix that."

"If it ever gets built." Barnes had come up to join the conversation. "We can't operate this temporary line over Rollins Pass much longer. Losin' too many men and too much money. But Moffat can't raise capital."

Susan knew from the newspapers that David Moffat was looking for financing for a tunnel at the 10,000-foot level. That would cut out the temporary roadbed above timberline, eliminate the need for the miles of snowsheds that protected the tracks and get rid of the notorious four percent grades and tight turns now necessary to get "over the top."

"That Harriman guy who owns the Union Pacific," Barnes went on, "he's got New York money squeezed tighter than a catalog corset." Barnes looked to see if his language had been too salty. Susan Anderson smiled back. She was enjoying their masculine attention.

Billy Woods cut in, "Teddy Roosevelt, he'll get old Dave out of the soup yet. Like he did in ought-four. Republican party's gonna bust them Eastern big shots." The woman kept silent, partly to keep from getting into an argument about votes for women; she didn't feel up to it today.

But she hoped Woods was right. Moffat was unlike the Guggenheims, the Hearsts and Tabors, who had gouged gold and silver from the beautiful Rocky Mountains leaving behind worn-out miners and a ghastly scarred landscape. Although getting along in years, Moffat pursued his faith that his beloved Denver would never be a great metropolis until it had a transcontinental railway as far as Salt

Lake City, linking it to the west where mineral and lumber wealth had barely been tapped. In 1907, rails stretched over the divide and through the Colorado River's Gore Canyon as far as Yarmony, but passenger service operated only 22 miles west of Fraser to Hot Sulphur Springs.

The air in the car was growing hazy; coal smoke accumulated with each passage through a tunnel. Susan tried to remedy the unpleasant taste in the back of her throat by filtering the air through her handkerchief.

She turned to Woods. "Did you just hire these men?"

"Yeah, see how they do. Swedes know their trees, but they ain't used to working up so high. Do better in Minnesota or Oregon."

"Do any of them take their families up there?"

"Some, but most is bachelors, come to this country to work, never marry. It's a rough country for women. You know much about the lumber business?"

"Not much. I've lived mostly among miners and farmers."

Woods explained that this was the season for cutting and limbing trees because it was easier for horses to skid logs over the snow and out of the forest. Logs were loaded onto sledges to be hauled to mills, or stacked at the head of a flume for floating down to the valley on spring runoff. Spring, when melting snow turned the forest into one huge bog, was when the same men gathered at the mills to saw logs into dimensional lumber.

A few seats ahead of her the husky blonde Swede was wiping his eyes and blowing his nose. For a split second she wondered if he was crying, but that was unlikely; Swedes were a stoic lot, not given to displays of emotion.

"He all right?" she asked Billy Woods.

Woods turned to the man. "Axel. You gotta problem?"

"Ina my eye. Dere's a spick."

Susan stood up and so did the Swede. Tossed left and right by the motion of the train, she had to grab seat backs to stagger toward him. The fellow loomed so tall that she was looking straight into his Adam's apple. "Sit down, I'll take a look at it." She could not keep from swaying against the lumberjack's shoulder as the rhythm of the curving roadbed pitched her back and forth. Ignoring his embarrassment, she looked intently, wrinkling her nose a bit because the Swede's breath indicated a considerable bender the night before.

George Barnes came to see what the problem was. "He has a cinder in his eye," she told Barnes. "I can take it out, but not while we're moving."

"We'll take on water in Rollinsville. Only about five minutes if he can wait."

She perched on the arm of the Swede's seat. As soon as Barnes leaned out the rear vestibule and signaled the train to a halt, Susan Anderson pulled a little pad of cotton cloth from her bag. Steadying her elbow against the man's firmly muscled shoulder, she expertly pulled his eyelid by its lashes, twisted it up, and told him to look left, right, up and down. She moved the cloth until the cinder stuck to it, then wiped the eyeball with one deft swipe as she pulled out the offending speck and showed it to him. Straightening up, she gave a reassuring squeeze to his shoulder. It was hard as granite.

"Tanks fery much missus, dat chur did hurt." After a moment, "I yam Axel Bergstrom."

"And I am Susan Anderson. You had quite a time last night, I think," she said matter-of-factly. Axel turned the color of a soda fountain cherry, from the part in his hair to where his neck disappeared beneath a woolen muffler. He was fumbling in his pocket, as though hoping to find some change left from the Larimer Street saloon where he had spent the last of his wages, "What I owe you, missus?"

She smiled, opened her hand and waved off his suggestion of payment.

"Some day I do somethin' nice for you, missus."

Barnes completed his supervision of the transfer of water from the tower to locomotive reservoir, the whistle blew and Train Number One was under way again. The roadbed left the canyon and climbed up the side of the mountain along the broad, sweeping switchbacks called Giant's Ladder. The train stopped again to take on water, this time just below timberline at Yankee Doodle Lake. Susan thought about how beautiful the lake had been last summer, remembered how gracefully the track curved around its shores. "More water so soon?" she asked.

"In winter you take on all the water you can hold," Woods explained. "If you get stranded by a drift and run outa water, you're cooked. You can't shovel snow fast enough to feed a boiler." He motioned toward the side of the mountain, "This is where the tunnel will be dug. From here on up it's a four percent climb and the curves are tighter than a Finn on a Saturday night."

As they started up again, she could hear and feel how hard the engine labored to pull this pitifully small load up the steep hill. Their progress was much slower now. The gnarled, twisted little trees on the hillside told her that they were at timberline. She gazed down, marveling at the lake they had circled a few minutes earlier, and imagined Sterling Way zinging straight down on his scoop shovel. Her view was cut off as they entered a short, untimbered tunnel. "They call this tunnel the Needle's Eye," Woods told her, "because the engineer can see a slit of daylight through it as he comes up the grade from Yankee Doodle."

When they emerged, her heart jumped into her throat; she was staring straight down 2,000 feet. Normally, heights didn't bother her, but it seemed that the only thing holding the train up was thin air. It was silly, she knew, but she suddenly wished she were sitting across the aisle, on the side closer to the mountain.

"Twin trestles over Devil's Slide and we're headed into a blizzard," called Barnes. The train crept over the trestles, seemingly alone in the cosmos. The side of the mountain was a crazy rubble of boulders that looked as though they would dislodge and tumble at any moment. Below her, a frozen lake was so far away that it appeared to be a tiny pebble. When her eyes lifted to the opposite side of the deep valley, great plumes of wind-driven snow rose hundreds of feet above the mountain.

As the snow swirled down angrily around the train they crept into the darkness of the wooden sheds. What little light came through the stacks showed timbers and siding. The train was moving very slowly; each clack, clack, clack of the wheels could be heard distinctly. Inside the car the smoke thickened.

In a few minutes, the train hissed to a halt. Outside a sign proclaimed: Lunch Room. "Corona!" intoned Barnes. "Passengers may detrain until further notice."

Susan Anderson picked up her bag and dog and stepped down to the level of the station platform. She felt dizzy in the thin, stinking air, but led her pet to the end of the boardwalk so he could lift his leg. When she turned back, she thought the dog was idling. Impatient, she pulled hard on his leash, then looked down to see the animal stretched on its side, unconscious. "My dog! My poor puppy!" She gathered him up and ran into the lunch room where the air was better. Near collapse herself, she held her limp pet across her lap and reached into her black bag for smelling salts.

"Leave him alone, he'll come to." Billy Woods was at her shoulder. She ignored him and wafted the salts beneath the dog's nostrils. He stiffened, slipped to the floor, then jumped up and down like a rubber ball, yelping madly.

"Guess I gave him too much," she said, relief in her voice. The dog chased his own tail around in circles, moving sideways across the floor until he ran into, and bit down hard on the striped canvas trouserleg of a man who stood at the lunch room counter. Susan's eyes followed the stripes up the legs of a tall man wearing an engineer's hat. Surprised, the fellow put down his mug of coffee in time to hear Susan say: "Isn't that wonderful? He's all right!"

Billy Woods laughed so hard that tears coursed down his leathered cheeks. "What kinda dog's that?"

"He's a spitz," Susan said proudly.

"Good name for 'im."

The engineer was laughing, too. The dog's nip could not possibly have penetrated his overall leg and thick boot. "By gar, lady. You got a dandy there." Woods introduced their engineer, George Schryer.

She was immediately impressed with Schryer's outsize nose. "Why, it's Cyrano!"

"Everbody keeps tellin' me about this Cyrano feller. Must be an awful nice guy. Gotta be, he's French." George explained that he was a Canuck. "Was workin' on the Great Northern. Had TB. Came out here five years ago to die. But I'm doin' plenty good, now." Susan brightened. She feasted on such stories of restored health.

Woods brought her a steaming cup of coffee, but it was only lukewarm to her tongue. Woods explained, "You can boil an icicle at this altitude without ever melting it. Fellow named John Quincy Adams Rollins built a road 30 years ago so Mormons could haul their wives over the mountain to Utah. Wives probably had to pull the wagons themselves so as to spare the horses. But everybody calls it Corona, because it's the top of the world."

The door banged behind Barnes. "They're turning the rotary around at the wye now. Should be outa here in fifteen minutes or so," Seeing Susan's confused look he added, "Rotary's the snow plow. They'll couple it in ahead of us on the downhill leg."

When they reboarded the train, Susan tried to avoid breathing the gasses and smoke that had built up while the engine idled. Billy Woods saw her wobble and propped his square body beneath her elbow. Axel Bergstrom saw her, too. He scooped her up as easily as he would a sack of beans and carried her to her seat, her dog nipping his heels in protest. Woods hollered to Barnes: "Get this thing outa here and find us some decent air."

As she sank back in her seat, she half heard Barnes saying to Woods, "Pump down at Pumphouse Lake is busted so there's no water in the Corona tank. No problem with our boiler, of course, but the Mallet pushing the rotary is arunnin' on spit. Only three miles to the first water at Sunnyside, but the snow is driftin' heavy at Ptarmigan Point after we pull outa the sheds. If she don't make it, we'll have to back her up clear to Yankee Doodle. That's if it hasn't drifted closed behind us." He looked anxiously at his ailing passenger.

Slowly, the train started downhill. Susan was choking for breath. As the severity of her spasm increased, Barnes prayed they had enough steam to plow a clean, fast path ahead. He averted his head because he didn't want to know if there was blood in her handkerchief. Though seemingly near strangulation, she waved away Woods and the others, indicating that she preferred to struggle alone. When she finally calmed, conversation was out of the question.

Brighter light and the sound of wind blowing snow aslant the car's wooden siding signaled that they were pulling out of the snowsheds. Susan's view from the window was quickly cut off by a sheer, vertical wall of snow as high as, sometimes higher than the train. From time to time, when the wall fell away, she could make out an astonishing sight just ahead. A plume of snow shot up into the air, arced over the railroad embankment and fell gracefully into the valley below. The rotary snowplow was at work.

The train moved slowly, almost at a standstill, chewing up well over an hour to go three miles. Twice it had to be backed up so a particularly dense drift could be charged at again by the rotary's cutter. When Barnes hurried up and down the aisle to adjust equipment, he was out of breath and sweating although it was now quite cold. The pot belly stove was no match for the fierce wind blowing against the uninsulated car. The passengers had long since donned their coats and jackets. The men leaned forward, as though that posture would help gravity pull the train downhill; their breath rising into the cold air looked like steam escaping from a big leaky boiler.

Susan was shivering uncontrollably. Even the fluffy warmth of her dog, snuggled next to her under her coat, was insufficient to calm her shaking body.

When Barnes finally brayed in triumph, "Sunnyside.

We made it!" a cheer arose from the passengers. "Soon as we get some water in her tank the next stop is Arrow."

Although it was no warmer in the car, palpable relief notched up the atmosphere. The train picked up speed; the snowdrifts weren't as deep now, and the snowplow was making quick work of them.

The roadbed had descended below timberline, into the big trees. Susan dozed as the train snaked through the Loop area where the tracks went across a trestle, around a mountain and doubled back through a tunnel beneath the trestle, an engineering feat designed so the roadbed could gain altitude in a short distance. It seemed just a minute before she heard Barnes call, "Arrow, next stop."

"Now you take care of yourself. We'll be seein' you around Fraser," Bill Woods told her as he, along with most of the lumberjacks, got off the train. From the platform, Axel turned back toward the train and waved up at her. She could barely see him through the frosty window.

She slept again, fitfully, on this last short leg of the journey. Barnes, passing by, heard her mumbling to herself, right hand clutching at her throat. "It was the diphtheria that killed them," she whispered. "The diphtheria. Nobody would listen to me . . . ."

Alarmed, he touched her shoulder, disregarding the snarls of the spitz. "Ma'am, are you all right?"

She sat up very straight, focusing him squarely in her clear blue eyes. "I won't cause you any trouble. I'm all right."

As the train slowed into the station she pinned on her hat, struggled to her feet, gathered her dog in her arms and picked up her black bag, no longer bothering to hide the gold lettering stamped into its side: "Susan Anderson, M.D."

CHAPTER 2

Physician, Heal Thyself

Flat flakes were falling, thick as feathers from a down comforter, when the train halted at the Fraser depot. Susan Anderson, peering through the sheet of white, practically fell from the steps of the train into Charlie Warner's butcher-sturdy arms, and a moment later enjoyed the comfort of Cora Warner's welcoming hug. Charlie, his jacket buttoned askew across his shopkeeper's apron, looked nervously at the mountain of barrels, trunks and cartons being unloaded from the baggage car. He surmised, correctly, that their guest had brought along all of her worldly goods and intended to stay. Motherly Cora, alarmed to see her friend looking so weak and tired, left Charlie to cope with the baggage and gently guided Susan across the tracks to the Warners' store. Their boots left a shin-deep trail in newfallen snow—through which Susan's dog hopped to keep up.

Throughout her first two days in Fraser Susan Ander-

son slept. Even so basic an emotion as curiosity was slow
to awaken. Finally she stepped to the window, wiped frost
from its pane and peered down to see a snow-clearing crew
energetically shoveling a path through waist-deep drifts on
Fraser's main street. Evidently it had not stopped snowing
since her arrival. Her train was the last to make it over the
top for several days. Cora brewed a pot of tea and sat
down for the little chat she had rehearsed with Charlie,
"Susan, this is no place for you. You can see how cold it is
now—it's only going to get worse. Why don't you take the
first safe train out, go to Oakland and recuperate with
your family in California where it is warm?"

"No. No. Never," answered Susan with quiet stubborn-
ness. "I am either going to die here or recover my health.
But I won't go live with my Pa and Minnie." The way she
pronounced Minnie's name made it sound like *Mean-uh*.
"They won't have the satisfaction of seeing me die, too."

Cora arched her eyebrow, but Susan did not explain.
"Surely they love you."

"That is not sure by any means." Susan changed the
subject. "I know what I'm doing. Please help me find a
little house where I can live, or even a room. I saved money
from Greeley so I can weather it through for quite a while.
And Cora, if you haven't already told people I'm a doctor,
I'd appreciate it if you didn't because I don't feel like one.
What kind of a physician can't even heal herself?"

Soon after Christmas Susan learned of a shack east of
the tracks—the depot side—about two blocks from Warner's store. Hoping the hovel's warm southern exposure
would compensate for the noise of living right by the railroad, she took it. A neighbor boy was drafted to fetch water and provide firewood for her little pot-bellied stove,
then to lug most of her trunks and boxes from Warner's
back storeroom. She was pleasantly surprised when, despite its single-wall construction, the little shack proved to
be warm; later she would learn that the snow piled around
it served as insulation. Cora presented Susan with an odd
house-warming gift—a rock, just the right size to heat on

top of her stove. Although rocks were the commonest of nuisances in summer, in winter when snows covered the ground they were notoriously scarce, even in the Rocky Mountains. Everyone kept a "spinster's friend" to warm feet at bedtime or to snuggle beneath toes during a long sleigh ride.

Susan was happy to have a place of her own where she could enjoy total solitude. During her six years as a nurse in Greeley she had been under the thumb of a hospital matron who dictated her nurses' lives, both professional and private. The hours she kept and even the size of her bank account had been closely scrutinized as though she were an eighteen-year-old trainee, rather than a graduate M.D. well into her fourth decade of life.

At long last she could focus on her own health. Rarely was she able to sleep through a night without awakening, soaked in perspiration. Compacted in her lungs, the cottage cheese-like matter that gave the disease the name "White Plague" refused to dislodge during her frequent coughing spells. When she rolled up her sleeve her bony arm revealed the ravages of "phistis," or the "consumption" of her own bodily tissue by the illness. The occasional sight of blood in a handkerchief was terrifying proof that one of her coughing spasms had torn a hemorrhage in her delicate lung tissue. Every doctor in Colorado had a theory about curing tuberculosis and she was no exception. Recovery would be promoted, she believed, by a cold, dry climate—one of the few commodities abundantly available in Fraser. She plotted a regimen which included rest, healthy food and fresh air, to be augmented by exercise when she became stronger.

First, she would catch up on all the sleep she had missed during nights on duty at the hospital and weeks of tending sick children. She found a narrow cot that on good days could be scooted through the front door of her shack out into the sunshine, where she rested and slept beneath quilts and comforters. At night and on snowy days she trundled it back into the shack. She was astonished to find sunny, warm days far outnumbering the stormy ones. When Charlie's store thermometer plunged to 20 or even 35 degrees below zero, causing the membranes inside Susan's nostrils to try to freeze together when she inhaled, the sun shone brightly. During those coldest January days she tied a clean rag across her nose and mouth to protect her respiratory system and snuggled with her hot rock beneath stacks of comforters, looking up to sky the color of gentian violet, gazing in wonderment at the pure white range of mountains that seemed close enough to reach out and touch with her left hand.

Each dawn and twilight she pulled on her big coat and carried a little jug a few steps to the barn of her neighbor, Broer Benson. The Swedish rancher, perched on his one-legged milking stool, executed an important part of her therapy—squirting milk from his cow's teat directly into Susan's bottle for her to drink on the spot. Susan rejected the whiskey-cure adherents who argued that alcohol acted as a stimulant to the appetite and as a relaxant; she maintained that it contributed to a TB patient's usual tendency to be listless and depressed. That kept her away from Fraser's only physician—jolly, middle-aged Doc Albers who prescribed whiskey for consumption as well as for a bewildering array of miscellaneous ailments. Plump and balding, an old-fashioned country doctor of inferior education, Albers was popular with patients. Children loved him for the candy he handed out of his big jar, adults for medications that guaranteed they would feel better—at least temporarily. He was not above administering tonics that were nearly pure alcohol, even to patients who were loathe to take a drink. To a physician like Susan, who prided herself on keeping herself abreast of the latest scientific advances, he was little better than a snake oil salesman.

Keeping up with scientific publications, and with reading generally, was a problem in Fraser. She went through Cora's small library, then borrowed books from anybody else who offered them. And although she seldom attended church, she read in the Bible every day, taking particular pleasure in the psalmic verse "I will lift mine eyes unto the hills from whence cometh my help."

A backlog of unscanned medical journals lay in her trunks and boxes, still largely unloaded. So, on a bright February morning she began unpacking. An astonishing array of miscellany tumbled into view; Susan was an inveterate hoarder, incapable of throwing away a sliver of soap: "Might come in handy some day." She assembled thread and yarn for her knitting, crocheting and tatting projects— "Idle hands are the devil's workshop"; grouped together a collection of magazines; then reached a pile of letters. One caught her attention. She looked at it, sighed and tucked it into a stack tied with ribbon. When it surfaced again she shuffled it to the bottom of another pile waiting to be sorted. The letter seemed to have a life of its own, constantly swimming into her hands, teasing her to read it. She was briefly tempted to burn it. Finally, she resigned herself and opened the envelope. Once more, she deciphered the crabbed handwriting of her friend, Frances; she remembered teasing her fellow medical student that her penmanship could be deciphered only by a pharmacist.

After medical school, Frances had married a fellow doctor. Dated June 30, 1901, the letter was mailed in Fairport, N.Y.: "Dear Susan: Yes Susan we are both very happy. We get along famously and think a great deal of each other. We have good practices and at present we are boarding at a place a block away but before long we intend to keep house . . . I am so glad I am married to a good man who cares for me and we are both wishing we had married when we first left Ann Arbor."

Bitter gall.

Frances had everything Susan ever longed for: a practice, a husband, a happy marriage, the prospect of children, her health . . . everything that had been yanked from Susan during a few fateful days in Cripple Creek the year before this letter was written. If it hadn't been for Pa's interference . . . Pa. Why had Pa done these things to her?

One of Susan's earliest memories was of a time when, all dressed up, she and her little brother Johnnie stood on the platform of a railroad depot, held firmly by the hands of a weeping woman. Suddenly Pa appeared and grabbed the two children from the woman's grasp and hauled them onto a train where they rode for hours and days and nights. An entry in the front of the family Bible said Susan was born on January 31, 1870 in Nevada Mills—a small town in northeastern Indiana—to William H. Anderson and his wife, the former Marya Pile. Beneath Susan's name was that of her brother John, born two years later. Susan never really understood why her parents' marriage ended in divorce in 1875. But she recalled a dim, constant childhood longing for her mother, someone who would smell good and would speak up for her against Pa.

Pa, who always got his own way. When he decided to homestead a farm near Wichita, Kansas, the rest of the family—Susan's grandfather, grandmother, Uncle John with his wife Lois and cousin Gary—all moved at the same time. The Andersons had been successful farmers in Indiana and continued to do well in the booming cow town that was Wichita in the '80s.

As a little girl tucked between Pa and his saddle horn, Susan rode down the straight, dusty road into Wichita, wide-eyed at the jumble of trail riders, cowboys, fancy women and gamblers who banged through swinging saloon doors. Located at the end of the old Chisholm Trail, Wichita owed its gaudy reputation to its temporary position at the railroad head. The prospering town dedicated itself to relieving cowboys of money they had earned during dusty, lonely months spent driving longhorned cattle north from Texas. When Pa walked down Douglas Avenue, Susan's six-year-old hand firmly clasped in his, he carried himself with a ramrod authority that lent inches to his otherwise average height. A curl in his upper lip, creating the appearance of a permanent sneer, was only partially concealed by a bushy, drooping moustache. He had a fine head of thick, dark hair which he combed up to add a little height; his square jaw gave notice that he was a man to be reckoned with. He always wore a black suit, vest, shoes and hat.

Pa frequently told his children that he had wanted to be a doctor, but had always been too busy to go to school. "One of my children," he sometimes said, "will grow up and be a doctor for me."

Susan's Pa was a capable barnyard veterinarian, knowledgeable about salves and poultices. Tagging along while Pa did his farming chores, his children learned to doctor farm animals in the corral. Or, John would have learned if he hadn't been more interested in lassoing the calves or pretending he was a toreador when he teased Pa's bull. Pa also set up cans on fence posts and taught Susan and John to become good shots, urging them to defend his land against coyotes and prairie dogs. Susan liked to carry a gun and was on constant lookout for snakes, particularly Kansas rattlers.

Pa bought her ribbons and pretty toys, took her everywhere he went and tried to pour every scrap of knowledge he had into her retentive brain. Very soon he was dismissing tow-headed John as a scatterbrain, in contrast to bragging about his daughter's stick-to-it temperament and quick mind. Before she went to high school, Susan was petted and spoiled. Susan loved to crawl up on her Pa's lap and snuggle in his arms while they talked about things, just about everything.

When, in her early teens, she learned Morse code and announced she'd like to be a telegrapher, her Pa brought home a book entitled: *What Women Can Do* and urged her to set her sights considerably higher. Obediently, she transferred her ambitions to medicine. Minding one's father came with the territory. In return William Anderson treated his maturing daughter as the woman in his life; he was proud of her good school work and liked to show off how pretty she was.

Pa's mother, a plain, kind woman—for whom Susan was named—ran the household. It was grandma who

taught little Susie her manners and showed her how to crochet, who as Susan said later in a letter to brother John:
". . . planted little seeds . . . inspiring us to be 'better than
common folks.' " Although Grandmother took pains to
teach little Susie the intricacies of fancy work, the arts of
housekeeping and cooking would never interest her. The
Andersons had a "hired girl" to perform such necessities.
Grandma Susan never cared much for Kansas; her heart
grieved over the loss of her beloved Indiana where the sum-
mers were cooler, the winters were warmer, the roses were
redder, the people were friendlier. Little Susan was raised
to believe in Indiana as some kind of paradise lost.

The Andersons lived in Pa's big, comfortable farm
house a few miles from Wichita, enviably rich by standards
of the Kansas prairie. From the start, Pa saw to it that Susan's education pointed her toward a future career. Grammar school was a one-room rural schoolhouse, but Susan
and John were promoted only after they passed stiff
county exams. For high school they would be sent into
Wichita. Pa anticipated that John—the dillydallier—
would need looking after, so he decreed that Susan should
interrupt her own studies for two years so the two could
enroll at the same time. Waiting for John, Susan taught in
the same grammar school from which she had just graduated; in those days, possession of an eighth grade diploma
was considered learning enough to turn around and teach
the same eight grades.

Wichita being too far away for a daily ride to high
school over muddy roads, Pa arranged lodgings in town for
Susan and John. There the two were drawn closer together
in alliance against paternal dictates that were becoming
increasingly arbitrary. Susan felt Pa was unreasonably hard
on her brother, failing to appreciate John's easygoing
charm, condemning his flights of independent thought as
wilfulness. And she no longer accepted Pa's opinions auto-
matically.

 Their high school curriculum was demanding, intended
to prepare them for college. Susan sailed through her En-

glish, algebra and geometry, physiology, geography, U.S. history and physics. She learned enough Latin to write simple phrases—and regularly tutored the blond, curly-haired scamp of a brother who would far rather make people laugh than impress them with his knowledge. When she told friends and relatives that she was planning to become a physician, they were not particularly surprised. In the '80s women physicians were not so rare a commodity as they became in the first part of the twentieth century. Just before great scientific leaps provided doctors with the technology to successfully fight disease and infection, the business of being a physician was hard work, smelly and badly paid—so women were welcome to try it. Later, as significant breakthroughs lifted the prestige—and earnings—of doctors, Susan saw all that change.

Susan and John were both graduated from Wichita High School in 1891 when Susan was 21 years old and John 19. Her graduation picture showed a solemn, comely young woman with chubby cheeks, light eyes staring off into the distance. Her grandmother had been dropping hints of Pa's growing restlessness, of his missing a young and feminine presence around the house; nonetheless, Susan was bowled over when Pa told her that after living a single life for over 15 years, he had decided to marry again—to a young woman named Minnie. Susan was indignant at the thought that her Pa would marry a girl only a few years older than she was. She saw right away that Minnie was equally jealous of herself and John, was determined to protect Pa's money for her own future family— Minnie would give Pa three more children.

About the same time, the *Wichita Eagle* was full of news about a place four hundred miles to the west—just over Pike's Peak from Colorado Springs—where the biggest gold strike in U.S. history had been made at Cripple Creek. Pa, fascinated, decided to leave the life of a farmer and move to the gold field so he could get in on the bonanza; once again the entire Anderson tribe packed up and followed their chief. Pa always bragged that he arrived early in 1892, one of the first hundred settlers in Cripple Creek. Actually, the Andersons moved to Barry, a little town that would soon be swallowed by a larger town called Anaconda, about a mile south of Cripple Creek at the foot of Squaw Gulch. Mines, tailings and smokestacks stretched up the hill toward the enormous Mary McKinney Mine.

But Pa didn't engage in the grimy business of prospecting and hauling ore from the earth. More lucrative by far were opportunities to buy and sell other people's stocks, shares, and fractions of claims. William Anderson made a stock-trading partnership with Fred W. Ford. Thanks to Pa's good business sense, the family continued to prosper.

The excitement of the gold rush was heady stuff to Susan, suddenly aware that Pa was not the only man who found her attractive. Everywhere she looked the streets were teeming with men. They far outnumbered the women who were either worn-out wives of miners or "ladies" who had drifted in to set up shop on notorious Myers Avenue, just a block below the respectable Bennett Avenue business section of Cripple Creek. Susan recognized them as the same sort of hard-faced beribboned women who entertained cowboys in Wichita. Pa ordered Susan to stick close to home, warning her constantly about the danger of falling in with the riffraff and sharpers who floated about the boom town. His daughter could hardly step out of the house without receiving what Pa considered unsuitable attentions. Pa had a poor opinion of mining people; in his book they were as unreliable as gypsies. Besides, Pa shared the feelings of many Victorian fathers who hoped their daughters would never marry—would remain virgins forever, thereby sparing themselves the degradations of sex, the dangers of childbirth and the drudgery of caring for children. However, keeping Susan confined to the house wasn't working out very well. Minnie and Susan were constantly at loggerheads, quarreling about household duties and the price of Susan's frocks, battling for Pa's company.

Susan folded the letter from Frances carefully and filed

it with a batch of others that bore exotic postmarks, most of them from female classmates at Ann Arbor who had gone on to become medical missionaries. Sending her off to medical school at the University of Michigan had provided Pa with several benefits. At Ann Arbor, she would be a safe distance from the young mining engineers who always seemed to turn up carrying the parcels she had shopped in Cripple Creek. Pa would no longer have to referee her stormy fights with Minnie. And he could brag that a member of his family was studying to be a doctor.

There was another reason for getting a young girl out of Cripple Creek in the summer of 1893. The streets of the gold camp were full of restless, unemployed miners—put out of work when the U.S. Congress voted to abandon the "bi-metallic" standard which backed paper money with silver as well as gold. Overnight, silver-mining towns like Leadville, Georgetown and Aspen were boarded up as miners packed up their gear and their families and fled to where the action was: Cripple Creek. In the face of an unlimited labor supply, mine owners tried to cut the men's wages; organizers of the militant Molly Maguires were joining the bristling new Western Federation of Miners to stand up to the mine owners. Violent conflict seemed likely to erupt at any moment.

Despite the troubles of "common folk" around him, Anderson's business affairs were on the upswing by the time Susan boarded the train for Michigan in early September, 1893. Within a couple of months Pa, Ford and E.H. DeVore would incorporate the Beacon Hill Mining Co. and the Cripple Creek Free Gold Mining & Milling Co., capitalizing them at a million dollars each. The huge sum was only on paper; Pa raised cash to finance her start in medical school by sale of a "fraction," an irregular plot of land where claims overlap. At the same time, Pa decided that John should become a civil engineer and sent him west to Oakland, California.

It wasn't difficult to gain admission to medical school. A college degree was not required; Susan's high school performance had been first rate and enrollment was open to all comers. The four-year medical curriculum at Michigan was designed to prepare students to become country doctors—in the eyes of most people a sure ticket to an impoverished future.

Susan's degree from the University of Michigan would always be a source of pride. She had been happy there, perhaps happier than she ever would be again. She loved Michigan from the Indian Summer of the first autumn, through winters when she skated on frozen ponds and lakes, into spring when the earth was so rich she could actually smell things start to grow. After living most of her life on the prairie and in arid Cripple Creek, she could never get over the greenness of Michigan, or next-door Indiana where she visited some of her father's relatives. Even in summer, roses bloomed. Susan loved going boating on the lakes and she marveled at summer sunsets that seemed to last for hours and hours.

Life on campus was like living in the midst of an ongoing Chautauqua circuit. Sometimes with other women, but often with male classmates, she attended concerts, plays, lectures or lantern shows of world travel. Several times she fancied herself in love but the romantic flurries petered out. She wondered if the men weren't looking elsewhere for wives, among women who would be domesticated stay-at-homes rather than partners in science. Each semester, when she handed over $35 for her out-of-state tuition, she swallowed hard. It was the most money she had ever spent at one time. She envied in-state students who paid only $10. She begrudged local landladies, in her opinion little better than robbers, for collecting the outlandish sum of $3 to $5 a week for room and board.

Her worries that she wouldn't be smart enough to pass the classes vanished as she plunged into her studies in the Combined Course with the Literary Department, which guaranteed she would get a college degree along with her medical certification. Since she had lively scientific curiosity, could memorize quickly, and was genuinely sympathetic toward sick people, she quickly proved herself an ideal candidate for a degree in *materia medica*.

Female students, who made up twenty-five percent of the student body, attended the same classes as men—except for anatomy where segregation of the sexes was considered appropriate. In the anatomy lab the women became fast friends; they depended on each other's support to overcome their repugnance for the cadaver into which they had to sink their bare hands. But Susan also enjoyed studying with men, and was thrilled when a casual touch seemed to offer future intimacy.

She thought back to the grinding hours spent on the wards of Catherine Street Hospital, learning first hand to deal with people who were sick and poor. Students were assigned night duty, sometimes treating patients from dusk until dawn, and were then required to attend day classes. She was certain that her illness dated from those agonizing months when she went for days at a time without respite, grabbing but an hour's nap here or there. Even when her feet were numb from standing, she never missed a chance to watch a surgeon operate on a live person, quite a different experience from carving up a cadaver. Once the patient had succumbed to ether and the doctor entered the body cavity, she wished she could get her nose in much closer so she could observe exactly how the surgeon performed each little procedure. Other students who watched her stitch up wounds marveled at her nimble fingers, fingers that had gained their skills from grandmother's fancywork lessons. She even recommended to a couple of her ham-handed male colleagues that they learn to crochet.

She was shocked and panicked when, halfway through her studies, she opened a letter from home and read that Pa was cutting off her support and ordered her to come home. The reason given was that since John was not applying himself to his studies the "only fair thing" was for both Susan and John to leave school. Instinct told her Minnie's hand was in this; she suspected that although he would be too proud to admit it, Pa's business affairs had taken a temporary turn for the worse causing Minnie, herself now a mother, to begrudge the money sent to Susan and John.

Fortunately, a fellow medical student named Mary Lapham—the daughter of a wealthy Michigan banker—offered to loan Susan money. Reluctantly, Susan drew at least $50 twice a semester to pay her bills. It wouldn't have been so difficult to accept the money if Mary had been able to study at Susan's side. But her young friend was in such serious danger from tuberculosis that her personal physician forced her to drop out of school and move far away to a warmer climate.

John, too, refused to return to Cripple Creek; although not as good a student as Susan, he decided to work his own way through school—at a pace leisurely enough to suit his temperament.

With the abrupt denial of her tuition money, Susan concluded parental loyalty was no longer an issue. For a long time she had secretly nursed a desire to find her mother. Locating Marya Pile presented no obstacle; she still lived near the place where Susan and John had been born in neighboring Indiana. Marya had remarried, to a man named William McLaughlin, so not only did Susan find a mother, she met three half-sisters and a half-brother. After twenty years the woman she encountered was a stranger to her, somber and dark with piercing black eyes and straight black hair. Susan's Grandma Anderson had sometimes hinted that her namesake inherited Indian blood from Louisiana-born Marya, something grandma didn't sound happy about. The only trace of such inheritance that Susan could detect in her own fair features was her classic high cheekbones; nonetheless, grandma notwithstanding, she liked to claim she was part Cherokee. Now, in adulthood, it seemed to her clear that Marya Pile had probably been helpless to fight for her two children against the wealth and domineering drive of William Anderson.

Susan came away with a feeling of foreboding. As she wrote to John on Sept. 25, 1896: "I went to mother's. She is

a queer woman. She is very quiet and seems so sad and bro-
kenhearted. I stayed only a little while for it was too melan-
choly & sad to stay long. She has four other children . . .
They all made a great fuss over me & I know I was welcome.
She [mother] gave me some pieces of her dresses, a roll for
each of us. She has your first pants & gave me a small piece,
I'll send you a part." Susan blamed her mother's air of sad-
ness on the pain Pa inflicted when he divorced her and took
her children away.

Susan had another problem, all her own. In her final
year she had developed a persistent cough, intensified by
frequent spells of weakness and dizziness. Probably her tuberculosis had been contracted from an impoverished patient. One of her professors had confirmed her opinion
and counseled her to leave Ann Arbor and return to the
dry air of Cripple Creek; the western climate should prove
favorable for "a touch of T.B." She would always wonder
how different her life might have been had the disease not
prevented her from accepting an internship offered by the
Women's Hospital of Philadelphia. She knew her disease
was a serious one, one which killed one out of every four
adult residents back in Colorado—where sufferers flocked
to take advantage of the climate.

Her anxiety about her illness, and its consequences for her
attractiveness, was reflected in her concern about her graduation photograph. Although no one from her family would
attend, she wrote to John of her preparations for the big day
on June 5, 1897: "I have had some pictures taken. I will send
you the proofs if I can find them. The ones in the black dress
were taken first and I didn't like the dress so I put on a white
waist and had them taken over . . . The cheek hollow does
not show so plain in it . . ."

A casual postscript noted: "One of my instructors will
be 12 mi. from [Cripple Creek] this summer & I expect to
see him sometimes perhaps." Perhaps.

When she returned to the gold camp in 1897, much had
changed. Two devastating fires the year before had burned
great sections of Cripple Creek, leaving thousands of

people homeless. Now that she was a doctor, when she saw fancy ladies on the street she didn't pay attention to how they dressed but rather to how they coughed, walked or even staggered. She spotted symptoms of their dependence on whiskey and laudanum, of the pain caused by venereal disease and bungled abortions. There were more of these women than ever.

What hadn't changed was the cool relationship between herself, Pa and Minnie. How grateful she would have been to have a little help buying expensive vital equipment such as a microscope and an apparatus for testing urine. She wanted to mend fences with Pa, but Minnie had other ideas. On July 12, John wrote to Susan from Oakland: "I rec'd your letter yesterday and was somewhat riled at Pa's conduct toward you. Does he not come to see you at all? . . . What have you done or not done that he pays no attention to you?" Well, Susan knew what she had done. She had committed the unforgiveable sin of visiting her own mother.

During the next three years Susan managed to establish a practice in Cripple Creek, but things never warmed up with Pa and Minnie. When John wrote from Oakland that he had promised to marry a woman there, Susan urged him to follow the dictates of his heart: "Pa has ruined one woman's life by his trifling or haste or change of heart or something & she is our mother."

In the same letter Susan confided: ". . . it makes me feel hard & bitter & sour when I have to go in old shabby clothes & scrimp & save & board off Grandma & Grandpa & Minnie gets new things for her & the babies & goes to all expense she needs & grumbles about not being able to treat me as she likes to on account of Pa & I know Pa would be glad to have things different & see me nicely dressed & comfortable."

Prophetically she continued: "Don't trust two-faced people with any affair that involves the happiness of your life & the life that should be dearest & most protected by you."

When Susan Anderson, M.D., first set up office in 1897 at Number 3, in the Bi-metallic Block of Cripple Creek, 55 physicians and ten dentists served a population of about 30,000 people, making for a highly competitive situation. Additionally, the established medical community was continually at the mercy of medicine men and dubiously qualified "physicians" just passing through, who advertised magical cures in the newspapers, sold expensive concoctions that were mostly alcohol, and then scrambled out of town leaving still-ailing gullibles to beg for charity treatment from resident doctors. Very slowly, word of the pretty young doctor's medical skills got around. She was proud that by dint of hard work and going without things she really needed, within two years she was able to repay the $500 she owed Mary Lapham.

One case helped establish her reputation. Some people called her to come to the gulch where their teenage son had by accident picked into "bad shot," unexploded dynamite. It blew up, breaking his arm, leg, and nose and spiking fine fragments of rock into his face. While Susan was cleaning the boy up, the parents sent for a surgeon who wanted to amputate the arm. Susan stood defiantly against it. Because of her skill in cleaning the wounds, infection failed to develop; the patient's arm was saved and restored to use.

Meanwhile, brother John was still half-studying civil engineering in Oakland. His letters were filled with his delights of bicycling down the West Coast and strumming his guitar, although he didn't see why the brother of America's greatest physician should have to put up with chronic catarrh.

Suddenly Pa decided that John might after all be handy for the Anderson fortunes. Pa's associate, Fred W. Ford, had abruptly decamped for the newly discovered gold fields of the Klondike, taking with him the corporation's technical expertise in geology and mineralogy. Pa, needing guidance on several business ventures, brought the family engineer home in hope that John might know a thing or two.

As the new century loomed, Susan became optimistic. Her dizzy spells were fewer, her practice was building steadily; people were actually paying cash for her services. Her beloved brother John had returned to Cripple Creek to bring brightness to her days and to become an ally against Pa. Most importantly, the man of her dreams, studious, intelligent "W.R.," had quietly slipped into her life. Johnnie was there to share the joy of a wedding planned for March. With happiness would surely come health, a cure for her tuberculosis.

So close. She had come so close to having everything cherished by Frances.

And then the nightmare, so painful that even now, eight years later, she could not force herself to open the pages of her diary to read words she knew by heart. Something had happened, she never knew what, between her father and W.R.—and without warning she was left at the altar. She had been haunted ever since by that mysterious exchange. What had Pa told W.R. that was so damning it would make a devoted lover leave town at the very moment when his bride-to-be was buttoning up her wedding dress? Was it the old canard about "Indian" blood? Had Pa warned that Susan would be disinherited if she married, or invented some fantastic falsehood about her health or her reputation?

She wouldn't have put it past him to make up a lie, just to get back at her for going to see her mother. One thing she was sure: W.R.'s sudden departure was caused by her Pa, the same Pa who used to say that nothing in the world was too good for his little girl.

Stinging from the loss of her lover, and his abrupt return of her photographs, Susan barely paid attention when she heard that John, who lived in a boarding house across the valley, had come down with influenza. Minnie and Pa didn't send for Susan until John was delirious from pneumonia. She was too late. All she could do was stand by helplessly as he suffered through his last few hours, gasping for breath.

Eight years had done nothing to erase the memory of those terrible few days in which she mourned the loss of her husband-to-be and the burial of her brother in Mt. Pisgah Cemetery. Not one to keep a regular journal, for those few terrible days she recorded, in terse sentences, the depths of her despair:

Sunday March 11, 1900: *John sick pneumonia.* **Monday March 12, 1900:** *Pictures returned by W.R. The end of a vain hope. No use to cast pearls before swine.* **Friday March 16, 1900:** *John died at 6:15 p.m. Was so strange to think of John dead but he has suffered all a mortal can. We are happy he died unconscious of his pain.* **Saturday March 17, 1900:** *Went to see John. Poor baby he is so sweet at rest.* **Sunday March 18, 1900:** *Saw John. Selected casket of black with silk cords.* **Monday March 19, 1900:** *John buried today. He is gone from sight but is not far away. I seem to feel that he is near me & knows all the troubles & how I feel.* **Tuesday March 20, 1900:** *Came back to Cripple Creek to live again. Life seems so useless & in vain. No one now cares much whether I live or die. John was my best friend on earth & now my best friend is in heaven.*

Since that catastrophic week, she had lived her life as best she could, an unremarkable blur, from day to day. Pa, disheartened by John's death, moved his brood to Oakland and forbade Susan to stay in Cripple Creek. She would have left anyhow. Her grief and heartbreak left her with very little desire to remain in a town where drunks staggered from honkytonk to saloon and greed dictated every transaction. Her immediate urge was to put the most distance possible between her father and herself, so she accepted a position as private physician and paid traveling companion to a wealthy man, also a victim of consumption. She accompanied him in his private rail car through the Eastern United States and Canada. When her patient announced he was feeling well enough to travel to Europe, she bowed out and returned to Colorado, thinking she could set up a practice in Denver, a town already tamed. She listed herself in the Denver Directory of 1901: "Anderson, Susan, Miss. Physician. 50 W. Maple," but waited in vain for patients to show up at her door. In 1901 Denver had one licensed physician to treat every 300 citizens, a very high ratio. Many were consumptive men who decided, just as she had, that they could cure both their lungs and bank account by practicing medicine in Denver. In Denver, being a woman was definitely against her.

She went west 150 miles to Steamboat Springs, but decided against settling there because the town had no railroad, nor prospect of one. She toyed with the idea of moving to another state, and obtained a license to practice in Carbon County, Wyoming, but didn't go there, either.

By the time she moved to Greeley, she was running out of money and ideas. Colleagues back in Ann Arbor had recommended her to Dr. Jesse Hawes, a respected Colorado physician and a fellow alumnus. Perhaps he could help her get established in Greeley, a thriving northeast Colorado farming community. Unfortunately, the elderly Hawes died soon after her arrival. She was too discouraged to keep looking for a position; most nights she woke up sweating, a symptom that her tuberculosis had taken a turn for the worse.

When she was offered a job as a nurse, she took it. In Colorado, trained nurses were as scarce as doctors were plentiful. During the six years she worked as a nurse in Greeley and in the nearby village of Eaton she never made any secret of the fact that she was an M.D. Mechanically, she went through the business of emptying bedpans, cleaning up wounds for careless doctors, and taking orders from men whose educations were inferior to hers. The blandness of Greeley wasn't to her taste; she was accustomed to boom towns like Wichita and Cripple Creek, where anything could happen. The respectable farmers and their upright wives couldn't compare to the flamboyant entrepreneurs she had known in livelier places. Even the establishment of Greeley's first-class hospital in 1904 did little to perk up her interest in life.

In Greeley, she had watched time pass dismally. Occasional letters from Pa pleaded with her to join the family in Oakland; she burned them. Gone were the dreams father and daughter had shared when she cuddled into his lap in Wichita.

Little by little her tubercular condition was worsening, aggravated in the autumn of 1907 by the stresses of a diphtheria epidemic. Perhaps, she feared, the illness was beginning to affect her mental faculties, clouding her judgment; a sharp dispute with the hospital matron over Susan's handling of the crowded children's ward had precipitated her departure from Greeley. As she admitted on arrival in Fraser, "I was about done up."

But not, she told herself grimly, quite washed out. Not so long as there was breath, however halting, left in her body.

Today she would finish unpacking. She reached for another box.

CHAPTER 3

You Gotta Save Dave

Each time a train passed, pictures attached to the walls of the shack danced up and down while enamel dishes clattered on Susan Anderson's little table. By now the rhythm of the trains had become her rhythm. An experienced traveler, she understood the language of whistle codes. An engineer warned when his megaton monster was approaching a road crossing by blowing two longs, a short, and another long. Months before she met the individual men who controlled the throttles, she could distinguish how each played his tune for the crossing three hundred yards south of her pillow. Some blew perfunctory little toots as though fearful of waking up babies. Others acted with the apparent conviction that anyone within earshot, day or night, would welcome a solo of long, lavish blasts played on an organ of immense resonance. She could even tell when a new hire came on the job. But most of all, she anticipated the rumble of the Mallets.

Plying the rails of the Moffat Road were some of the most powerful locomotives ever built. Designed by a Swiss mechanical engineer named Anatole Mallet, American railroaders always called them Mallets. The behemoths boasted four sets of triple drive wheels in the configuration known as 2-6-6-0. They owed their power to a system which consisted of two engines beneath one long boiler. First, steam passed through the rear engine which was rigidly bolted in place. The same steam then passed from the exhaust of the rear set of cylinders to the front engine, which was hinged into place so it could swing laterally. In this way, the huge engines could maneuver the roadbed's tight curves. No speed demon, a Mallet could not exceed thirty-five miles an hour. But the Moffat Road demanded raw power to drag freight up four percent grades. So demanding was the grade that often five or six Mallets would be interspersed throughout a complement of coal cars in order to haul it "over the hill."

When a Mallet headed downhill out of Fraser, gaining speed for its four-mile romp along the straight-a-way toward Tabernash, Susan's little shack shook like an avalanche was crashing into it. The noise was as loud as a thunder clap when lightning strikes the roof. When a locomotive labored uphill, its gasping struggle for momentum belched out clouds of smoke; a fine shower of cinders besmirched the snow. Yet Mallets became her friends—powerful, strong, dependable. She smiled when she wished to herself that she could find a man like that, even if sharing a bed would be somewhat awkward. Their whistles never kept her awake at night, although in daytime they were so loud that people had to interrupt a conversation and plug their ears until the train passed. She was alerted only when there was a change in their pattern. That spring of 1908 she noticed that more and more work trains were headed west, pulling track-laying equipment and crew cars so that rails could be laid through the Colorado River's Gore Canyon into the Yampa Valley. Work would begin just as soon as the spring run-off slowed and crews were no longer at the mercy of dangerous rapids in the chasm.

As her strength increased, she found herself less and less interested in brooding about the past. She concentrated on her self-prescribed exercise regimen and ventured forth on snowshoes, learning to waddle with her knees apart so she didn't step down on the edge of the opposite shoe, a mistake guaranteed to stop forward progress until she could figure out how to untangle her own feet. One day, when she heard water gurgling noisily beneath the ice on St. Louis Creek, she recognized a sign of spring in the high country.

"I declare, Susan Anderson, your cheeks are so tanned that you look like a lumberjack," joked Cora Warner one day. Faithful Cora checked daily to satisfy herself that Susan was eating properly. "Maybe you'd like to get out, see a few people. Come down to the store and clerk for me occasionally. You can be there as much or as little as you like."

"I might not be much use to you, but I'd like to help out," said Susan, grateful for the suggestion of a way to return Cora's manifold favors.

A pretty woman working in a public place like a general store could hardly go unnoticed. The "Swedish" bachelors sought her out. "Good Americans," whose ancestors had arrived on these shores one or two generations earlier, lumped all Scandinavian newcomers into the category of "Swedes," whether they came from Norway, Finland, Denmark or even Iceland. A man would ask, "Which is da best coffee?" or make up other excuses to talk to her. She was flattered to observe that most of them would wash and shave before coming to the store, but it seemed their chats always ended up as English lessons. Most of the brawny lumberjacks were disappointed to learn that her name, Anderson, was English rather than Svensk, but because she was always kind and helpful, if a bit distant, they liked her. Cora Warner noticed that it was only when railroad brass or mill bosses—machinists, foremen and office managers—dropped by, that Susan extended herself to flirt.

Springtime in the Rockies does not live up to its romantic reputation; the intermittent melting of snow piled several feet deep produces a prolonged mud season. By late April Susan had been forced to hang her snowshoes on a spike on the side of her shack because in many places soft slush and sticky mud would no longer support her weight. By mid-day there was no way to get from her front door to Warner's store or Lemmon's Post Office without slogging through a bog, avoiding rivulets that ran deep enough to pour icy water into her galoshes' cuffs. But on glorious spring days the breeze blew so bracingly that the sweet air was like a tonic rushing bubbles of oxygen to her brain and through her recovering lungs. Her spirits sagged only when spring blizzards blew in with a cargo of heavy, wet snow, plunging Fraser back into winter. She discovered that the only dependable way to ensure getting her quota of exercise was to awaken when the sun first peeked over the Continental Divide, and to walk out while the ground and snowpack were still frozen.

The town was full of new faces. Mud season forced all of the lumberjacks to come down from the woods to work as mill hands. Not until the spring run-off subsided in late June or early July would they be able to return to the forest to fell trees and skid logs out of the woods. In the meantime, they bunked at the mill and strolled around town as the days lengthened. Unless a blizzard closed Rollins Pass, Number One disgorged more men looking for work at the mill every day. Each evening the saloon keepers on Fraser's "skid road" poured a lot of drafts as men smoked, played checkers and shot pool to pass the time. When Susan strolled forth to stretch her legs, she assessed them as possible husband material. The town was full of Scandinavian bachelors who were often too shy to show much interest in "nice" women. For feminine company they usually waited until Saturday night when paid companionship was part of their weekly bender.

Mill business wasn't the only thing that picked up in the spring. Cowboys who had gone to Texas or Mexico to work through the winter returned to the mountains, looking for jobs when calving season began in April. They loved the high country and preferred to live there, but through winter a homesteader could usually manage to fork hay to his herd himself and mend his own tack. Besides, there was no money to pay a hired hand.

In Warner's store canned foods, such as sardines, vegetables and fruit, were bought by those bachelors who had money to spend. Milk and fresh dairy products brought by rail from the East Slope would remain very expensive until summer, so poor people bought canned milk for their children. Susan wanted to tell them to save their money because canned milk was nothing but water, fat and sugar. But she realized the mothers of Fraser wouldn't have credited a spinster store clerk with any special expertise in nutrition. She quickly won their respect, however, when she advised them on sewing matters. She could show them how to save a quarter of a yard of calico and a dime by repositioning their patterns on a length of goods.

Mr. Warner knew how to entice a few extra coins from the pockets of his customers. Colorful jars and bins of penny candy were positioned to guarantee children would beg their parents for licorice, horehound or cherry drops from rows of colorful jars and bins. Charlie Warner also roasted peanuts, teasing the noses of even the stingiest rancher or lumberjack to take along a fresh, warm bag of nuts to shell and munch on his way home. But best of all was the soft stick candy, chewy and studded with popcorn, that Mr. Warner made himself.

One indispensable item carried in any general store was gossip. "Just heard that the Eastom Company, fellers who own the sawmill, are about to sell," Charlie told Susan one morning.

"Can't think why," said Susan. "Seems to me they are doing a good business. Of course, maybe the Eastom family is tired of being beholden to so many investors. My Pa always said to sell while the books look good."

When a transfer of the Eastom Company to the Omaha Lumber Company took place on March 19, 1908 and $255,000 changed hands, people wondered what the new ownership would mean to their jobs. But as long as so many virgin trees in the forest were needed to build houses in cities back east, they weren't too worried.

Sometimes town gossips tried to pump Susan about her past. Susan told them as little as possible. But in a small town the only thing harder to hold onto than money is a secret. It was inevitable that someone would fall into conversation with a friend or acquaintance from Cripple Creek who said Susan Anderson was a doctor, or one from Greeley who said she was a nurse. Word passed quickly from mouth to ear to mouth that the pretty stranger was actually a physician. Good news doesn't make much progress without the spice of scandal, so at the same time it got around that she had been a nurse in Greeley, but was forced to leave because she made a terrible error that caused the death of a newborn infant. Some even said she was hiding out from the law or the medical society.

One morning, as she was pushing a broom over pine planks moistened with sawdust, Susan looked up to see a thin young cowboy hurrying toward her with a worried look on his face. His old, tattered denim jacket suggested no great prosperity. The hand that held his hat in front of him in a gesture of supplication was scarlet with fresh blood. Alarmed, she gave him a professional once-over, but could see no obvious injury.

"Ma'am, ma'am, Dave . . ." she was afraid he was going to cry as he waved his hat back toward the door. "Dave got cut up in barbed wire and he's butchered pretty bad. Ma'am, they say you're a doctor and I need help real bad. Could you please come, fast. Dave's all I got."

It was the moment she had dreaded. Responding to his plea meant revealing her secret and destroying her privacy forever. Yet in view of its urgency, her Hippocratic oath forbade turning him down. She really didn't have any choice.

"My bag is at my house, just across the tracks." She whistled for her dog, leaned her broom behind the counter, untied her canvas apron and hung it on a peg. Cora Warner could hardly suppress a smile, watching Susan's transformation from clerk to doctor. People in the store stopped their shopping and stared.

She walked purposefully out of the door, the young cowboy at her heels. "Where is your friend?"

"Down at the corral."

She stopped. "Can't he be moved from there?"

"No ma'am."

She stopped and looked him in the eye. "Is Dave your partner?"

"No ma'am, he's my horse."

It was a good thing she had assumed a professional air because it prevented her from showing the anger she felt. She felt tricked, but she had given her word and knew she'd have to make good on it. All frontier doctors had to work on animals from time to time. From Cripple Creek she had rueful recollections of her difficulties in treating horses; her small stature didn't supply the strength required to deal with their unpredictable movements. But the truth was that doctors were plentiful and veterinarians scarce.

So she told the cowboy to tote a fresh bucket of water to the corral, build a fire and set it to boil while she fetched her bag. As she assembled a kit, she said to her dog, "Well, if I'm going on my first professional call in Fraser, I might as well look the part." She tied up her hair and tucked it into a white turban, then pulled a clean white apron over her dress. As an afterthought, she packed her sewing kit with its big carpet needles and some tough canvas thread. She was angry with herself for being so gullible and did not minimize the situation she was going to face. When a steer or a mule gets tangled in barbed wire it will stand quietly until someone comes to cut it out. But most horses will thrash and struggle trying to break free, the wire cutting deeper and deeper with every effort until wounds bite into an artery and the poor creature bleeds to death or someone is forced to shoot it to put an end to the agony.

She shut her dog in the shack. Her feet crunched along the ice on the still-frozen street as she headed for the corral opposite the depot where livestock were penned before being herded up through chutes into cattle cars. Children too small to be in school began to follow. News had spread fast from the store to the women of Fraser, whose days normally offered nothing more exciting than splitting kindling and hanging out the wash. They dropped their scrub brushes and flat irons, grabbed their babies and hastened to the corral to watch the store clerk sew up a bloody horse. Loafers who hung around the depot waiting for a job call saw an opportunity for a little sport in the morning sunshine. "A woman Doc is going to sew up a horse? By golly. What's she gonna do, embroider the alphabet on his hide?"

When she arrived at the corral she saw the cowboy holding a rope to her patient's halter. The gelding limped, his fine head bent low with pain. He looked to be about a three-year-old, a beautifully spotted pinto who would probably develop into a good roping horse. She could see the cowboy had told the truth when he said, "He's all I got." Besides being his friend, the pinto had probably cost him every penny he had ever saved.

Quite a crowd had gathered. She stood over the boiling bucket of water, washing her hands meticulously with soap, inspecting her fingernails. She ordered the cowboy to wash up, too.

"Now you take this hot water and rinse it through every single cut. Then press these pads against any cuts that are still bleeding. That's first." She was glad that the wounds were relatively fresh.

Several of the women nudged each other when she unwrapped a bundle containing shiny instruments and dropped them into the boiling water. The sun melted brittle ice from ruts in the corral floor, releasing the stench of ammonia from accumulated manure. Susan ordered the cowboy to tie the horse in one corner, hitched up her skirts into her belt, took a deep breath and stepped into the muddy corral to inspect the wounds. Many were deep, dirty and serious.

The frightened, lathered animal turned his neck to watch her approach. His eyes rolled up in his head with fear. "Ho boy, ho big Dave," she crooned, sounding calmer than she felt.

She turned to the cowboy, "I've got to pour carbolic acid into these wounds or they'll get badly infected. He's not going to like it at all. Can you hold him down?"

"I'll try, ma'am."

"My name is Doc Susie. And you're going to have to do better than try."

Suddenly the onlookers got into the act. Nearly everybody in the audience had a helpful suggestion or two: "Rub manure in the wounds, it brings out the infection"; "Blindfold him"; "Put some arnica up his nose." Susie ignored them; her sideways glance let them know who was in charge.

A couple of loafers, clearly impressed, stepped into the corral to help. One held the horse's tail out of her way while another brought her a box from the depot to stand on so she could examine wounds on the horse's back that had been inflicted while he was on the ground struggling. Doc Susie's first rule was never to hurry, figure out a plan in advance. Always a deliberate practitioner, she carefully picked dirt from each wound. Then she reached under the horse's hide, right through its cuts and pulled muscles together, painstakingly reconnecting severed sinews and blood vessels, layer by layer, moving as quickly as she dared along and down the jagged cuts. Finally she pulled thread through his hide to close each wounded area. The young horse was skittish and at unpredictable intervals shied away from her in pain. Once he stepped down hard on her toes. Wincing, she fought off her instinctive anger.

"Can't you give him somethin' for the pain, Doc?"

"I have nothing to give him. I never keep dope and besides, anything that would be strong enough to kill the pain would probably kill him, too."

Dave lurched suddenly, kicking over the bucket of hot water and scattering her instruments into the manure. She stepped back, put her two hands on her hips, looked up at the sky and bellowed, "Hek-a-roon!" By the standards of those watching, her oath was mother's milk, but it was uttered with such raw feeling that its impact was forceful. Quickly, she took a few deep breaths and regained her composure. Gathering up her mired implements, she methodically rewashed and resterilized them.

She eyed the cowboy again, "You've got to twitch him."

"Twitch Dave? I hate twitches."

"If you ever intend to ride this horse again, you're going to have to twitch him."

She didn't like twitches either, but she saw no other way. Reluctantly, the cowboy looped a strap around the horse's upper lip, inserted a stick and twisted. If the horse moved, the pain to his sensitive mouth and nostrils was even more intense than if he stood still. It was a trick she had seen farriers use when an unruly horse refused to stand still to be shod. She wished she had thought of it sooner.

Taking advantage of the twitch, she kept sewing. The sun moved higher and hotter. The cowboy grimaced. Obviously his arm ached from holding the twitch at an angle, and he would be wondering if she would keep this agony going for man and beast until sunset. Bored kids stuck their fingernails under little scabs of bark on the corral poles and peeled them back. The housewives began to worry about whether the fire had gone out under the clothes they left boiling at home. Didn't she realize they needed to get back to their chores? Couldn't she hurry up and get the job done? They didn't want to leave and miss anything, but they hadn't reckoned on the fact that this little doctor didn't know how to do a bad job, and that her professional pride required her to be as meticulous when she sutured a horse as she would be attending a human. Finally, as cowboy, horse and doctor all sweated and steamed in the hot, early afternoon sun, she straightened up and wiped the back of her hand across her brow to clear a lock of hair that had fallen in her eye, "That's the best I can do. I hope he doesn't pull all of the stitches out."

A cheer went up from the bystanders sitting atop the corral fence and peering through its poles. Doc Susie would be the topic of conversation over every pot of beans and schooner of beer in Fraser that evening, animated conversation that would usually end up, "Well, horses is one thing, humans another. Women wasn't meant to be doctors. It ain't natural."

"Hek-a-roon!" The women and children in town tried out a new word, one they could utter without being accused of swearing. "Hekaroon." They liked it.

The cowboy came up to her as she cleaned her instruments and packed her bag. "Uh, Doc, I ain't got no money 'til pay day end of the month. Uh, could I owe ya?"

"Tell you what you can do for me," she said. "Stay with Dave and pull him through. He's going to need to be kept clean, on his feet, out of the mud and manure. He'll get awful stiff and he'll need to be walked around town three to five times a day. Those wounds have to be cleaned and tended. I can wait for your money. What I need right now is a little success."

"Sure will, Doc Susie. Sure will. And thanks."

For the next week, several times a day she strolled down the street to the corral and checked on her patient. When the cowboy attached a rope to Dave's halter and walked him up and down the streets of Fraser the pinto pony was like a billboard, inviting people to examine his new seams and advertising that there was a lady doctor in town. As she told a reporter nearly fifty years later, "Everytime I stitched up his worst wound, the horse yanked out the stitches with his teeth, but I pulled him through."

It was an era when house calls were common. But Doc Susie's first medical case in Fraser was a horse call.

CHAPTER 4

The Price of Canned Milk

Doc Susie's practice didn't blossom all at once like golden dandelions in a June hay meadow. Her figure was regaining its attractive curves and her stamina increased daily, but she knew better than to pronounce herself cured and retreat to a lower altitude. She had known many TB sufferers who left a beneficial climate when they seemed to be recovering only to suffer a relapse, sometimes fatal. So she continued her routine of vigorous exercise, rest and fresh warm milk.

Finally, she wrote to her Pa and Minnie to tell them she was living in Fraser. She knew Pa wouldn't be pleased; her medical career hadn't gone according to his plan. He replied, pleading with her to join the rest of the Anderson family in Oakland. When she read his directive she said, "Pooh!" and tossed his letter aside.

That summer, people began to drop by the store and seek out a quiet corner to ask Doc Susie for advice. It usually went like this, "Doc Susie. A friend of mine has this problem," then the inquirer would proceed to describe a gall bladder condition, hernia or pain in the belly, pointing to the exact spot where the pain occurred, giving specific details that only a sufferer could relay. Some people wanted a little free advice; others were testing her to see if she knew the right answers. She treated all such inquiries with dignity and professional confidentiality.

For the most part, they took their ills and their money to Doc Albers or to the railroad doctor down in Tabernash. Occasionally, when the men weren't available she was summoned to a bedside, but most of her first patients suffered from minor woes, of which Gertrude Arkell's was typical.

Doc Susie had made friends with the Arkells, a prosperous ranching family who had sold a farm in Kansas to buy the Diamond Bar T Ranch in the verdant Ranch Creek basin east of Fraser. Their daughter Gertrude, a seventh-grader, had a little sore on the outside of her cheek, the kind of blemish that drives a young girl crazy but that most people dismiss along with normal growing pains. Thirteen-year-old Gertrude didn't mention the sore to Anna, her mother, because she had been picking at it and she knew she would receive a lecture about keeping her hands off. But the blemish persisted so one day when she rode her pony four miles to town to fetch the mail, Gertrude dropped by Dr. Anderson's little shack. There was no mistaking which shack was Doc's because on the front she had mounted a small box with a red cross painted on it. If she was out on house calls or errands, she left medications her patients were expecting in the box so they could be picked up in her absence.

Gertrude was curious about the educated woman who often called at the family ranch, socially, to chat with her mother. Anna Arkell had been a school teacher; she and Dr. Anderson enjoyed conversations that rose a notch above standard gossip. Loneliness was one of the worst diseases to afflict mountain women, especially those whose schooling made them aware that there was more to life than colicky babies and butter churns. Gertrude liked to trail along behind and eavesdrop as the two women identified wildflowers or hunted berries. She was fascinated by the attractive visitor who was truly a real doctor.

Although Susan always asked people to call her "Doc Susie," the mothers of Fraser never allowed their children that level of informality. Gertrude wouldn't have dreamed of addressing her as anything but Dr. Anderson.

The doctor examined the eruption and pinched it a little, then motioned that Gertrude should follow her to the hen house. Gertrude had great respect for Dr. Anderson's ability to get hens to lay all winter when fresh eggs were prohibitively expensive at the store. In less knowledgeable hands, a chicken that escaped the frying pan in autumn would surely freeze to death in winter; Doc's not only survived but kept on laying. Dr. Anderson took a compound from the shelf that Gertrude recognized because it was used to disinfect the chicken coop, and poured a little into a bottle. She instructed the girl to wash her face with some of her mother's good homemade soap and then to apply the substance; Gertrude wrinkled her nose at the smell of creosote. But the chicken medicine cured Gertrude's sore.

In those days, Doc Susie used medications interchangeably between humans and animals. That was before pharmaceutical houses discovered a fundamental economic principle. Label a medication for human consumption, and a higher price could be charged. But the sore was more an excuse than a problem. Gertrude looked for reasons to hang around and watch Dr. Anderson. Each time Gertrude stopped by, Doc Susie would say, "Let's have a look at that cheek. I can see you are keeping it very clean because it looks fine."

That formality accomplished, Gertrude would stay to "neighbor with Dr. Anderson." She helped to draw buckets of water from her well in the yard, or in winter she scooped up snow to melt. She was mesmerized to watch the thoroughness with which the doctor prepared sterilized dressings for use in emergency calls. People discarding old sheets or rags saved them for Doc. She would wash and boil them, then dry them outside on the line. In winter, the items would first freeze stiff and then dry out. She heated flat irons on her stove and pressed each strip of dressing to sterilize it, then rolled it. Finally, she boiled her instruments, wrapped them in the homemade dressings and prepared ready-to-go sterile bundles.

Her meticulous approach to cleanliness sometimes caused problems. One day, while visiting at the Diamond Bar T, Doc Susie volunteered to help Anna Arkell prepare strawberries for dinner. They weren't the tiny wild berries that grow on moist slopes around Fraser, so small that the fruits of an hour's picking won't fill a teacup. No, they were a special treat—berries from the East Slope, big ones still muddy and mixed with straw. Susie, with typical precision, approached her task as though she were preparing fruit for surgery rather than eating. She rinsed each berry several times, held it to the light and removed the slightest speck, then she turned it to inspect the other side. Anna was afraid that the cleaning of one box of berries might delay the dinner bell. After that, Anna tried to arrange her cooking chores so she could refuse Doc Susie's offers to help. After all, there was only so much time that could be allotted to the preparation of each meal. But that same insistence on detail served her well when she treated wounds. "Nobody ever got an infection from a wound she cleans up," her patients said. Doctor Anderson gave the Arkells considerable information about nutrition and preventive medicine, advising them to supplement their diets with vitamins because for most of the year fresh vegetables and fruit were not available in the mountains. She believed that the minerals in the watershed around Fraser percolated enough iodine into the water supply to prevent goiters, those ugly globes so common on the necks of people whose nutrients lacked essential minerals. She was ahead of her time in perceiving that iodine was necessary to healthful nutrition and she prescribed a lot of it—to be slathered on injuries as an antiseptic, or to be taken by droplets to prevent thyroid conditions.

"Anna, you must bake brown bread for your family," she insisted. Anna Arkell occasionally complied, although she didn't rank common brown bread with the fluffy white loaves she prided herself on. "And you should cook cracked wheat mush for your family for breakfast. No eggs after you are thirty."

Papa Arkell wasn't convinced, "You can grain a horse, but I never heard how it improves people," he grumbled. Still he liked Doc Susie and was glad of her visits to the ranch.

Doc Susie confided to Gertrude, "The main thing I hate is waste." It made Susie sad to see the big, virgin trees cut down, an attitude she wouldn't have shared with lumberjacks. But she knew her opinion was safe enough with a rancher's daughter. When they chatted, Dr. Anderson preached that sooner or later everything would be needed and to never throw anything away. Gertrude admired Dr. Anderson's display of the little green bottles that many patent medicines and cooking ingredients came in. Susie picked up discarded ones and took them home, arranging them in a window where the sun streamed through. Gertrude thought their green reflection on the linoleum floor looked pretty and started her own collection. Gertrude never did figure out what Dr. Anderson intended to do with some of the items that were stacked around, such as the huge pile of broken ax handles that she had gathered on her forays into the woods. Whenever Doc Susie came along a trail and found a splintered ax handle, she picked it up and took it home. In a pine forest, they were one of the few objects made of hard wood. They would have kindled a long-lasting fire, but Gertrude never knew Doc to burn any of them. A couple of times she thought she would ask, but just then the conversation suffered a "Fraser skip," the pause necessitated by the deafening noise of a passing locomotive. In Fraser, nobody tried to yell over the noise of a Mallet.

Gradually, requests for Doc Susie's services increased. House calls were the normal way a rural doctor did business. If Doc Albers and the railroad doctor down in Tabernash were out on their rounds or "on confinement," as everybody referred to childbirth, they might be unavailable for a period lasting from a few hours to a couple of days. In that case someone suffering from an ache in the belly or tooth would seek out Doc Susie.

Most husbands remained united in their disapproval of "a woman Doc." After all, who would want to be treated by some female who didn't even believe that whiskey could cure what ailed you, and refused to give you a "snort" even to deaden the pain when she pulled a tooth?

But their wives were glad to have someone to tell about their "female troubles." Husbands usually viewed such wifely complaints as nuisances that interfered with the productivity of a good work animal. Male doctors often treated women as though their ovaries were located somewhere above their eyebrows, advising that a better attitude would compensate for a tipped uterus or abnormal bleeding.

Children provided a steady supply of cuts, bruises, nails in the feet and broken arms. They dreaded the medication that she used to swab throats and treat sinus conditions. One patient described its taste "like a cross between motor oil and Tabasco Sauce."

One evening, as Doc Susie was reading her Bible, she looked up to see the station agent's boy hurrying toward the house. "Doc. Billy Woods called down from Arrow. There's a baby awful sick up there and he wants you to come see her. There's a freight coupling on a helper engine at Tabernash, going up the hill in about 15 minutes," the boy gasped after delivering his important message all in one breath.

A baby. She didn't really want to treat a baby. "Can't you get Doc Albers?"

"He's out fishin'. Besides, Bill Woods said he wanted you to come." She had seen Bill Woods a few times around

Fraser. Upon learning that she was a doctor he reminded her, "No wonder you was so good gettin' that cinder out of Axel's eye that day on the train."

She resigned herself to the summons, grabbed her bag and tucked a sterile kit into it. She wished Bill Woods had been a bit more specific about what was wrong with the child but she moved fast because she knew better than to keep an uphill freight stopped on the main line. She stood in front of the yellow depot, watched the engineer grab the message to stop the train from the agent "on the fly." (The note had been tied to a string, laced between the tines of a huge fork with a long handle, and held in position for the engineer to grab.)

The train slowed down, barely stopping as the conductor leaned down to scoop Doc up the caboose steps. She smoothed her skirts and followed him through the door. All cabooses smelled the same, like coal dust and stale tobacco. She wrinkled her nose, speculating how often and under what circumstances the spittoon might be emptied. The conductor was a friendly fellow who offered her the only hospitality a caboose affords, a cup of coffee. Idle chat was out of the question, she knew, in the caboose of an uphill freight. Coupled right behind the caboose was a Mallet helper engine engaged in the noisy business of digesting coal and belching steam. She reached into her bag, pinched off a little cotton, rolled it and stuck it in her ears.

As she sipped her coffee and stared out the window at the autumn aspen leaves, shining like pure gold in the last light of day, she wondered what was wrong with the child. Her thoughts returned to that other baby. No clear diagnosis had ever been made of the baby's death in Greeley. It died while she was solely responsible for 26 diphtheria patients. She had been working as long as 22 hours at a stretch. She confided one day to Gertrude Arkell that she had quarreled with the physician in charge about how the children were being treated. At the time there had been much controversy over Dr. Frank Waxham's method of intubation, a drastic procedure which allowed children who

were near death to breathe again. Dr. Waxham had tried in
vain to seek money for diphtheria antitoxin from Colorado's legislature. Susan was outraged when she learned
that legislators at the current session found funds to gild
the capitol dome with pure gold and spent $65,000 to "pre-
serve game animals," yet appropriations for the serum
were defeated.

The rumor persisted that while she worked as a nurse
Doc Susie had accidentally put boric acid instead of water
into an infant's formula and the baby died. Thus, she left
Greeley with her reputation under a cloud. Actually, her
attempt to serve as a nurse was doomed from the start; fellow nurses resented her knowledge and physicians were
wary of giving orders to someone whose education was superior to theirs. Doc Susie told Anna Arkell that when she
left Greeley she was convinced her mind had snapped and
she was in the throes of a mental collapse—little wonder,
given the strain she was under and the state of her tuberculosis. The rumor was a rare blot on her professional reputation.

When she stepped down from the caboose in Arrow, she
found a couple of "Swedes" huddled in the depot. The
husband was tall, blond, his fair nose perpetually peeling
from high altitude sunburn. His woman was thin, her gray
eyes very old in her uncreased face. She was probably not
yet twenty and pregnant. In her arms she held a tiny bundle, and with her calloused hands, rough from working in
the woods, she unwrapped it. Only Doc Susie's profession-
alism kept her from gasping. Although she had never before seen an advanced case of scurvy, the textbook
symptoms were all there: swollen eyelids, emaciation and
dehydration, thin bones and rapid respiration. When she
put her fingers into the little mouth she found spongy
gums. Susie donned her stethoscope and listened for a
heartbeat, it was faint and very fast.

Because they spoke scant English a woman from Arrow
was there to translate for the Swedes, whose name was
Knutson. Doc Susie asked, "How old is your baby?"

She learned that the infant had been born the previous October, nearly a year ago, delivered without assistance by her mother in a tent in the forest. Neither mother nor child had ever seen a doctor. Dirt-poor immigrants, far from family advice, they held themselves apart from other workers.

"Was the child healthy at birth?"

Yes, while she sucked from her mother's breast she had been bright and normal. The young woman held the universal, and erroneous, idea that a woman cannot become pregnant while she is nursing. Although rare, it does happen with the consequence that the mother's lactation ceases.

"Then what did you feed your baby?"

"The milk from cans," was the reply.

In a lumber camp in the woods fresh foods were difficult to come by even in summer. The parents bought cases of milk to feed the child, and for awhile she seemed to be all right. They suffered from another fallacious myth, that canned milk was a good substitute for fresh. But after a couple of months the baby became very fussy and frequently ran a temperature.

"I'm sorry," said Doc Susie, as gently as she could, "but I can't do anything for your baby." She instructed her translator to tell the mother she must be examined. Although pregnant, she had obviously been working side by side with her man in the woods. Susie sent everyone outside and performed a thorough examination of the mother on a hard bench in the waiting room. Her tender touch was the first contact the poor girl had had with another woman for months. Because she had been eating venison and elk poached from the forest, and had supplemented it with dried apples and berries, her condition was not as bad as Doc had feared. But she was thin and her abdomen lacked muscle tone.

Doc Susie took the girl's two hands into hers and held them tightly. For probably the first time in the New World, tears coursed down the woman's cheeks. She looked at the tiny bundle on a depot bench, *"O min stackars liten. Agnes."* she sobbed.

"My poor little thing," echoed the translator, wiping her nose. Doc Susie motioned to the translator to bring in the girl's husband.

She started out her lecture gently, explaining the importance of obtaining fresh vegetables and fruit on a regular basis, even when they stayed in the forest. She suggested several ways the mother could get vitamins, including eating dried fruit and sprinkling lots of hot pepper sauce on her food. They winced; Scandinavians weren't accustomed to eating spicy food. Doc warned them to abstain from sex until after the next baby was born, until he or she was six months old. "If her mother's milk dries up, get a goat," she ordered.

Then she turned to the husband and looked up straight into his blue eyes, "This woman is not a mule or an ox to be worked to death. You were wicked not to bring the baby to a doctor. If your woman continues to work in the forest, she will die and you will have no wife and two dead children."

In English he said, "I haf no money."

"You must call me to help when your baby is born. If anything happens to her or the next baby, you will be held responsible and you will go to jail." She held her hands in front of her, as though she were holding onto two iron prison bars. "I don't care if you don't have money. I will be there."

The threat of a jail sentence wasn't true, but she was learning that dire warnings were occasionally necessary to cut through the nonsensical pride of poverty. She was furious that a young man's stubborn refusal to seek medical advice because he couldn't pay could cause his baby's death. She sent the Knutsons on their way, warning that little Agnes had but a few hours to live. She was glad to see that the lumberjack took his wife's arm protectively, as though he realized for the first time her true worth.

"Remember," she called after them, "Doc Susie will be there, wherever you are."

In the light of a coal oil lamp Susie sank onto a depot bench. She waited for a downhill freight, her shoulders sagging in discouragement. She tried to nap a little, but each time her head nodded the baby's swollen eyelids rose in front of her eyes. A hand touched her shoulder and she looked up to see Bill Woods' weathered face. "I told you this was terrible country for a woman."

"And you were right."

"You could help, you know. You should stay here. Those people listened to you." Bill slipped her a dollar. Her usual charge for a house call was 25 cents. "Don't tell them I paid you," he said.

She took the money. Woods could afford it and he ought to pay. If he had been a little more generous with the price of logs the baby might have lived.

The Knutsons moved away, but Doc Susie was occasionally reminded of them when she glimpsed a small marble headstone along the tracks near Irving Spur. She visited the lovely spot on foot occasionally; nestled at the foot of a circle of towering, protective Englemann Spruce, a tiny white gravestone said:

Agnes Knutson
Oct 20, 1907
Oct 6, 1908

She often wondered why they chose to put the grave at that spot; it would have seemed logical to bury little Agnes in a graveyard at Arrow or Fraser. "Waste," Doc muttered to herself. "Waste."

CHAPTER 5

Beat the Reaper

Westbound from Arrow the downhill train chattered along, sprinting over the same roadbed the uphill train had labored so hard to climb. The Greek trainman in the caboose had been surprised when the engineer stopped to take on Doc Susie, but he was happy to have some company for awhile.

"Looks like our first big snow tonight," he said, as soon as she was comfortably settled with a mug of coffee—extra strong, the way he liked it.

"Oh?" she said. "But the moon is so bright." She had spent the last few hours in Arrow, deep in the forest with no view toward the mountains.

"Wind was blowin' somethin' fierce up on the hill, the snow sheds were just shakin' with it. It'll drop to the valley 'fore long. Looks like there's lotsa moisture in those clouds."

"But it's still September!"

"Don't matter. The snow will melt in the valley for the next month or so, but winter's almost here for sure."

When she climbed down from the caboose in Fraser she looked up toward the front range, sighting the notch where the trains crossed the Continental Divide at Rollins Pass. Sure enough, the moon was ducking in and out of huge clouds that were moving so swiftly it seemed the moon itself was speeding across the sky.

She was weary, bone tired. It was the longest day she had put in since quitting the hospital in Greeley—and a discouraging one. She would be glad to stretch out on her cot, and regretted that she had not stoked the fire before she left so she would have a nice hot rock to warm her feet.

As she pressed her thumb on the latch, her little dog capered in a spasm of joy, jumping up and down on his hind legs, wagging his tail furiously, and licking her hands. She lit a lamp, roughed the fur behind his ears and gave him a piece of dried deer hide she had been saving as a treat. He hunkered down to chew on it.

When she set the lamp on the table, a letter fell to the floor. Postmarked Oakland, California, it had arrived that morning. Her father congratulated her on her improving health and urged her to come west to the coast before winter. She had been thinking about it, knowing the coming winter would be severe and long. She picked up the letter. Maybe she *should* get out of Fraser before the blizzards hit.

She unpinned her long hair, loosened it and pulled a brush slowly down its length while she talked to the dog. "Pooch, I saw a baby tonight and she is going to die. What a waste. But I'm glad I went, maybe I did some good." She undressed, threw her clothes onto a chair, pulled her nightgown over her head and toppled onto her cot. With just one flutter of her eyelashes she was sound asleep.

A loud banging on the door, accompanied by ferocious barking was the next thing she heard. "Who's there?" she called cautiously.

"Dr. Anderson, Dr. Anderson. It's Harry Hollingsworth. Our neighbor boy is real sick with pneumonia. You gotta come."

She pivoted out of bed, pulled a bedquilt around her shoulders and was jolted instantly awake. Pneumonia! The terror of the Fraser Valley, the scourge that had taken the life of her brother John. The last burden she wanted to take on was to treat a young man with pneumonia. She raised her voice, "I just came back from a call up to Arrow. Can't you get Doc Albers?"

"He ain't there ma'am. Dalton Irby is real sick, breathin' awful hard and just burnin' up. His pa sent me to get a doctor, any doctor. You gotta come!"

Later, she figured out that she had slept only about 15 minutes when Hollingsworth banged on her door. She knew from her practice in Cripple Creek that the chances of saving a pneumonia patient at this altitude were no better than 50-50.

"I don't even know where they live," she protested. It was a lame excuse but the only one she could think up.

"Mr. Irby sent me in his buggy. It's just outside of Fraser about a mile. Not far, I'll take you there." Susie allowed herself the luxury of one huge yawn, extending her shoulders and arms in a lengthy stretch. "Wait for me in your trap. I won't take long."

She quickly wound up her hair, slipped in a few hairpins, and pulled on the clothes she had cast aside; remembering the flickering moon, she added an extra petticoat and flannel shirtwaist. This time, she took not only her sterile bundle and medical bag, but scooped up her dog. If it was really pneumonia, she knew she wouldn't be back very soon and she didn't want to be worrying about her pet.

As they headed out of Fraser, Doc Susie questioned Harry, "How long has he been sick?"

"Just a couple of days. We went out fishing and he fell into a beaver pond. Walked home after dark, all wet. Wouldn't eat any supper. Said he had a headache and drowsed off. Went right to bed and woke up yesterday, coughing. I been tryin' to help Mr. Irby do the milking."

As they rode into the wind, autumn's leaves scurried toward them. The wind bit into her cheeks so she drew her scarf across her nose and tucked her dog beneath her big coat where he served the useful purpose of keeping her hands warm. She was very tired but the only place she really felt it was the pain in the back of her neck, between her shoulders.

When they arrived, a sudden patch of moonlight revealed a cluster of fat dairy cattle. It was a promising herd; she guessed most of the Irby family's worth was tied up in those bossies. Doc Susie knew that besides cattle, the Irbys had a lot of little human mouths to feed. She looked to the cabin where a light was shining; as with most ranches, the cabin was modest compared to the barn. The Irby dogs did not bark at the approach of a familiar horse, but stiffened and growled when Susie set her dog down on the ground. The spitz growled back bravely, staying near the safety of Doc's skirts as she swept into the cabin.

Her eyes adjusted slowly to the coal oil lamp light. On a cot in front of the cook stove was a boy of sixteen, shivering beneath a mound of comforters. He was coughing hard, as though trying to clear his lungs and throat, a dry, racking cough. Susie laid the back of her hand across the lad's brow. She didn't need a thermometer to know that his temperature was dangerously high. Around his flushed pink cheeks, on which sprouted the first fuzz of a beard, were curly blond tendrils that framed a young face in the last stage of boyhood. She took out her stethoscope and listened. As she moved it around his chest she sniffed a boy-man smell, a smell that was simultaneously just a little sour like dirty socks, and fresh as hay.

That smell—when she looked up to Dalton Irby's face its contours faded into another young face. She saw her brother John, as she had seen him one night asleep in Wichita during their high school years when she had the responsibility of looking after him. "Take care of your brother," she heard her father say, from a long way off.

In that same moment she realized that she must be very careful. Was her mind playing tricks on her again? She stood up, slowly removed her big knitted coat and looked purposefully around the room. She didn't think she was having hallucinations, but the memory of the visions she had suffered in Greeley still made her cautious where her own feelings were involved. She quickly grounded herself to the reality of standing in a rude cabin outside of Fraser in the midst of a large, anxious ranch family that included a hard working father, an exhausted mother, a very sick boy, his younger brother and several sisters. All had their eyes bolted to this diminutive woman doctor.

This wasn't Cripple Creek, and her patient wasn't John. She didn't have to fight with Pa and Minnie about how Dalton Irby should be treated . . . and it looked as though they had sent for her in time to help. She was a stranger to this trusting family, who would do anything she asked without question . . . because she was the doctor, trained by the finest medical school she knew of. The thought of the University of Michigan made her stand up straighter and to feel something warm and expansive in her chest and shoulders, something she would later come to realize was power.

There was another feeling, too. Outside the log cabin there was a force trying to grab this boy; she thought of the ominous clouds she had seen earlier whipping across the sky and thought of them as death. No, call it the Reaper, like in Longfellow's poem. Yes, the Reaper wanted this strong young boy and her anger flushed blood into her cheeks like a blush. The dark Reaper clouds weren't going to get Dalton Irby if she could help it.

She had a theory about how pneumonia should be treated. Judging from Dalton's ominous symptoms, she didn't have anything to lose by putting it to the test. He would be dead within 24 hours unless something changed—drastically, and almost immediately.

To the astonishment of the Irbys, she reached down and swooped all the comforters from the lad's thin body. His mother leapt forward protectively while his father, who had been leaning quietly against the cabin wall with his thumbs hooked through his overall straps, stood up straight.

Now that she had their attention, the first order of business was to turn these exhausted people, numb with despair, into a life-saving team. She turned to the dazed Mrs. Irby, "I need a cup of coffee. We must boil a lot of water. Do you have a big wash tub?"

Mrs. Irby blinked with bewilderment and confusion at the rapid-fire orders. Doc Susie put a hand on her arm and laughed, "I do need a lot of hot water, but I'm not going to drink a tub full of coffee." The tired woman managed a thin smile.

Susie addressed herself to the entire family, "Now listen carefully. If we are going to save Dalton, I need all of you to help. You may think what we are going to do is strange, but Dalton is very sick and you must trust me."

Her assumption of command met no resistance. Members of the family gladly stepped forward in turn to receive orders. To the father, "Do you have a well? No? Then dip buckets of water from the irrigation ditch and haul it to wherever you boil the clothes."

To C.L., the next oldest son, "Go bring me your mother's biggest wash tub and put it here on the floor."

To Ella and her sisters, "Help your pa split armloads of dry wood to make a hot fire under the wash boiler. I want gallons and gallons of boiling water."

To Harry Hollingsworth, "Bring in small, dry kindling to the cook stove. I want some hot water as fast as possible."

To Mrs. Irby, "Find me a clean wool blanket that you don't care will shrink because we have to pour boiling water on it." Then she sent one of the girls to the barn to fetch a milking stool, placed it smack 'dab in the middle of the tub and poured boiling water around it.

"Undress him," she told Harry.

"Open all the windows and doors," she told the father. He looked at her as though she were crazy, but only for a moment. When the windows and door were opened, wind blew fresh snowflakes into the cabin.

She asked Harry to help steady the boy, wrapped a wool blanket around the lad's skinny frame and commenced pouring hot water over it, so water dripped down into the tub. By now it was freezing inside the house and everybody was very uncomfortable. At any attempt to close a window to cut out a draft she would yell, "Air, we need lots and lots of air. Air, Air."

Dalton whimpered and protested; he just wanted to sleep.

"I don't want you to sleep. I want you to breathe this fresh air as deeply as you can." She reached repeatedly beneath the wet blankets and thumped his chest and back hard, trying to dislodge the phlegm that was threatening to fill his lungs. Harry Hollingsworth was miserable, soaked and cold as he steadied Dalton on the milking stool. The cabin filled with steam mixed with snowflakes. The only creature who wasn't suffering was Doc Susie's dog, snoozing behind the cookstove.

Susie asked the boy if he had been constipated. He said he was. She turned to his father, "Which do you sell, milk or butter?"

"Butter."

"What does your family drink?"

"Milk skimmed from the separator."

"No wonder this boy has pneumonia. It's a miracle all of your children aren't sick from drinking nothing but skim milk. You're taking away most of the vitamins when you separate out the butter to sell and give them that stuff. It's nothing but blue water. Give it to the hogs. Save some rich, whole milk for your children. They're worth more than cows."

She kept Dalton's attention by talking about fishing, about baseball, about how he would probably bag his first

bull elk this fall. She made the drowsy youth answer her
and give sensible replies to her questions. She talked guns,
fishing lures, anything to try to interest him, then thumped
him hard on the chest. She told him about her brother
John's adventures, how John rode his bicycle all the way
down the coast of California from San Francisco to the village of Los Angeles. Her patient brightened to hear of
such a fine adventure. She didn't tell him that John was
dead.

Everybody in the family was busy: bringing hot water,
pouring it over the blankets, taking away the tepid water—
and trying to stay warm. From time to time the Irby parents would look at each other and shake their heads. Once
Mrs. Irby said, "Are you sure? I never seen anything like
this before. . ."

Doc Susie answered curtly, "If you want to save him, do
it my way. If you want to bury him, I'll leave." They said
no more.

In that cold, terrible hour just before the sun comes up,
Dr. Susan Anderson looked at her patient and saw the sign
she was hoping for. Little drops of sweat popped out on
Dalton's forehead. Soon, rivulets of perspiration ran into
his eyebrows and down his cheeks. She stuck a thermometer in his mouth. His temperature was dropping. First to
103, then 101.5, finally to below 98.6. On the last reading
she held the glass tube triumphantly in the air and cheered,
"We did it. He's going to be all right now. You'll see."

Finally, she allowed them to close the windows, dry
Dalton off, and put him back on the cot with just one
flannel sheet covering him. She sat beside him in a homemade willow rocking chair. The emergency over, Papa Irby
took C.L. and Harry out to help milk the cows. Mama
Irby made toast from her good homemade bread and
scrambled some eggs which everyone ate heartily. Then one
by one, children, parents and Harry plopped down wherever they could, and slept.

Doc Susie sat, only half asleep. She looked at the boy,
and was relieved to note that now the only face she saw was

covered with Dalton Irby's scruffy chin hairs. She was glad
of that. But the sound of a rooster, crowing in the distance,
somehow triggered thoughts of her diary:

> *John sick pneumonia . . . John died at 6:15 p.m. . . .
> suffered all a mortal can . . . happy he died uncon-
> scious of his pain. . . . Poor baby is so sweet at
> rest. . . . John buried today . . . gone from sight but
> not far away. . . . I seem to feel that he is near me &
> knows all the troubles & how I feel. . . . Life so useless
> & in vain. No one now cares much whether I live or die.
> John was my best friend on earth & now my best friend
> is in heaven.*

Her face was buried in her hands while she suffered the old
agony. But when she opened her eyes she saw that this boy,
Dalton Irby, wasn't in heaven. He was breathing regularly
and normally, here in his bed; he was going to live to grow
his beard and bag his first bull elk.

She dozed again, peacefully now, and when she awoke
an unnaturally bright light streamed in the window. Rubbing her eyes she stood up, stepped out the door and was
nearly blinded. She had forgotten about last night's storm,
but now the sun reflected across the stubble of hay meadows covered with autumn's first fresh snow.

She pulled on a sweater and stepped outside. Papa Irby
was splitting wood. He looked up to ask, "How is he?"

"Shouldn't wonder but what he'll want chicken and
dumplings for dinner." She looked a little ill at ease.

Pa Irby asked, "Can I help you?"

She glanced up toward the hill, and spotted what she
was looking for. "No. I just need to shed a few tears," she
said as she made her way toward the privy. Papa Irby
smiled. She had a way of saying things.

When Susie came back she checked Dalton again, then
poured herself a cup of coffee from the back of the stove
and gave Mrs. Irby a serious lecture about the Vitamin A
carried in the fat of whole milk, about protein, fresh

fruits, brown bread, vegetables and minerals. The woman listened carefully. Doc reached into her medical bag, took out a few brown pills and gave them to Mrs. Irby, telling her when to give them to Dalton. And she told her she must check regularly to be sure nobody in her family was constipated, fortifying the advice with a bottle of cod liver oil to be administered to the whole family immediately.

"I'm going home now. Dalton will be all right, but I will look in on him tomorrow. Just keep him quiet for a few days if you can. If he runs any more fever, send for me immediately."

Mr. Irby appeared at the cabin door. "I'll hitch the horse. . . ."

"No," said Susie. "I want to walk home. I know I ought to be tired, but I'm not." She packed the last of her gear. Just before she lifted the latch to leave she turned to the Irbys. "Isn't it glorious to be alive?"

Pa Irby pulled an old bandana out of his pocket and noisily blew his nose in an unsuccessful attempt to hide his tears. He looked toward Dalton, sleeping as peacefully as a baby. "Such a good boy," he said. "Thank you." He slipped a half dollar into her hand.

"Thank you." She hated to take it, knowing the Irbys needed it. But she respected their considerable pride. She whistled to her dog, lifted her medical bag and stepped out into the splendid sunlight. As they walked away from the Irby place, the dog gleefully dashed about in the fluffy new snow, running ahead, doubling back to kneel playfully on his front legs. When they were out of sight of the house, Doc Susie dropped her bag and ran at the dog, throwing fluffy snow into the spitz's face. She laughed and laughed, chasing him, skidding sideways in the slushy snow and jumping as lightly as a child.

"He's going to live! We're going to live! We beat the reaper."

On the way to her shack, she stopped by the depot and filled out a Western Union blank. "Pa. Stop. Have decided to make Fraser my home. Stop. Love Susie. Stop." The agent read it and smiled.

"Now you know messages are supposed to be confidential. You are officially forbidden to read and understand them," she teased. "I want to listen to you send this, to be sure you've got it right."

"Would you like to send it yourself?" The agent knew she had learned Morse code.

"By golly I would." She slipped into the agent's cage.

"Tap, tap, tapatatpatatap." She grinned as she hit the key with growing confidence. Finished, she paid the agent a quarter. He smiled at her from beneath his green eyeshade. "I'm sure glad you're staying, Doc Susie."

She looked him in the eye, "I came here to die, but since I didn't get the job done, I guess I'll just have to *live* here instead."

CHAPTER 6

Life in Lapland

Through that winter, more and more people banged on Doc Susie's door, summoning her to tend the ill and injured. She no longer worked at Warners' store because she couldn't promise Cora that when she came to work she would be able to stay.

In a tentative concession to Twentieth Century progress, Doc Susie had a telephone installed in her shack. Anderson, Susan, M.D. was the first name on a page-long list posted next to the phone in lieu of a phone book. People responded to a pattern of rings. To contact Doc, a caller turned a crank to ring a bell twice, "two longs." Other people on the line responded to as many as five varied rings. All twenty-five subscribers were on the same party line and everybody heard each other's rings. If the constant ringing wasn't annoyance enough, the phone soon became a community listening post, bad business for a doctor whose contacts had to remain confidential. Subscribers were on their honor to keep track of their calls and pay ten cents for each. That was a stiff tariff in the days when the best-paid logger made only twenty-five cents an hour.

Before long, she had the phone taken out and she never owned another one. She knew that if anyone needed her badly enough, they would get word to her. Most of her patients lived in the forest or on ranches where decades would pass before phone lines would be installed. Usually, when she was needed somebody came and got her. She never owned her own horse or an automobile.

Although she wasn't getting rich, her reputation was spreading. The Swedish lumberjacks loved her and accepted her at once. Many had migrated to Colorado from camps in the Pacific Northwest where medical care was all but unavailable. Behind them they had left too many of their friends buried beneath giant redwoods, dead from injuries they might have survived had a doctor been available.

One summer morning as Doc Susie clucked to her chickens while she gathered eggs, she heard a horse coming up the road on a dead run. She looked up to see a lad, not more than 14, riding bareback on one of the gigantic skid horses used to drag trees out of the forest. His skinny legs seemed to stick straight out, too short to wrap around the massive horse's girth. He reined the animal sharply in front of her door, dramatically raising a cloud of dust, and shouted, "Dr. Anderson, Dr. Anderson! You've got to come to Lapland. Elof Nielsen hurt his arm up St. Louis Creek when a tree fell wrong. There's a bone sticking out of it. They're bringing him down to Lapland."

She was always just a little amused at the heroic way most messengers entered her life. Screaming, yelling, impressed with the importance of summoning a physician on an emergency call, almost every courier seemed to have rehearsed his or her entrance; a message just wasn't worth delivering if the speaker didn't shout the lines breathlessly at the top of the voice. But she noted that the horse wasn't lathered, so the lad had apparently obeyed its owner's injunction to walk to Fraser; a good skid horse was worth a lot of money. Swedes were somewhat cheaper.

But there was no doubting the urgency of his summons. Lapland was one of the temporary lumber camps up St. Louis Creek, one of the busier logging locations that summer. Doc Susie told the boy to go over to George Smith's livery and drayage and get a horse or a buggy or whatever was available while she assembled her supplies. A compound fracture would be a painful, mean thing to treat. She would have to stay with her patient long enough to see him out of shock, and that might require a couple of days in the forest. But she didn't mind, the St. Louis Creek basin was lush and green this time of year. Besides there was a new boss man up there named Ben Jones, a good looking fellow who had flirted with her at a dance two weeks before.

Presently, the boy reappeared leading a horse hitched to a small trap. She loaded her black bag, a valise containing personal items, a couple of bundles of dressings, some smallpox vaccination serum she had just received and her dental kit. She knew that the injured man would not be her only patient. When she visited a lumber camp, sufferers took advantage of her presence to save themselves a trip to town.

Doctor, boy and her white dog headed southwest out of town on a road that was rough and seasonal. But it didn't have to be very good because most of the logs from the St. Louis Creek basin were floated to the Fraser mill in a V-shaped flume, supported by an X-shaped brace into which water had been diverted from the creek.

"Good morning," she called out when she met one of the mounted flume riders who constantly patrolled the flow of logs, poking with a cant hook to break up log jams. Some of the flume riders were women because the strength needed to nudge a log back into the current wasn't great and the job didn't pay very well. In places her buggy wheels bumped over "corduroy road," where logs had been laid to keep wagon wheels from sinking into the marsh.

She headed toward Byers Peak, whose series of gentle shoulders rise out of the forest and climb above timberline to define the western side of the Fraser Valley. Along the road the yellow sweet peas called golden banner were fading, and blue lupines, white yarrow and wild roses bloomed in their stead. In damp, shady aspen groves blue columbines flowered against the white of aspen bark. Next to Indiana roses, they were her favorite flower.

She came upon some children playing in the flume. They had built themselves little boats to float when no logs were in sight. With sleeves rolled up they happily dipped into the flume water which was a few crucial degrees warmer than the icy creek behind them. She waved and called, "Mind you, I don't want to catch any of you joy-riding on those logs in the flume."

"Not us Dr. Anderson." She realized her warnings would probably be in vain. Most children ventured to sit astride a log and ride at least once. It was dangerous, and although most of them got away with only bruises and scrapes, others came to her to have broken clavicles set and bleeding lips stitched.

As the road took her higher into the basin, the trees gradually became larger. The thin lodgepole pines—used to make telephone poles, fence posts and railroad ties—gave way to immense Englemann spruce and Douglas fir trees. Although small when compared to redwoods of Washington and Oregon, these Colorado giants were sought after by lumberjacks for sawing into dimensional lumber. She hated to see these ancients come crashing to the earth, destroying virgin groves, just so city people could order their board feet of lumber.

As she drove through one particularly dark thicket the hypnotic pattern of alternating sunshine and shade caused her to doze. Her gentle mare contentedly followed the boy's skid horse so there was no particular need to rein the animal. She awoke with a start when a limb brushed her forehead. That brushing motion barely grazed her hair, but it sent goose bumps shivering down her arms and legs. Suddenly awake, she decided to shake her sense of foreboding with a little target practice. To help relieve the boredom of long rides, rural doctors often resorted to shooting. As she pulled a .38 Iver/Johnson revolver from her doctor's bag, the boy showed interest.

"Got to keep my aim steady." She pointed to a large aspen tree. Eye-shaped scars, where aspen limbs had been shed during the growth cycle, made excellent targets. "See that big tree over there?"

Bang. The boy saw bark fly loose from the center of the tree. "By golly!" said the lad. "You're good."

She then pointed to some survey flags that had been tied to a tree limb. Bang, bang. Her shots riddled the fabric. But bullets cost money, so she never practiced longer than it took to satisfy herself that her aim was still true.

Like most boys, her guide liked guns. He reined his horse back and rode next to her. She showed him another gun she carried, a smaller five-shot Iver/Johnson. "Tell you something," she said. "There are two things I'm really afraid of. One of them is mountain lions."

"Yeah," said the boy. "Last week I seen a couple of them. Saw a mama and her cub and boy did I high-tail it outa there. I'm skeered of them myself. What's the other one?"

"Dope fiends. You never know where you'll find a dope fiend. I never keep any dope. No morphine, no opium, no laudanum, no cocaine. Better to have a doctor without dope than no doctor at all. Back in Cripple Creek, dope fiends broke into my house a couple of times. Doctors have been killed by people out to get that stuff. Me, I can't fight off a big man that's trying to get at dope. Or a woman, either. I've seen women having the cravings till they're clear off their heads. Whiskey's bad enough, but there's nothing a fiend won't do to get his dope. Anybody ever asks you, you tell them Doc Susie doesn't carry dope in her bag **or** keep it in her house. No kind, never. Tell them I do carry a gun and I can shoot."

At long last, guide and doctor arrived at Lapland. As they entered the rough camp the boy's dramatic flair returned and he flapped his reins against the horse's flank and bellowed, "She's here. Doc Susie is here!"

From behind the cook tent a couple of lumberjacks stepped forward to take her horse. Children swung down from tree limbs and came out of hastily constructed log cabins. Women emerged from shacks and lean-tos, wiping their hands on their aprons and waving to her. Her arrival was an event.

Lifting the flap of a wall tent was someone she knew; it was Axel Bergstrom, the Swede who had a cinder in his eye on that first train trip from Denver.

"Hello Axel. Not working for Billy Woods anymore?"

"Naw. He get a bad cook. Bunch of us quit." She knew that men who shoveled in food at two to three times the rate of ordinary workmen set more store by an outfit's grub than by its wages; sometimes even one unsatisfactory meal could cause a lumberjack to tell the boss, "Make 'er out," meaning he wanted his check. An unscrupulous logging boss would lure a good cook from a competitor, just so he could get the other man's entire crew in the bargain.

Axel looked serious, "You gotta help my friend Elof. He's hurt awful bad. I got him here in the tent." He led her into the hot tent where light shone brightly through the white canvas. The wall tent was used for a bunk house and smelled strongly of new canvas, neat's-foot oil used to waterproof gear, and sweaty underwear.

She hadn't met Elof before; he was probably new. He looked to be about thirty years old, and until today was probably as strong as the oxen used to pull logs out of the forest. From his upper lip sprang an inch-thick growth of flourishing moustache, bushy and so large Susie wondered how he ever curled that mass around the lip of a coffee mug. His pale gray eyes stared at some flies caught in the canvas above him. Doc Susie went to him, and took his good hand in hers. "Do you know who I am?"

"Ya, Doc Susie. I'm chur glad you come."

"You got yourself in a fix, yes?"

"Chur did. Tree, she fall da wrong way. Widow-maker hitted me." Doc knew that "widow-makers" were loose limbs, flying from a falling tree in no predictable fashion.

One of the men who had carried Elof from the forest had donated the undershirt from off his back, which was wrapped around the injured arm. Doc Susie removed it carefully to see that fragments of Elof's broken forearm were sticking at an awkward angle from his body. The shirt was soaked with blood; the bone, as well as nerves and flakes of skin, protruded from the flesh. After she had checked to be sure he was not losing too much blood, she put her hand on his forehead. He didn't seem to be feverish; if he had previously been in shock, that crisis had passed for the moment. As a precaution, she asked Axel to lift Elof's feet and put a log under them so they would be higher than his head. "Axel, I need your help. Will you assist me?"

"Me, missus? Don't you vant one of the vimmin?" His W's still all turned into V's, but his English was clearly improving.

"No, I need someone strong who won't faint. You know what faint means?"

"Ya, pass out cold like drunk."

"Well, something like that. Now go rustle me up some coffee and tell Mrs. Johnson in the cook shack and the other women to boil water for us."

"Dey do dat already. Efferybody know Doc Susie vant lota hot vater." She smiled, glad to know that people anticipated her orders.

The camp boss, Ben Jones, came in. Doc Susie greeted him expansively, reminded him of their encounter at the dance, but noted that he seemed nervous and ill at ease. He took her hand in welcome but she saw that his eyes wandered around the tent, looking at everything except the injured man. She understood at once that boss man Jones was squeamish when it came to the sight of blood; some people just never got used to it. "Do what you can for him Doc. He's a good man. Don't suppose he'll ever be able to work in the woods again." Just then, Axel came back into the tent, and Doc Susie saw his jaw stiffen at the sight of Jones.

She made a note to speak to Ben later about pessimistic bedside comments. She could also see the boss was relieved when she suggested he leave. She got busy at once, pulling a clean white apron from a sterile bundle, putting her hair in a turban and dropping clean rags into a kettle of water. Then she started washing her hands in a tin basin, telling Axel to do the same thing in another. Axel always kept himself clean, proud of his neat appearance and tidy gear. To survive the generally deplorable conditions in the lumber camp, he carried a little tent, spreading his bindle on the ground so he could sleep away from the other men. Lumberjacks washed rarely through the week, not minding being dirty, unshaven and even lousy. Cleaning up was a Saturday chore.

Axel washed his hands carefully, up nearly to the elbows. "Take off your shirt and your undershirt, too, Axel. I want you to wash clear to your armpits." He was surprised, but did as he was told. Shirtless, his musculature was as well defined as she had suspected that day on the train. His stark white arms were big around as telegraph poles and when he bent over the wash basin, pumping soapy water up and down his arms, his biceps rippled in sequence. Maybe Paul Bunyan stories got started with Swedes like Axel, she thought. She had rolled her own sleeves as high as decency allowed. She paid special attention to her fingernails, checking each one to assure herself there was no dirt underneath.

Her stint as a school teacher impelled her to teach people the whys of how she did things. "Axel, I can set this man's arm and sew him up. But if I don't clean everything very carefully, he's far more likely to die of germs than he is of getting hurt. If my hands are dirty, I might even put germs into the wound myself."

Axel's cheek twitched; he looked dubious. She continued, "In every drop of water there are thousands of little critters that you and I can't even see except through a microscope." She winked one eye shut, and pantomimed using a microscope. Axel seemed to know what she was talking about. "They're alive and trying to find warm, damp, dark places to hide. When Elof hurt his arm, little germs came right off the tree and he picked up more from the dirt where he fell on the ground, and from this undershirt which isn't very clean. Did you know that germs make pus? You know about pus?"

His wrinkled nose showed that he did, and he looked thoughtful. Little creatures in drops of water had never occurred to him. And he had never tried to figure out what made pus. Now Doc Susie turned to her patient and fingered his collar, "You've been wanting a new shirt, haven't you Elof?"

He nodded, trying to be agreeable, and she realized he didn't understand what she meant until she took out a sharp little pair of scissors from her bag and carefully cut Elof's shirt away from his arm. "Ya, I tink I want a red one." Poor fellow, he was trying to show good humor through his ordeal. Axel gently removed what was left of Elof's shirt, then helped Doc Susie wash his friend's torso thoroughly.

As they moved closer to the wound, Doc Susie sniffed Elof's breath. She looked up at Axel who said, "I give him big dose of whiskey, missus."

"I wish you hadn't done that. But don't give him any more until I say you can."

Doc Susie looked down at Elof, "You know much English?"

"Chust a little." She told Axel to speak to his friend in Swedish and to translate Elof's replies for her. She needed for Axel to explain that she had no painkiller to give her patient, that Elof would have to grit it out. The patient nodded, trustingly. Although she was uncomfortably hot, she was grateful to have the good light that radiated through the white canvas of the tent.

She poured hot water over the wound again and again, irrigating it into a basin. She picked carefully around the exposed bone, looking for dirt, tree bark, lint from the shirt, anything that didn't belong there.

"You OK?" she asked Axel. She was glad to see that her assistant had survived the shock of working with Elof's terrible wound and was absorbed in the task of bringing hot water and emptying wash basins. Axel watched her every move, fascinated. She told him how to turn Elof on his side so she could work on the wound from a different angle. The only time her patient winced was when she poured on iodine. These Swedes had a reputation for being stoic; it was well deserved. But sometimes she wondered whether some of the Greeks and Italians she had treated, who howled, wept and cursed at their pain, weren't better off. She didn't think they drank as much whiskey later.

She sent Axel off to round up some extra hands to help set the bone, and to tell them to wash up. When she stepped from the tent to explain the procedure, she smiled to see that her assistants looked more as if they were ready to row a Roman galley than to assist in setting an arm; Axel had made them all strip to the waist, too. She explained to the lumberjacks how she was going to pull the bone back into Elof's arm and then position it to join together again. She told each of them where he was to stand, and made sure they understood what she meant when she said "Pull, twist left, twist right, and relax." She was glad to have the men, because without them she might not be able to set the bone properly. To retract the bone far enough to ease it into position was going to require some brute strength. She smiled when she looked at their scruffy beards and burly backs. These were just the brutes to get the job done.

When they all came into the tent, Elof's eyes showed that he knew what was going to happen next. She ex-

plained through Axel that she was going to knock him out
for a few minutes. She took a small bottle from her bag
and at arm's length poured a little ether onto a pad. She
placed the pad over Elof's nose and said, "Look for the
gold balls, Elof." His eyes rolled up into his head.

As the men began to pull Elof's arm in accordance with
her orders, she checked her patient to be sure that he was
still unconscious. She snapped out commands to the men.
"Don't worry about pulling too hard. Retract, retract." It
did not take long to realign the bones in Elof's arm.

When Elof opened his eyes, his arm was straight again
and he could no longer see the bone. Doc Susie was pulling
a curved needle through his arm, stitch by stitch, and had
sent Axel to round up cardboard boxes from the cook and
find shims in the tool shed to fashion into a cast.

As she stitched, she was singing: "There'll be a hot time,
in the old town, tonight." Somehow, the cheerful song in a
half-understood language comforted the suffering man.

"Is dat a baby song?"

"No," she said. "It's a dancing tune." Elof managed a
little grin. By now it was midafternoon, and very hot in the
tent. Doc Susie had unbuttoned the top of her shirtwaist as
far as she dared; she was perspiring and thought her back
would break from leaning over the injured man. The oily
smell of canvas intensified with the heat.

One of the women sent in a venison sandwich; after
sniffing it for freshness, she consumed it ravenously. Her
guide had stood by, anxious to help; she ordered the boy to
kill all of the flies he could reach, and to keep the tent as
free from them as possible.

Together, Doc Susie and Axel managed to construct a
solid splint for Elof's arm. She tied it firmly in place, then
checked his pulse, heartbeat and temperature. All were
normal. She was grateful for his strong young body and
robust health. "Tell him I will stay here at Lapland tonight."

Elof said something in Swedish to Axel. "Elof wants to
know when you are going to cut his arm off."

Doc Susie chuckled, took the man's good hand in hers and smiled straight into his wide gray eyes. Slowly, so Axel could translate, she said, "Your arm will be a little shorter than the other one, and until it heals it will hurt a great deal. The rest of the summer you will have to help the cook or be a flume rider. But I guarantee that by winter you will be strong enough that you can be a faller again, and swing any kind of ax." Elof smiled and slept.

She removed her bloody apron, let her hair fall out of her turban and stepped out of the tent—her hand on the small of her back because it hurt so much. The intense afternoon sunlight made her blink and sneeze. Her sneeze seemed to send a signal because suddenly she heard music. The lumberjacks had assembled a camp band for her bene- fit: a guitar, a fiddle, a concertina, a harmonica and a washtub base. The tune was a lively schottische.

The still shirtless Axel grabbed her waist and whirled her around a flat, dusty space in front of the cook tent. Delighted, she giggled and said, "Whoopie!" The lumber- jacks roared, pleased with her enthusiastic response. The few women in camp were quickly claimed for partners, but lack of a member of the opposite sex didn't stop the lum- berjacks who hooked arms with each other and charged about in their cleated boots. Children danced with each other and one little boy picked up Susie's dog by his front paws and they danced, too. By now, other lumberjacks were coming in from the woods, grabbing instruments and partners. "Put your little foot," polkas, "Daisy, Daisy," foxtrots. There were Scandinavian songs and dances, Irish jigs and "Sweet Betsy from Pike." Discreetly out of sight, because they knew Doc Susie disapproved, some of the lumberjacks were passing a jug. She knew they were doing it, but didn't say anything.

Ben Jones appeared to claim a dance. In contrast to the exuberant lumberjacks fresh from the forest and redolent of perspiration, Ben wore a necktie and vest, looking as though he had just slicked himself up to go to town. Even his thin moustache looked freshly trimmed.

Doc thought to herself, "I ought to be very, very tired but I've never felt so well."

"You are the most interesting woman," said Ben. "I like the way you walk. You carry yourself so straight, like a little queen."

"How about my dancing?"

"Play us a waltz," he shouted.

With his arm around her slender waist he told her how very happy he was that she came to help, although it was terrible how Elof had been so careless as to get himself hurt in the woods.

"Elof wasn't careless," she replied. "That tree got careless when it refused to fall the way you ordered it to." Ben laughed. He wasn't able to keep her as a partner for long. Lumberjacks claimed dances as Doc whirled from man to man.

When the musicians struck up one of their tunes, Doc Susie stopped in her tracks to listen. "Why, they are playing Chopin!" She was surprised to hear a classical piece. She asked the man with the fiddle, "Where did you learn that song?"

"Oh, in the old country."

"Did you know it is a famous sonata by Frederic Chopin?"

"Naw, just sometink my uncle learned me."

Chopin in the woods. Well, now she could boast that her lumberjacks had some culture.

Finally, Mrs. Johnson rang her triangle, summoning the lumberjacks to supper. Families went to their own lean-tos and tents; the bachelors trooped into a big wall tent. Ben Jones, tucking Doc Susie's hand onto his arm, steered her to a long table covered with oil cloth, a neat row of upside down mugs ran the length of it. Axel looked disappointed; perhaps he had hoped to be her dinner companion and had to settle for sitting opposite her. As the food arrived, she smiled, "You were right, Axel. Mrs. Johnson spreads a fine feed." Doc Susie had been in cook shacks where flapjacks were nailed to tent poles to protest the poor quality of the food.

Not a big eater, Susie's dainty manners made the men suddenly aware of their usual "grab it and growl" behavior. It was difficult for them to show restraint in the face of roast pork, sauerkraut, mashed potatoes, fresh bread, and stewed tomatoes. For dessert, Mrs. Johnson had baked beautiful cherry pies made from canned fruit. "I can see that I had better check Elof frequently," she said with a wink to Mrs. Johnson after the meal. The woman glowed with pleasure. "Dat chur was good," was the most elaborate compliment she ever received from the lumberjacks.

"Oh," said Mrs. Johnson modestly, "if you give them enough gravy, they'll eat anything."

Susie had been invited to spend the night with the Willhite family, so Ben Jones walked her the short distance to their log-walled, canvas-roofed home in the woods. "I hope you didn't mind the boys kicking up their heels a bit this afternoon."

"I loved it." Suddenly tired, she said, "I think I'll turn in. It's been a long, long day."

A hanging blanket marked the only privacy between the Willhite parents and their children. On the children's side Estelle, the oldest daughter, had to surrender her cot for Dr. Anderson to sleep on but she didn't care. It was an honor to brag to the other kids the next day that Doc Susie had slept in *her* bed. Everybody fell into the sack when the sun went down, which was nearly nine o'clock so close to summer solstice. As Doc Susie pulled her nightgown from her valise she said, "Now children, pull the covers over your head and hide your eyes while I put my nightie on." Obediently, they covered their eyes until she slipped into bed. They were secretly hoping that she might tell them a story, or describe something gory, and were disappointed when she immediately fell asleep.

The next morning Doc Susie was very happy to see Elof sitting up and demanding flapjacks and cackleberries for breakfast. So she went back to join Hattie Willhite for toast and coffee. Women of the camp, delighted by Doc Susie's presence in the woods, dropped by to visit. Life was rough for wives who packed up their children and followed their husbands into the forest. Each day the women were forced to tote water in buckets from the nearest creek for drinking, cooking, washing clothes and bathing. All of their food had to be hauled up from town; since the lumber company usually charged outrageously for freight, they tried to order as little as possible between family supply trips. Cooking was done over an open fire or, if the wife were lucky, on a small sheepherder's stove or atop a converted oil barrel.

Although tough for mothers, life in the woods was pure heaven for children. Kids were allowed to roam and romp, wade in the creeks, hunt for bird nests, sneak rides atop logs in the flumes. It made some women feel better to see their little ones enjoying youthful freedom before they accepted the drudgery of the workaday world.

Sunday was a day off for the men. The bachelors usually left on Saturday night to spend their week's wages in a saloon. But married men often used the day to poach a deer. A haunch of venison could feed a family for ten days or so if it didn't rot. Although officially illegal, the hunters had little to fear from game wardens who were rarer around logging camps than "a curly headed Swede"; no one could ever remember seeing one. The problem of how to preserve venison was frequently solved by digging a hole next to the creek, lining it with boards to frame a small locker and hanging the meat in it. Then planks were put on top of the pit and water diverted over it. The stream, running about 34 degrees owing to its proximity to the glacier from whence it sprang, kept the meat very nicely. Children of those days, now grandparents, swear they became so tired of venison that they never ate it again if they had a choice.

Worse than their limited diet and hard work was the loneliness women suffered in the woods. Their men labored from dawn until nightfall, returning at twilight with just enough energy left to wash up and chow down before collapsing into bed. The camp resounded to the snores of big men, sleeping the deep sleep of exhaustion. Left to tend the children and provide the basics of living, women were starved for gossip. Doc Susie's arrival in camp brought relief in that department. She circulated through the camps and town spreading news, and although she never violated a professional confidence she was ready to share news about who was spooning, who was having trouble with their kids, who was moving away.

Little William Joseph Willhite, Jr., known even then as Bud, sat on the ground in front of the women as they drank coffee and basked in the morning sunshine. The child studiously poured dirt and pine needles from one tin can into another, his neglected nose streaming from the effects of a mild cold. His mother was an experienced hand whose success was evidenced by four older children; in the process, the importance of a dribbling nose had been considerably downgraded. But Doc noticed and said, "Sonny, blow your nose."

Little Bud looked up thoughtfully, sniffed mightily and noisily, then said, "I blowed it up!"

Doc Susie sputtered in her coffee cup, laughing so hard she held her sides. "I blowed it up!" she repeated, over and over.

She looked pensively from the child to his mother, "I would hate it if nobody ever called me *mother*" she said. Unsure how to reply, Hattie ducked into the cabin for more coffee.

Soon patients came looking for Doc Susie. "Doc Susie. I haf had a tooth hurt for two weeks." In the woods, dentists were even scarcer than veterinarians. Often her biggest problem was trying to figure out which tooth to pull because people could not pinpoint the pain. Some folks said she pulled the wrong ones occasionally, but with no X-ray to guide her mistakes were inevitable. Nobody held it against her. Occasionally, the patient himself would have to provide the final yank to extract a molar when she couldn't manage enough leverage to budge it.

Doc Susie always made it a point to examine the babies and young children in camp to be sure that they were developing properly. She lectured women on nutrition and insisted that fresh milk be made available. Some camps kept cows, others had goats. Because she had never seen a child at the breast suffer from a nutritional deficiency, she encouraged women to nurse their babies as long as possible.

There was nothing she could do for children allergic to mosquito and gnat bites. She urged their mothers to give them hot "sody" baths, despite the difficulty of hauling water; the soda water immersion soothed the itching. She knew the tykes would eventually outgrow their sensitivity, but she felt sorry for them, the way they scratched until their sores became infected. Huge pus-filled sores caused by impetigo were also a constant problem, not restricted to children. She had seen big Swedes with impetigo sores in their beards, men who protested mightily when she ordered their whiskers off and generous layers of gentian violet on.

To children whose ailments were minor, Doc Susie symbolized stinging iodine and castor oil, neither of which was pleasant. But children who were chronically ill or broke bones would remember her as a kind person. Some people accused her of liking sick children better than healthy ones.

Whenever she had a supply of serum, she took it to the camps and vaccinated children against smallpox. Sometimes their mothers wondered if the huge sores produced by vaccinations weren't worse than the disease. To overcome their resistance, Doc Susie told them lurid but true tales about people with pox and scars all over their bodies, about mining camps filled with dead people. There are still plenty of Doc Susie vaccination scars on the arms of Fraser's oldest residents, but the town never suffered an epidemic.

A woman shyly brought her tiny baby so Doc could look at its herniated navel. Doc examined the baby, cooed over how cute he was, got the mother's confidence and then said, "When was this baby born?"

"Last month."

"Why didn't you call me?"

The woman turned bright red, and admitted that she had delivered the baby herself because her husband was out of work after being injured and they had no money. Doc gave her the standard lecture that she had first given the Knutsons, threatening the parents with jail if they didn't call her when the next baby came, then taped the baby's navel so its abdomen would form properly. But she eased the rebuke by lingering, kissing the baby's little toes, gaining his mother's trust. How grateful Doc was that the Knutsons had sent for her when their second baby was born; fortunate because he had difficulty breathing during his first few hours.

As she handed the baby back to his mother, Doc heard some children giggling and saw one pointing at her spitz: "Your dog's trying to go in the woods," said a freckle-faced little boy, tugging at Doc's skirt. It was becoming a joke around Fraser that in spite of Doc's wonderful medical skills she had been completely unable to cure her own dog of constipation. The children were laughing, imitating how the animal sat down and pulled its hind end along the grass with its front paws. Doc was aware that most people thought her little spitz was something of a pain in the neck, but she loved him and didn't care.

"Don't worry, I'll give him something for that," she told the children, briskly.

While in camp, she made it her business to check the privies. She wanted to assure herself that they were not sitting upstream from where people drew drinking water, that plenty of lime was available and in use and that a basic level of cleanliness was being maintained. While the men were off working in the woods, she took a self-appointed inspection tour. When she emerged from the privy area, Ben Jones stepped out from behind a tree and grabbed the startled woman around the waist. "You sure do stick your nose into everything," he chuckled as he hugged her, so tightly that it hurt her ribs.

"Ouch," she said. Pulling herself free she turned to him. "You'll thank me for it when your crew doesn't come down with typhoid."

"Typhoid, clear up here in the woods? Look down at that stream. The water is as pure as the driven snow," he said.

"Fiddlesticks, that water was pure just until it came to the first place where a horse defecated in the stream or someone rinsed a deer carcass. I lived through several typhoid epidemics back in Cripple Creek, and I never want to see another one. Don't worry, your situation looks pretty good. It's well away from the stream."

"Good. I pay men to cut trees, not to dig holes." Ben Jones looked just a little less playful as his steely eyes met hers. "You are here to treat a broken arm. And that is all."

He was new in these parts. Perhaps he hadn't heard that she could make things rough on a boss who resisted her orders. The Swedes had a way of getting real stubborn and work went slower than a team of oxen headed uphill when Doc's suggestions were ignored. For the sake of a friendship she hoped might develop she was glad that she wouldn't have to rag Ben about the location of the privies. Although she liked to be hugged, she wondered why he squeezed so tightly.

Early in the evening, Doc finished treating patients and checked Elof one more time. He was recovering very nicely, but she delivered a stern warning to take it easy. She promised to return in a couple of days; she needed to get back to Fraser before it got dark.

"You sure you want to start back so late missus?" asked Axel.

"I'd better get George Smith's horse back to him. He might need her."

"You be careful. All da horses been actin' up, dey got bad nerves. Somethin's botherin' dem."

It was later than she had planned to start, but the horse

knew the way back to the corral. Doc slacked the reins and gave the mare her head.

Tired, as usual, and a little lonesome now that the camp was out of sight and the road was so deserted, she hugged her dog for comfort. As the twilight faded into darkness, she realized just how late it was. Driving along, she sang a little song to reassure herself, "I'm afraid to go home in the dark."

She was feeling moderately brave when, from not too far off, came a terrible yowl. The hair on her dog's neck stood straight up and he snarled, looking off into the woods. The skin on the back of Doc Susie's neck tightened, too; goose bumps on her arms felt as big as goose eggs. She was breathing quickly and her horse was shying, sidling off to her right with every step.

Then she heard it again—a squalling sound, like a scream, even closer. She couldn't tell how far away the animal was but she and the horse got the same idea simultaneously. Nearby was a hungry mountain lion with fresh meat on his mind.

So intent was she on listening that she wasn't paying much attention to the road ahead. Suddenly something brushed her hat right off her head. "Yow-eee," she screamed, "He's got me!"

The horse took off at a gallop. Susie pulled at the reins, holding onto the buggy seat for dear life. So sudden was the horse's movement that the dog fell off the seat and was yapping along behind the buggy. Convinced that a mountain lion was after her—would grab her dog and eat him and then go after herself or the horse—Susie reached into her bag, pulled out her .38 and fired it twice into the dark trees above her.

It was many seconds before she realized that the only thing that had "attacked" her was the overhanging limb she had encountered the morning before. Little matter, she pulled her dog up into the buggy by the scruff on his neck, slapped the mare's reins across her back and off they went on a bumpy, wild ride to town. Emerging from the dark forest into open meadow land helped, but her heart was still knocking against the wall of her chest. She knew that if she stood up her legs would buckle under her.

When she pulled into the drayage, George Smith was alarmed at her pale face, her wild loose hair and the condition of his quivering, lathered horse. When she told him what had happened, he nodded his head gravely, "Next time I'll take you."

Not until Susie had collected her bag and dog and was safely home did she realize that the only serious danger to her person was caused by her own nerves, and by the foolishness of running a horse over uneven ground in the dark. But when she crawled into bed she muffled her pillow over her ears because the sound of that lion's screaming echoed all night long.

CHAPTER 7

A Roof Like in Indiana

When a big Ford automobile pulled up at Doc Susie's house she left her washboard in mid scrub. The automobile wasn't on the road; instead, it came to a halt on the railroad tracks. She had seen such cars before, flanged wheels installed instead of tires so the car could be driven on the rails. Generally such vehicles were the transportation of choice for railroad executives who rode the rails on inspection trips, or took prospective investors sightseeing. Amid the standard racket set up by her rooster and dog, a bona fide Big Shot appeared at the door. Impressively portly, he wore a pin-striped suit, vest, a necktie, and a look of annoyance because a handful of cinders had poured into his city shoes when he slipped down the slope from the level of the roadbed to Doc Susie's front gate.

Almost immediately, neighborhood children hung on her fence gaping at the expensive car, curious to know what kind of a man actually got to drive an automobile that needed no steering wheel.

The man's self-important air softened a little as he sized up Doc's shack, which looked more like a gypsy's caravan than a dwelling. It was so small that she had been forced to hang many of her belongings on its outer walls: snowshoes, washtubs, tools. Several other little shacks had sprung up around it to serve as storage for her beloved salvage. In the midst of the clutter stood Doc herself, dressed appropriately for a woman who was laundering bandages. She held her small hands in front of her, and shook water from them with a flourish, as though she were scrubbing for surgery rather than interrupting a session on the washboard. Ill at ease, the portly man removed his felt hat from his balding pate. His eyes, set closely together beneath thin eyebrows, refused to meet hers squarely.

"Are you Dr. Susan Anderson?"

"I am, but you knew that already."

"My name is W. R. Freeman, General Manager of the Denver and Salt Lake Railroad. Did you know that your house sits on the D&SL right-of-way?" In 1913 the official name of the railroad had been changed, but everybody still called it the Moffat Road.

"No. I don't know that. Nobody ever showed me a survey."

"Well, we don't think you are safe here, so you are going to have to move."

"Move? Where would I go? I can't afford to move."

"Don't you worry little lady. The D&SL means to be reasonable about this. We will hire a man and a wagon to cart your things. But you can't stay here. We're going to put an access road right through where your house sits." She could see that in his mind's eye a dusty road would be an improvement over her home.

"Are you going to pay me for my place?"

"The way we see it, since it was built on our right-of-way, the land already belongs to the D&SL. The house is yours."

If Freeman expected tears and protest from Susan Anderson, who was far more attractive than she had been described to him, he was disappointed. In the face of her stoic failure to respond, he babbled on, "Down in Denver, we appreciate it that you help a lot of people up here and we don't mean to make it tough on you. You've got some time to think it over, but you've gotta be outa here by next spring."

She remained silent, seeming to grow taller by the minute. He had come prepared to argue, not to recite a monologue. "Now if there's anything else we can do, just say so."

"You could make me the railroad doctor. That way you can furnish me a place to live, move me to Tabernash and pay me to look after your men."

He inhaled rapidly three times; Doc feared he might hyperventilate. She had seen many flatlanders try to compensate for the lack of oxygen at Fraser's high altitude by inhaling too frequently, overloading their brains with oxygen. To the untrained eye, symptoms of the condition were like a heart attack. The man was trying hard to act as though he hadn't heard what she said. It occurred to Susie that to Freeman she was a preposterous woman. The notion of giving her a respectable stipend to tend people she was already caring for had never been considered by the railroad management; the position of railroad doctor was reserved for well-connected young men who arrived in Tabernash and departed on a fairly predictable schedule—usually about the same time that they had gained some skill at their craft and people were learning to trust them. Gesturing that he couldn't keep his automobile parked any longer on the "main," the panting tycoon scrambled up the cinder embankment and jumped into his car.

"If you breathe into a paper bag for a few minutes, Mr. Freeman, you will feel better," she called after him. The flanged wheels on the Ford squealed faintly as they sped away, down the tracks toward Tabernash.

So that was the great William R. Freeman. She had

heard from the railroad men that Freeman was muscling his way into the company; some said he had taken great advantage of the confusion that resulted when David Moffat died while on a business trip to New York City, on March 18, 1911. Moffat had been trying to secure financing from Edward H. Harriman's bank. Harriman, President of the Union Pacific, had died in 1909. He had always perceived Moffat's railroad to be a threat to his empire although the two rail lines served vastly different areas. Even after his death, Harriman was able to thwart Moffat from his grave when Moffat's attempt to work out a deal fell through. Moffat died the same day, some said from a broken heart; others hinted darkly at suicide. Into the void stepped William R. Freeman. Every month Freeman seemed to gain more power, and stock, for himself.

Doc Susie had little time to reflect on Freeman's ultimatum that morning because she was summoned into the woods to treat a lumberjack. On such a beautiful morning in late June the thought of leaving the Fraser Valley seemed preposterous. Yet—she began to make a mental list of reasons why she might leave. Her tuberculosis symptoms had long since vanished. She hadn't been able to save much money, but it was enough to move and start a practice in a more hospitable climate.

Life was so very hard here in the Fraser Valley; although many people swore by her, there were others who swore at her, not trusting her as a doctor—probably because of the woman thing. She had noticed that fewer and fewer women were becoming doctors these days and that when people used the term "woman doctor," it was almost as though they were describing a freak. Her shack was so small that she couldn't examine patients there and was forced to conduct all of her business on house calls. From time to time she asked close friends if they thought she should leave.

But such thoughts were put away when she arrived at a place called the Bear Tree to work on the injured lumberjack, Pat Leonard. The father of a large family had been hacking mining ties with a broad ax and cut his knee, causing a serious wound. "Your Pa is going to have to stay down three, maybe four weeks," she told two of his young children, Jim and Edna. They knew what that meant—the family diet for the next month would be limited to any deer they could poach, and they were already heartily sick of venison.

On the way home, Doc Susie took a little detour into the neighboring Meadow Creek Valley to check on a child who had suffered from measles a couple of weeks earlier. She rode down a lane between buck and rider fences, made from slender lodgepole pines resting atop X-shaped supports. As she approached the ranch house its owner loped up on his big buckskin gelding.

When he spoke, a stem of timothy grass held between his teeth bounced up and down beneath his Stetson in rhythm to the horse's gait, "Doc, I'm selling my spread. Them measles was the last straw. The missus says it's too rough up here for her—she was afraid she'd lost the boy when he was so sick. Now she wants to be near her family in Ft. Collins. I feel pretty bad about it. Another year or two—it mighta worked out good."

Doc looked around. "I'm sorry. I know how much you wanted it." Ranchers were a tenacious breed, but making a living at 8,500 feet, where the growing season is so short that only one crop of hay can be harvested each summer, is a tough proposition. Susie looked toward his barnyard where a solid barn, dating from prerailroad days, stood amid extensive corrals. "I always admired your barn, one of the best around here. Too bad you have to leave it behind. They don't build nice barns like that since the lumber mills started up."

The rancher thought a bit. "Yup, it's a dandy. Don't suppose the new owner will want it. He's doing a cow/calf operation in the meadow, won't be putting up hay in the barn. Told me he might bust it up for firewood. Tell you what. I'll tell him I gave it to you to settle a bill. He won't care. Maybe you can move it some day."

Log buildings were frequently moved. The chore of se-

lecting the straightest tree trunks of the right length, hauling them out of the forest, peeling them and hewing them
to notch snugly at the corners was so exacting that it was
easier and cheaper to tear down an existing log structure
and move it than to build a new one. After the coming of
the railroad, when sawmills began spewing out boards, log
buildings were rarely built because they were too much
trouble.

Together, the rancher and Doc went into the barn,
walked around it, paced it off. Her quick eye told her that
the logs had suffered very little rot. She had seen quite a
few log buildings and recognized this one to be well made.
The tree trunks had been carefully chosen, then assembled
in round notch fashion like a child's set of Lincoln Logs.

"Roof's sagging pretty bad, heavy snow load I suppose," she commented when she saw sunlight streaming
through gaps between boards.

"You'd have to tear off the roof to move it, put on a
better one," said the rancher.

"I'll sure think about it," she said. She knew she would
give it a lot of thought.

When she returned to town, two men she knew as su-
pervisors from the Fraser sawmill—now owned by the
Stevens-Barr company—were sitting on an old bench out
in front of Doc's fence. They were chewing tobacco and
spitting toward the road. As she approached, they stood
up. The taller one stepped forward, tipped his hat and said,
"Doc Susie? We hear Freeman is going to make you
move." He paused, hoping his next statement would ap-
peal to the little doctor's legendary thrift, "Would you pay
a buck for a place to live?"

She blinked, baffled by his strange suggestion and he
continued, "We want you to know that Stevens-Barr will
give you—well actually we will charge you a dollar so as to
make it legal—a nice lot in that plat we laid out west of the
tracks. We owe you that."

"News travels fast," she said. She stood for a moment,
surprised they knew of her plight, then remembered the

children who had been hanging on the fence that morning. Across her mind passed the scores of difficult trips she had made to logging camps to treat injured and sick lumberjacks and their families. The lumber mill was under no obligation to pay her; after all, the men didn't work for Stevens-Barr. They worked for individual jobbers who might or might not pay her; usually it was left to the injured or sick person to make good on the bill. If Stevens-Barr wanted to help her out to show gratitude for all those logs her patients cut from the forest—well, she could see her way clear to accepting a little piece of land.

"And, we'll be glad to move this old shack over there, too, although you surely deserve better."

"I guess I wouldn't mind getting a little distance between me and the Malleys." They walked to the lot which was about a half block from the depot—in Doc's estimation a very nice location. She accepted their offer with pleasure.

Word of something as sensational as an eviction gets around a small town fast. That day, Doc's misfortune had been all the talk at Warner's and at the Fraser Mercantile. Gossips remembered how she had been talking about leaving the valley. From there word spread to Hulda Wilson's house, where townspeople often dropped by in the middle of the afternoon for coffee and a sweet roll. Heads were shook and chins were pinched at the shabby way in which the railroad, Bill Freeman in particular, was treating Doc Susie. Everybody, whether they claimed her as their personal physician or preferred Doc Albers, agreed that it would be terrible if she were to leave because she had no home.

When Doc went for her mail the next morning, the aroma from Hulda Wilson's yeasty cinnamon rolls drifted down toward the Post Office. Doc followed the scent into Hulda's kitchen. Slender, attractive Hulda spoke English with just a trace of an accent, enough to add a pleasant lilt to her conversation. She had come to America to work as a domestic and had held a position of responsibility in the household of the governor of Colorado before she married Gustaf Wilson. She held her firstborn, little Glenn, on one hip while she stirred a pot of stew on the stove. It was at the Wilson house that Swedish people in the community celebrated Christmas with Lutefisk and all the trimmings. Her open kitchen door provided a natural contact between the Swedish lumberjacks and the rest of the community.

Hulda's husband Gustaf, who worked in Carlson's Saloon, didn't entirely share his wife's high opinion of Doc Susie. Not that he begrudged Doc a sweet roll and coffee, he just grumbled about how she looked going about her rounds in multiple petticoats and thick boots. "If she's a doctor she ought to look like a doctor," he opined. His idea of a doctor, Susie suspected, was someone who always wore a white jacket and slept with a round mirror affixed permanently over his eye.

Doc started telling Hulda about the barn, quietly at first, then with growing enthusiasm, "It's not a large barn. I could just see it under a real pretty roof. They had such pretty roofs on the houses in Indiana." Doc's eyes focused out the window, a long way off. Dreamily, she told Hulda she'd sure like to move the barn and make a house out of it, but couldn't figure how she'd ever be able to afford to hire it done.

Hulda smiled when Doc mentioned Indiana. So often had she heard how superior everything was in Indiana that she shared a private joke with her husband. Whenever Gus complained about anything, Hulda said pertly, "Yah. Iss better in Indiana."

A few evenings later, as Doc was running a flat iron over strips of dressings, her spitz set up a fuss out front. Looking out, she was surprised to see a group of lumberjacks which included Axel, Elof Johnson, John Escola, Gus Severein as well as some other Swedes she didn't know as well. They stood outside the fence in a little clutch, their caps and hats in their hands as if they were in church, staring at the yapping white ball of fluff that jumped up and down on his hind legs like a trick dog in the circus.

Axel, since he knew Doc best, had been delegated as spokesman. He cleared his throat twice, "Missus. Da boys an me. We wanna help you to a new house."

"I really appreciate that, Axel. But Stevens-Barr and the railroad are going to move my house for me."

"No, missus. We're gonna make you a real house, move dat barn from up at Meadow Creek and put a nice roof on it. Stevens-Barr, dey gif us a team and wagon and planks for da roof. We get a lot of dese dumb Swedes together and it'll go fast. You see."

Doc Susie looked into a sea of sincere blue eyes. She knew these men, knew their word was as good as money in the First National Bank in Denver, knew that trying to change their minds—well, some said it would have been easier for the Captain to turn the Titanic around before it hit the iceberg than to change a Swede's mind. If these men said they were going to move a building, you might as well stand back because you might get hurt if you stood in the way.

The next few evenings, Doc sat with Axel at Hulda's kitchen table, working beneath the light from a single bulb hanging from the ceiling. On this particular occasion power from the sawmill's generator was pretty steady, although it faded and surged occasionally.

First, Doc Susie drew a little sketch for a floor plan. "These front rooms should be for examinations." Axel nodded. She showed Axel how she had planned a scheme of interior partitions to provide load-bearing supports for a second story and to divide the ground floor space into small rooms for storage, cooking and living. Upstairs, she wanted two large, airy rooms. Her bedroom would have a dormer opening out to a view of the front range. The other would provide space to string clotheslines indoors, so she wouldn't have to freeze her fingers when she went out-of-doors in winter to hang up medical dressings.

Axel drew the plan in more detail, showing her where he thought a stairway should be. "It'll be steep, but you can make it."

"I want a pitched roof, Axel. I just can't manage to shovel it by myself." In Fraser, unless a roof's angle was very steep it had to be shoveled several times each winter to prevent collapse under the weight of snow.

Axel thought for a minute. Then he took his stub of pencil and made a sketch of a two-story building with a roof that had not one, but two slopes to the pitch. "In Sweden, dey make a lotsa houses and barns with a roof like dis. Snow scoots right off and it's real pretty."

"Why that's beautiful," said Doc Susie, a thrill in her voice. "I remember seeing a roof like that in a picture in a book once. It was on a beautiful stone house in Virginia—near Williamsburg I think." Her blue eyes glittered with excitement.

"Yah, you never hafta shovel dat roof."

"Gambrel. I think they called it a gambrel roof. Oh, and I've seen roofs like that lots of times in Indiana."

Hulda, who was behind Doc's back wiping dishes, winked at Axel at the reference to Indiana.

The next evening, Doc Susie and Axel drove a buckboard out to look at the barn. Together they measured it from every angle to be sure their plans were accurate. Axel didn't seem to mind when she bossed him around, demanding that he climb here, stand there, hold his arms straight out from his sides to give her an idea of this or that dimension. For her part, she was pleasantly surprised that the young lumberjack knew so much about carpentry. She thought to herself that it was too bad he hadn't been trained for a skilled craft.

While riding or walking to house calls she had plenty of time to think, and it occurred to her that she had spent many nights sleeping in log cabins thrown up hastily in lumber camps, perhaps by the same men who were offering to build her house. The experience was generally an unpleasant one; often little skittering and chewing sounds made her aware that her sleeping companions included squirrels, chipmunks and pack rats. The roofs tended to sift dirt or leak mud, depending on the weather. She had better figure out a way to supervise these generous lumber-jacks. After all, their business was to make tall trees fall to the ground, not to set them up straight again.

One morning she tacked a note to her door saying she was out on calls. She packed odd nails she had gathered into some sugar sacks and thrust them into saddle bags, then tied an apple and some biscuits into another sugar sack, hung a hammer from the saddlehorn of a borrowed horse and spurred him toward Meadow Creek. Her dog ran joyfully along the road, happily wagging his tail and look-ing up at Doc who wore a sunbonnet to protect herself during the coming day's work.

As she dismounted she said to the dog, "Looks lone-some, doesn't it?" Anything of value had been carted off by its former owners; tenants had not yet been found to occupy the ranch house. The barn roof sagged worse than ever. "Never you mind," she said aloud in a soothing voice, almost as if the building were a patient. "When we're finished you'll be better than new."

She grabbed her hammer and set to work. On the cut end of the log nearest the ground she hammered one nail clear into the wood so that only its head showed. Next to it she hammered another halfway in, then bent its head to-ward the outside wall. The nail pattern would show her workmen that this log would be the closest to the ground on the east side of the building and also showed which side of the log should face outward. Into the next log she ham-mered two nails to signify it would be the second log up from the ground, then pounded in another nail and bent it the same direction as the one in the log beneath it. And so she worked up one stack of log ends until she had to stand atop an empty barrel to affix eleven nails to the top log. Neatly, almost daintily, each log end was decorated with a precise little row of nails that could be immediately deci-phered by the workmen. When one column of log ends had been marked, she went to their opposite ends and marked them to match.

All day long, Susie counted and pounded. Finally, she

put her hands on her hips and looked at the barn with great satisfaction. She walked with her dog around the building, reaching out to caress the logs with her sensitive fingertips. She knew the building could be reassembled exactly the way it was built, with the hand-hewn logs stacked in proper order. Homeward bound, riding toward the sunset, she felt like a child who skipped school for a day. How wonderful it was to spend a little time away from everyone else's blood and pain—it was her own back that ached and her own thumb that throbbed from a blood blister that arose after an inattentive moment when she swung her hammer with more gusto than accuracy.

On the very next Sunday Axel and the boys appeared in front of her shack; they were in reasonably good shape considering they had survived their usual Swedish Saturday night. "Hey missus! Let's go get your house."

Doc skirted ahead of the team of horses and climbed up to the wagon's seat, next to Axel. The men were in a holiday mood; behind her, Elof Johnson played his accordion as the wagon bumped along the road. Axel told Doc Susie how the men had hatched up a good plan to move the building. "And we will take down the logs, one by one, and load them on the wagon with the top ones first so they will be at the bottom, then chain them up just like we was hauling logs from the woods . . ." He paused, as though awaiting her objections to the scheme. From their previous dealings, Axel knew that Doc was a woman of firm convictions; so firm that he told her she would have made an excellent Swede.

"That will be just fine, Axel." Her easy agreement made him downright apprehensive.

When they arrived at the barn, Axel shouted, "Dat's a fery fine barn we're gonna tear down today. It gonna make a swell house for Doc Susie!" As he looked it up and down, a glint at the end of a log caught his eye. He went closer, examined a neat little row of nails, counted them, then quickly glanced around the corner to see more nails in each log end. He deciphered the code immediately, then looked to see Doc Susie grinning at him. He said, "I allus knowed you was a smart lady. You figured to fix it so us dumb Swedes couldn't bollix it up." He winked and thumped a finger to his skull in appreciation.

Although some blue eyes had been pink and bleary as the wagon pulled out of Fraser, no Swede would ever admit to being felled by a hangover, especially when tests of manhood were in the offing. Vigorously they attacked the roof with an arsenal of lumberman's tools including pry bars, pickaroons, wedges, even peavey heads. "Timber!" they shouted when the rafters fell down.

It wasn't difficult to dislodge the logs; the major reason the building stood was because log ends were notched to dovetail at the corners. They encountered a few spikes and pried them out; mud that had been chinked between logs to keep out the wind and snow just powdered and fell to the ground.

The mighty woodsmen were showing off for Doc, tossing thirty-foot logs as easily as they would two-by-fours. Sometimes an entire log would be lifted and hurled toward the wagon by just one man; she tried not to think about such occupational hazards as hernias.

Sitting atop the first wagonload of logs to be hauled back to Fraser, she waved triumphantly to curious townspeople as her future home was freighted down the main street, across the tracks and up one block. "Hurray, they're hauling Doc Susie's house down the street!" she heard a neighborhood ragamuffin yell out.

When they arrived at her lot she suddenly became very picky about the order in which the logs were unloaded and stacked. As a practical matter, she knew that the area's labor force changed so frequently that the put-it-up crew could be a totally different one from the tear-it-down crew. It would just depend on who showed up next week.

A crowd of curious townspeople gravitated toward the lot. Among them was Ben Jones, the handsome boss from Lapland. As Doc walked Ben around the lot, showing him where doors and partitions were to be placed, Ben was full of expensive suggestions, "You oughtta add this, you shoulda bought that . . ." But he didn't offer to stay and work. By nightfall, the barn had been completely removed.

Every evening that week, Axel rode into town after he got off work. He and Doc Susie pounded stakes and stretched lines from balls of twine she had saved to delineate the foundation and partitions. Using a shovel and hoe, Axel dug foundation trenches. It seemed that every time he sank his spade into the ground he was greeted with an unpleasant klank, indicating he had hit yet another rock. Doc and Axel sorted through crates and boxes and nail kegs, gathering serviceable hardware from among the cast-offs she had gathered with her "waste not, want not" zeal. "By golly missus you've got a lot of stuff," he said frequently. When work was done for the day, Doc would brew up a cup of coffee and they sat together on a pile of logs, sipping from tin cups and gazing toward where her house would be. Then Axel rode back to the lumber camp in the dark.

When Saturday morning dawned Doc sprang out of bed even before her rooster crowed. Although it was July, there was frost on the grass as she hurried toward where her house would be built. She had expected a goodly contingent of Swedes but was very surprised when it seemed that everybody in town wanted to help. Normally a work day, on that Saturday trees in the forest were safe from the broadaxes and crosscut saws of the lumberjacks. The men had declared themselves a holiday so they could work on Doc's house. Mill hands from Stevens-Barr arrived with a load of dimensional lumber for interior stud walls plus subflooring. The section foreman from the railroad brought some windows, good windows originally purchased for a station that the railroad never got around to building—windows that had somehow disappeared from the D&SL inventory list.

Ranchers arrived in their buckboards. Dalton Irby and Harry Hollingsworth had grown into strapping men. Ranchers sported hammers dangling like sidearms from loops in their overalls. George Schryer, the railroad engineer, and his wife Grace built a roaring fire in the corner of the lot and rigged a big hook over it. The first thing to hang there was a huge enamel pot; water was heating for coffee.

"It's been a month of Sundays since I seen you!" "You're a sight for sore eyes!" "Where've you been keepin' yourself?" rang out whenever new workers arrived because people from isolated corners of the valley were so pleased to see each other. It seemed that everybody had big news to confide to Doc. Karl and Adella Just came in from their Pole Creek ranch. Della whispered that she was expecting another baby next winter; Doc promised to put it on her calendar. Harry Hollingsworth told Doc that he was "seeing" Gertrude Arkell; she would be returning soon from Denver where she had graduated from high school. And wasn't it wonderful? Dalton Irby was "seeing" Gertrude's young cousin, Rose. Doc was reminded how swiftly time had passed since she arrived in Fraser.

Axel led each new volunteer around the lot, proudly showing him how Doc Susie had marked the logs with rows of nails. A crew got right to work shaping floor joists and nailing down subflooring. Once they began lifting stud walls into place, things went quickly. The Swedes insisted that they be the ones to reassemble the logs. They were dubious that mere carpenters from the mill could appreciate the intricacies of working with logs.

Doc Susie was pulling splinters from one Swede's fingers when she looked up to see Axel unbuttoning his shirt. She watched as he released his cuff buttons, peeled the sleeves of his plaid shirt from his arms, then crossed his arms in front of his chest and lifted his knitted, longsleeved undershirt over his head. His shoulders were just as she had remembered from the day in the tent when they set Elof's arm—broad, snugly molded over bulging biceps that were bigger around than most of the logs he lifted. His white skin was like marble, and she thought for a moment of a Greek statue she had seen in Chicago at the

Columbian Exhibition of 1897. But she smiled when she remembered that Greek busts didn't have brown lines around the neck where Axel's collar stopped, his skin exposed to the sun. Picking up the cue, the other lumberjacks shucked their shirts, almost in unison like a corps of ballet dancers.

So mesmerized was Doc by the sight of these beautiful men—stripping and pounding—that it was a few minutes before she realized they were putting themselves in danger, "You will be sunburned terribly. Please, at least put your undershirts back on."

"Hey missus," yelled Axel. "It's a beauteous day and dere's no skeeters here." Again she realized the folly of trying to argue with a Swede, but made a mental note to insist that they keep their shirts on after lunch. Besides, she was loathe to deprive herself of the sight of those strong men-machines, lifting their hammers, pounding nails like the heathen Norse god, Thor. She noted that other women, especially the teenage girls, also appreciated the show. She promised herself to introduce Axel to some of these nice girls. It was time for him to be finding a wife.

George Schryer was also impressed by the sight. "By gar I was going to play this later, but now I feel inspired." He reached into the boot of his Hudson and pulled out his fiddle. He tuned it, then affixed his magnificent nose over his instrument and broke into a Cajun air. Smiling mischievously, he played the "Anvil Chorus" while all the Swedes pounded in unison.

Axel was doing his best to keep everyone organized. "How green is dem boards?" he asked the men who were pounding sub-flooring.

A mill hand responded good-naturedly, "These are aged. Sawed them last week. Nobody's been squirted in the eye with sap yet so they must be dry." Fact was, green lumber was the only kind available because nothing stayed around the lumberyard long enough to be "cured." Even though the men used a level and did their best to make dimensions square, in a few weeks boards would find their own shape. It was just a fact of mountain building that everyone accepted. Later generations would label the warped results "rustic."

Late in the morning someone came up behind Doc and put his hands across her eyes, "Guess who?"

"I guess it's you, Ben Jones," said Doc excitedly.

For once, Axel didn't come forward to greet the newcomer and assign him a task. He could see that Jones was not dressed to work on the house. "I'm awful sorry, Susie, but something came up and I've got to go to Denver, goin' by the noon train."

Doc's annoyance showed in her voice, "We must all do what is important to us," she said and strolled away. Axel grinned.

At noon the women laid out a feed, on planks balanced across saw horses, that was fit for harvest hands. No one could remember a church social to match it. There were ham sandwiches, fried chicken, cold joints of venison, trout pickled in vinegar and lots of potato salad. Someone unfamiliar with the valley might have thought they had stumbled across a rhubarb pie baking contest because there were so many of them. Rhubarb was the only fruit that could be grown in abundance at that altitude, so throughout the summer women turned its red stalks into jam, sauce, syrup and tarts. By fall, almost everybody was sick of the sandpapery feeling rhubarb left on their tongues and teeth.

Doc knew that the men would politely don their shirts when they ate, so while they mopped up bean juice from their plates with homemade bread she made them promise to keep their shirts on. After the pies had been reduced to crumbs, the work area fell silent. The only sound was the clank of tin plates being gathered by the women. Hammers and saws rested while the men lolled with their backs against logs, napping a little with their hats pulled over their faces for shade. After an hour, almost as though a work whistle had blown, it was back to work. Although the Swedes were not as frisky as they had been that morning, their determination to raise her house in a single day kept them pounding. The afternoon chore was to lay flooring upstairs, build roof joists and hoist them into position.

Now the young people had an important assignment. They mixed plaster with water and chinked spaces between the logs, smoothing the surface with a trowel after the filler was packed into place. The white plaster between dark logs made the house look as if it had white stripes painted around it.

It was a good thing that the days were long that time of year because the men worked well into the evening. Just before dark Axel produced a little pine tree that he had brought from the forest. He climbed with it to the top of the roof and waved it triumphantly in the air. When he pounded it into place a great cheer went up. Doc looked a little puzzled until someone explained that in Scandinavia, nailing a tree atop a newly framed building signaled that it had been "topped out."

Doc Susie chose that moment to produce a flat, crated parcel. Very carefully she pulled nails from cross braces and unwrapped brown paper that protected it. High above her head she held a diamond-shaped pane of glass, etched with the curlicued figure of a rose. One of the carpenters cut a hole into a door and Axel fitted molding around the window. "That's an Indiana rose," she said. "I bought it a long time ago. Never thought I'd have a home to go with it."

One of the reasons the house went up so quickly was because Doc Susie didn't want any newfangled conveniences. When it was suggested that she install wires for electricity she asked, "What for? Every time you really need electric lights around here—like when there's a storm or it's snowing—the generator is broken or the wires are down." That was true enough. It would be many years before Roosevelt's REA provided a dependable source of power. "I'll stick to my kerosene lamp."

Indoor plumbing? Well, all the pipes she had ever seen

in this country froze up every winter. That would take even longer to remedy.

Telephone? If she had one of those things she'd never get any rest. She had learned her lesson the first time around. Besides, if anybody needed her all they had to do was come get her or phone the depot and the agent would relay a message. She feared that if she had a telephone she would be at the mercy of every runny nose in town.

At sundown tired lumberjacks, mill hands, carpenters, railroaders, ranchers, women and children pulled stumps around a fire in front of the house where stub ends of two-by-fours and other construction trash was being burned. Tired as everyone was, they sang songs: "Home on the Range," "Long, Long Trail A-winding," "Tipperary" and "Bicycle Built for Two." George played his fiddle gently, less urgently than that morning; Elof struck some nice chords on his accordion. As people packed up and started home, one by one they approached her, "Will you stay now?"

"I never said I wouldn't," she replied. Until then, she had wondered whether or not anybody cared.

It was several weeks before Susie could move into the house. Until then, she mopped linseed oil onto raw boards and supervised as cupboards were installed—both for her personal use and for the office. She hired a man named Tom Smith to build a large, beautiful fireplace to her specifications; it was rumored to include secret hidey holes where she put money rolled up on adhesive tape spools. It would have gone against her grain to abandon her old shack so eventually it, too, was hauled to the lot to serve as an outbuilding behind her house.

Axel frequently commented about how much stuff she had, and how unnecessary most of it seemed. After all, he could load most of his own possessions onto his back and move in a moment if he decided to change jobs. From her old place he hauled, rolled, trundled, carried, dragged and staggered beneath a bewildering assortment of what most people would consider junk. Every time he protested, Doc

Susie would say, "Waste not, want not," and remind him of how useful many of her castoffs had proved during the construction process.

The only thing she lacked was a well, deep enough to provide dependable clean water. They don't call them the Rocky Mountains for nothing. Now Ben Jones finally volunteered. "I know just where to dig," he claimed. He arrived one day with a local douser whose job was *not* to find underground water—it was everywhere—but to carry his forked stick around the yard until it dipped toward the place that had the fewest rocks. Doc didn't put much faith in dousers. The raggedy fellow finally called out, "Dig here!"

Doc sputtered, "Right by the outhouse? And you claim to know what you are doing." She invited the fellow to pack up his stick and hit the road. Ben Jones sulked because his advice had been ignored; she thanked him, invited him to stop by again another time.

It took another crew of volunteers another long Sunday to dig the well in a safer location; maybe the fellows who did that job worked the hardest. Fortunately, at a depth of about 18 feet the diggers hit water that satisfied her—but not before she had tasted it, looked at it through her microscope and put some strange chemicals into it. From then on, the only problem she would have with her well would be to keep the surface free from ice in winter. It never occurred to her that it was any real inconvenience to carry pails of water fifty feet into the house. No, lots of people had to break a hole in the ice in the creek to get their water. A well in the yard was a genuine luxury.

Eventually Doc began sleeping in her new house and although it would never really be finished, she began to think of it as home. She was very surprised when, one day, the mail brought a nice clock to put on her fireplace mantle—from Pa. Her Pa visited her from time to time and she wrote letters to him. But they were never what she would call close. His generosity was the first he had showed in many years. She was very proud of the clock, and explained to everyone that it needed winding only once every eight days. It chimed the same tune as Big Ben in London, every quarter of an hour.

Axel kept helping with little improvements. Siding here, spading a garden there. One day he leaned a ladder high up on the front of the house and nailed on siding in a diamond-shaped pattern above the door. He found some special white quartz rocks that she liked, and arranged them among the columbine flowers that she had transplanted from the forest to her rock garden. Doc Susie praised everything he did, but she was growing uneasy; after all it was *her* house. Sometimes Axel acted like he was the man of it. When Hulda warned Doc that people were beginning to ask if there was anything between the two of them, she grew apprehensive.

"He's just a friend. And he's so young . . ."

"And ignorant?" ventured Hulda. Doc Susie ducked her head, trying not to meet Hulda's gaze. "Ten years isn't so much difference. You could do worse," said Hulda.

One Saturday evening Doc glanced through her rose window to see Axel coming up the walk, holding something behind his back. He was wearing a dark suit, tie, shiny shoes and a derby. Beyond getting cleaned up, Swedes didn't ordinarily dress up to go drinking at one of Fraser's "skid road" saloons or to visit the nearby crib of a soiled dove.

As she let him in, she couldn't help thinking what a fine man Axel was. He was so tall, and always kept himself so clean and neat. But she feared the seams of his store-bought suit jacket would burst from their attempt to contain his bulging shoulders and arms. Her eyebrows arched with surprise when he presented a bouquet of red roses. Real roses. "Dey come on the train. I sent for dem for you. Just like Indiana."

"Oh Axel, you've done so much for me already. How can I ever repay you?"

"Dat's all right missus. I allus said I'd do somethin' nice

for you, after you took the spick outta my eye on the train."

"You are a man of your word."

She motioned for Axel to pull up a chair and sit down in front of the fireplace. "Are you going to Denver, Axel? You are all dressed up."

He blushed. "No, missus." The clock ticked very loud but its two hands seemed stuck. Doc Susie began counting knots in the floorboards.

"I come to call on you."

"Call on me? But . . . oh."

The easy intimacy the two had shared for so many weeks ended as suddenly as if they had stepped from bright sunshine into the damp of an ice house. The sound of her chair rocking on the pine planks thundered like a wagon being pulled across a bridge. Doc's hands, normally graceful, flailed in thin air; desperate, she grabbed into a bag at her side, pulled out a ball of string and set to crocheting furiously, her hook grabbing in and out at the helpless thread. Silence stretched for minutes that seemed like hours. "I'll make us some tea."

As she busied herself fussing over her kettle, Axel stood up and rested his elbow on the mantle of her beautiful fireplace. For the first time she realized that this huge lumberjack was a very quiet man.

"What did your father do, Axel?"

"He was a peasant."

"A peasant? Don't you mean a farmer?"

"Yah."

"Did you go to school in Sweden?"

"Oh yah, missus. In Sweden efferybody learn to read, write, do sums."

"What did you read?"

"About Martin Luther and the Diet of Worms. I allus thought dat was a funny thing. Worms." His "W's" would always melt to "V's."

Why, she wondered, when she tried to talk to him about anything other than the house, was it so difficult? Sweden.

She would talk to him about Sweden. "I've always enjoyed the works of Strindberg. Ibsen the Norwegian, too, of course. They were practically the first to realize that women . . . Miss Julie . . ." her voice trailed off.

"Yah. They was a bunch of Strindbergs lived down the road from us. Don't know if any of dem come to America."

Susie's exhaling breath echoed around the room. Pa's big clock clanged each quarter of an hour, and both looked at it each time it rang as if they didn't already know exactly what time it was.

Finally, Axel stood up. He reached for his hat and said, "Well, Saturday night and I gotta get drunk again."

"You don't have to get drunk, Axel. You make it sound like a duty."

"Yah. Maybe so," he said as he walked through the door.

"Axel," she called after him. "I don't think there is any way I can ever repay you."

"Tink nothink of it," he called over his shoulder.

She leaned against the doorjamb, watching his dark figure retreat into moonlight as he walked toward the row of saloons. She banged her fist against the door frame so hard it scuffed her knuckles. "Those I want I can't have. And I don't want those who want me."

CHAPTER 8

Pride of the Rockies

When Karl and Della Just announced they were throwing a barn dance at their ranch on Pole Creek, Doc Susie was as excited as everyone else; a good barn dance was always the social highlight of summer in the Fraser Valley. At the Post Office one morning Ben Jones grabbed her by the waist, his eyes roving over her full figure, then promised he'd see her at the party. Fiddles and banjos tuned up in her head as she hastened home to rummage through her trunks for something special to wear.

Her gait was somewhere between a lope and a skip as she sped down the rutted road, but she slowed to a walk when she saw two women hanging up clothes and heard clipped bits of conversation, "So I sez . . . and she sez . . ."

"Well, I never . . ." shrilled the other.

Doc could never quite understand why people wasted their time repeating stories, why they needed to talk,

Susan Anderson, M.D.
University of Michigan
Ann Arbor, 1897
photo courtesy of Colorado Historical Society

Gentleman enjoys early spring view of Yankee Doodle Lake from Rollins Pass road-bed near Needle's Eye Tunnel.

photo by L. C. McClure, courtesy of Western History Department, Denver Public Library

William H. Anderson, Susan's father

Susan's mother, Marya Pile, with two of her children from her second marriage: Louis and Cuba McLaughlin
photos courtesy of Roger Brady

Doc Susie's grandmother, also Susan Anderson. She raised Susan and her brother John.

Susan and John in Wichita, 1876.
photos courtesy of Roger Brady

Graduation
Wichita High School, 1891
photo courtesy of Roger Brady

In 1891 the Andersons moved from Wichita to Cripple Creek, Colorado to seek their fortune in the gold boom. A buxom, healthy young Susan looked forward to her new life.

photo courtesy of Roger Brady

Doc Anderson House

St.tut in.

Susan Anderson's first house in Fraser. The identity of the young man "playing soldier" is unknown.

Freight coming in Fraser

A Mallet steams past Doc Susie's house, directly behind the locomotive.
photos courtesy of Laura Jean Welty

Powerful skid horses were kept sleek and fit in lumber camps like Lapland, shown above.

Sturdy Swedish lumberjacks—like these shown posing with a cat, accordion and tools—moved Doc Susie's log cabin to a lot in Fraser.
photos courtesy of Grand County Museum

In the lumber camps, Swedes did not wait for women partners when they were in the mood to dance.
photo courtesy of Grand County Museum

It took many years to finish Doc Susie's log cabin.
photo courtesy of Minnie Cole and Hazel Briggs

Occasionally, William Anderson came from California to visit his daughter in Fraser. They are shown with Susan's step-brother.

In a happier moment, Doc Susie poses with a friend and her child on the main street of Fraser in front of the Opera House, 1917.

photos courtesy of Grand County Museum

Summer tourists enjoyed their excursion trains to the summit of Corona.
photo courtesy of Western History Department, Denver Public Library

But in winter, avalanches could impact a mighty rotary snowplow to the extent that it had to be taken to the Tabernash shops to be picked free of ice.
photo courtesy of Western History Department, Denver Public Library

This picture of William R. Freeman appeared in the *Denver Post* at the time of his retirement in 1934. He saved the Denver and Salt Lake Railroad and built the Moffat Tunnel, but his heavy-handed tactics were frequently criticized.

photo courtesy of Western History Department, Denver Public Library

George Schryer, shown at the throttle of his locomotive in 1950. The engineer was one of the heroes in the war against "The Hill," as the railroaders called Rollins Pass.

photo courtesy of Grand County Museum

Even when excavation was completed and the tunnel was being shored, its cavernous interior was impressive.
photo courtesy of Grand County Museum

Although she is not among the people in the photograph, Doc Susie was responsible for this sign of protest that greeted the Official First Train to emerge from the Moffat Tunnel.

photo courtesy of Western History Department, Denver Public Library

Wearing a fur coat and hat, Doc Susie posed with the crew of the first train. She is fourth from the right.

photo courtesy of Western History Department, Denver Public Library

In 1941 a troop train was halted in Fraser so Doc Susie could sew up the arm of a sailor, Roger Richards of Brooklyn, New York.

photo courtesy of Minnie Cole and Hazel Briggs

wanted to believe the worst about each other. Probably it was because so little of real interest ever happened in the Fraser Valley. Its women rarely had an opportunity to leave their homes. Homes? Hovels was more like it. Mountain life was so harsh; a woman's waking hours had to be spent keeping the family fed, warm and clean. The same drudgeries awaited them week after week: boil the clothes on Monday and hang them on the line to be showered by cinders raining from the sky each time a train passed, iron on Tuesday, bake on Wednesday, mend on Thursday, split kindling, split kindling, split kindling. The only recognition these drudges got for their efforts was to be yelled at if things didn't get done.

Suddenly the idea of going to a barn dance wasn't as attractive. Doc saw herself as likely grist for the gossip mill. Her every movement—especially where Ben Jones was concerned—would be noted and repeated, her every wink stored up and savored for future speculation.

Doctors, she mused, were particularly favored subjects. She had learned over the years that rumors were as much a part of a doctor's life as the black bag she carried. For some odd reason people were a lot more interested in the love lives of doctors than in those of, say, mill hands or store clerks. Maybe it was because a doctor was usually the best educated person in town; people wanted to believe that a lot of schooling didn't offer protection against foolishness. They were certainly right on that score. And doctors, supposedly, harbored titillating secrets. Her professional oath of confidentiality forbade her from revealing what happened when she went into someone's house and told them to take their clothes off. The gossips knew they had told Doc Susie things they wouldn't tell their own husbands. Susie couldn't help but reflect that the secrets she kept were a lot less interesting than the chatterboxes could have imagined. Doc also suspected that Fraser women envied her freedom to come and go as she chose. How they would love to walk out the door, not telling anyone else where they were off to! Men didn't approve of

Doc's freedom, either; running around in the woods the way she did, alone. It set a bad example for their women, might give them ideas.

She knew that the gossips kept tabs on Doc Albers, too. They made sure that Doc Susie heard about how Doc Albers drank too much whiskey and loosened himself up by taking some of the pills he kept around.

Gossip about Doc Susie was in particular demand. Some said Doc was "man crazy," that she preferred to treat men over women, liked to do that "pneumonia cure business," feeling under the comforters while a man sweated out the poison.

She didn't go to any lengths to conceal the fact that she did want someone to share her life, someone who would always be there, who would put his arms around her and squeeze away disappointment. She wanted a husband, and held out the hope that Ben Jones might be the man. And she wanted children. The sight of a child whose cut lip she had just sewed up running to the comfort of his mother's open arms left her own arms feeling empty. But if it wasn't too late already, very soon all possibility of ever having a child would be past.

From time to time Doc daydreamed about how wonderful it would be if she could simply have a child and not bother with the husband part of it. But that was merely wishful thinking. Such a woman would not be allowed to stay in a "respectable" town, let alone practice medicine there.

Doc had seen the pathetic little dramas that played themselves out after she was forced to confirm a young woman's worst fear—pregnant. Pregnant because some young man pleaded, begged, urged and promised. Then, faced with a hasty marriage, the same fellow would accuse the girl of luring him, ruining his promising future. She had seen men who treated their horses better than they did their wives. Worn-out women, old before thirty, sat home on Saturday nights dreading the moment their drunken husbands came home from the saloon to force yet another unwanted child, followed by another and another. Usually, the whole terrible scenario started with a pre-marriage pregnancy.

With Doc, marriage was a prerequisite to family. She hoped nobody ever knew how much she suffered when she saw Karl Just sneak a secret nibble on Adella's ear while they danced.

How ironic! These woods were just full of men; they far outnumbered women. Often Doc thought of the lines from *The Rime of the Ancient Mariner*: "Water, water, everywhere,/And all the boards did shrink;/Water, water, everywhere,/Nor any drop to drink." Only in the Fraser Valley it was men, men everywhere . . . none suitable, or willing, to become her husband. Sometimes it seemed there were handsome, strong, beautiful men behind every tree. Unfortunately, the pastoral illusion vanished the moment these he-mountains opened their mouths. After an evening of trying to make conversation with some muscle-brain she found herself yearning for the stimulation of a good book. Sometimes she found herself attracted to raw masculinity; usually the man in question vanished from the scene very quickly, intimidated by her authoritative ways and superior education.

Ben Jones was different. Tall, slim, cleanshaven except for a moustache, he kept himself slightly aloof from townspeople and his fellow lumbermen. He never dressed like the rough workers he bossed, wearing a vest and bow tie every day. In the woods he barked his orders with arms crossed, rarely stooping to give a hand with physical labor. Nobody asked questions of a competent overseer. Doc wondered if Ben was among the men who "got lost in the woods," the black sheep son of a good family, a bankrupt businessman, maybe even a romantic robber like Jesse James, running from the law.

At the Stevens-Barr mill they liked Ben because he had a reputation for wringing a good quota of work from his men—even new hires. Arriving workers, raw, broke, needing a job and not knowing the territory labored more out of fear that the sharp-tongued Ben would fire them than out of loyalty. He ran a tight camp. Lumberjacks loved to grumble about the cold, so Ben never allowed a thermometer in his camp. Most of the best men, like Axel, wouldn't work for Ben after the first few weeks. When Doc asked Axel why, he said, "We didn't see eye to eye," then kept his mouth shut.

Ben could explain how locks worked in the Panama Canal, talk about music (he had actually attended a performance of Carmen) and literature—he said he had read everything that Lew Wallace had ever written. He never talked about his education much, but Doc gave him credit for being interested in material loftier than the contents of the *Police Gazette*, the reading material of choice for most lumberjacks.

And he was exciting. The first time Ben Jones kissed her, they were in the woods. When Ben turned to help her scramble over a log, her long skirt snagged on a branch. She stumbled and very nearly fell into his arms. He looked at her, sighed, and kissed her very hard. It was not a gentle invitation to explore, but a demanding, insistent kiss which she was only too happy to return. After she grabbed a hank of hair on the back of his head and squeezed it rhythmically he reached for the top button on her shirtwaist. At that point she pulled away and said, "Ben! I'm not your hanky-panky kind of woman."

"You're a tease, Susan Anderson. Like most women you lure a man and then say, 'I'm not your hanky-panky kind.'"

She remembered walking away breathless—thrilled, but threatened. He was a dangerous man.

Another time he asked her to take a little walk with him. They followed a fisherman's trail up a little tributary of St. Louis Creek called Byers Creek. There, Ben pointed out a series of white-water cascades spilling down the mountainside, forming little golden pools bordered by magenta flowers called King's Crown. They sat down on the bank, alive to the roar of crashing water. Ben put his arm around Susan, then turned her chin toward him so she was looking up into his eyes. "If you were to show me how a proper wife would act," he said, "it might influence my decision to acquire one." Angry at his suggestion and the way he phrased it, she turned and hastened down the trail to camp, returning to the patient she had been summoned to tend. She did not believe in casual liaisons, thought only a wanton woman would agree to such an arrangement. If she ever did such a thing her Pa . . . wasn't it silly, to worry about what Pa would think after all these years?

Strangely enough, Ben reminded her of her Pa. He was so demanding, always ordering her around, never there when she needed him.

Maybe the barn dance was just the opportunity she needed to get Ben Jones to think seriously about marriage. Their flirtation had gone on for months now, and although he didn't show up often enough to suit her, he had left no doubt that he liked her—a great deal. If he wasn't the professional man of her dreams—well, he was a *boss*, and a mature woman in the country was forced to choose from among what was available. Although not particularly practiced in feminine wiles—winks, bats of the eyelids, inviting smiles—she would declare the barn dance night open season for flirting.

Despite her forty-plus years, choosing a costume took hours of schoolgirl-like indecision. She discarded a gingham dress as too youthful, a black silk frock as too mature. Eventually she settled for her tried and true favorite—a lacy shirtwaist tucked into a full black skirt. Beneath it, she would wear a gray moire taffeta petticoat, which she hoped would swish provocatively. She planned to tie one black velvet bow high on her tatted collar and fix another one atop her hair; ratted up on her head, it might make her appear taller. The outfit was chosen far in advance of the event because Doc Susie knew all too well that if she left her decision until the last moment she was sure to be called to someone's bedside. If she even managed to get to the party, she would be reduced to dancing in the clothes on her back—serviceable enough to wear in the woods, but that was about all.

As the night of the dance neared, Doc Susie was looking forward to a relaxing social evening. Her calendar revealed no pregnant women likely to go into labor, no injured foresters who might develop infections. Spring epidemics of measles, whooping cough, mumps and chicken pox had passed. With luck she would be able to spend hours near Ben. Her optimism rose as the Saturday of the dance passed uneventfully.

Early that evening she dressed and fussed with her hair, brushing it out, re-rolling it and poufing it around her face, affixing hairpins, checking the results in a mirror, then brushing it out again when the hairdo failed to pass muster. The process was repeated several times while she waited for the Arkells to pick her up. She knew it would be quite late before their 1910 Cadillac, loaded with Tom and Anna, young Gertrude, Grandma and cousin Rose, pulled up at the door. No rancher could leave his spread before he had milked the cows and taken his Saturday night bath.

The lumberjacks worked late on Saturdays, then waited to be paid. The Warners had to close up their store. People from neighboring towns who took the train wouldn't arrive in Tabernash until evening. Nothing would really happen until after nine, about the time the summer sun went down.

Most families were already on their way out of town, loaded in spring wagons pulled by horses. Circulating among them loped young cowpokes on their best ponies, showing off for the girls. Their favorite trick was to ride up behind a group of girls, toss a rope and lasso at least three of them as they would a calf—then revel in the resulting giggles and squeals and false protestations, "Oh, we can't get loose!"

Every year more and more people drove cars. Popular in summer because they were comparatively speedy, in winter tin lizzies and other heaps were as useless in the mountains as other wheeled vehicles. Ineffectual in heavy snow, automobiles were set up on blocks because their tires would freeze flat and ruin the rubber; radiators had to be drained. Nobody could even picture a day when automobiles would supplant dependable draft animals pulling sledges and sleighs in mountain country. Doc was not particularly fond of automobiles, but she was glad enough to accept a lift from the Arkells. When Tom Arkell announced their arrival by softly squeezing the bulb of his horn, "honk, honk, honk," she scurried out the door.

"We've got to get there before dark," called Tom. "I finally gave up trying to fuss with these carbide headlights."

They sped northwest along the Four-Bar-Four Road (named for the brand of one of the ranches), the route built for stagecoaches before the coming of the railroad. The Cadillac slowed only to pass wagons; Tom Arkell wouldn't commit the unpardonable sin of frightening the horses or showering road dust on the passengers. When he wanted to resume speed Tom had to lean out the door—the driver's side was on the right—to shift gears. Anna never drove the car because she couldn't reach the gears; Doc wondered to herself what good a car was if it stayed parked by the barn while Anna rode a pony into town to pick up groceries and fetch the mail.

As they passed the Johnsons' wagon, Doc pointed to their daughters' starched petticoats, standing up in the back of their wagon like little teepees. Petticoats were carried to the dance because their cardboard consistency scratched the girls' legs; besides, they wouldn't want to wrinkle away any of their precious, carefully ironed stiffness before the dancing started. It was a good thing starch was cheap because girls soaked their homemade underskirts in pots of the viscous glue, hung them to drip from the clothesline, took them down while still very damp and pressed them in steaming kitchens for what seemed like hours until they were glazed so stiff they could stand unaided in the corner.

They rounded the bend at twilight; the Just place came into view, kerosene lanterns shining from the barn beckoned the cars, wagons and ponies toward the huge log barn which sat in a tall grove of virgin pines. The evening was unusually warm, perfect for dancing. Off somewhere Doc could hear a fiddler practicing a new tune. Panicked chickens and geese, fleeing for cover ahead of the cars, sought the safety of their nightly roosts.

Doc helped the Arkells unload. Carrying baskets of fried chicken and potato salad into the bright interior of the barn she admired the clean-scrubbed pine plank floor, sprinkled with corn meal so dancers could spin and shuffle even faster than if the floors had been newly waxed. Evergreen boughs and wildflowers were strung between stall braces. At one end, a planked platform for the musicians had been laid over tree stumps. Walking across the crunchy barn floor Doc enjoyed successive waves of smells: fresh pine, hay, rotted manure, neat's-foot oil used on tack and harnesses, cinnamon cookies, lemonade.

She greeted the fiddler, her friend George Schryer, who could stroke his violin with the same gusto he used putting steam to his Mallet. George's wife Grace clutched some sheets of piano music. But very few tunes would originate from printed sheets of music that evening; the Swedes who strummed guitars, banjos and bull fiddles, as well as Elof Johnson on his accordion, all played "by ear."

Seeing Axel in the shadows, Doc hastened to him and extended her hand. It had taken great tact to reestablish their friendship. He was still protective toward her, in a good-natured way. If he had other feelings, he kept them to himself.

A quick glance around the barn revealed that Ben Jones had not yet arrived. Nobody thought of getting a particular "date" to go to a dance. But close watch was kept on who paired off with whom; enough gossip could be generated off a good barn dance to chew on for months to come. When Ben's lean form appeared at the barn door, Doc's back straightened just a bit; she smiled prettily as she cocked her head toward Della Just, moving a tad to the side so Ben could spot her easily. Ben's sharp eyes scanned the room. He looked sleek and confident in his striped shirt, dark bow tie, shiny black boots and a leather vest. He had slicked his hair straight back with Macassar. "Dat's a real fine dude," Elof Johnson said, jabbing his elbow into Axel's ribs. As usual, Ben did not immediately greet Doc, just smiled and nodded. His reticence annoyed her; she could see no reason why he was so reluctant to acknowledge her in public.

But as soon as the musicians led off with a polka, Ben strode across the floor and grabbed Doc Susie by the waist. She reached both hands up to his shoulders and off they sped at a gallop, spinning around the dance floor like synchronized tops. Ben leaned into her ear, "The roses in your cheeks bloom as fair as those in Indiana. You smell just as sweet!" Doc knew Ben must have practiced that speech. She would have been embarrassed if anybody else had overheard it, but she liked it well enough.

If Ben Jones hadn't been such a good dancer, Axel might have stood a better chance with Doc. When Ben put his arms around Doc Susie she was glad to hand control to someone else for a change; he led them through tricky dance steps, giving interested bystanders a good excuse to keep an eye on the pair. They danced exuberantly, prancing in perfect time to the music.

Gradually the dance gathered momentum. Young girls in their stiff petticoats stayed near their mamas for a little while, then gravitated toward each other to stand in little groups, admiring each other's dresses. For a time young cowboys, loggers and railroaders stood apart, their nervous Adam's apples bobbing up and down in frequent gulps. Finally, bolder ones summoned up courage to "cut a girl out of the herd" and ask her to dance.

Della Just stood near the punch bowl with her five sons. At her side were a few thin-looking strangers, T.B. sufferers who boarded for the summer at the Justs' spacious ranch house. Patients of Doc, they marveled that anybody could dance so fast at that altitude, let alone someone who had recovered from consumption.

When the musicians slowed to a waltz, Ben propelled Doc with more precision, extending his long right arm to twirl her under his armpit. Particularly handsome was their execution of the varsoviana, a Polish folk dance more commonly called "Put your little foot." When Ben shunted Doc back and forth in front of him, little girls noted carefully the exact angle at which Doc extended her leg and pointed her toe, then sought an area behind the musicians' stand, where lanterns didn't burn so brightly, and mimicked Doc's steps.

There was very rarely a break in the music; musicians spelled each other so that everybody had a chance to play and dance. Doing schottisches, waltzes and polkas, the ladies in their calico dresses over full petticoats spun around the floor like mountain buttercups. Over the din of the band and the stomping of cowboy boots came the stentorian voice of the square dance caller: "Alemand left with your left hand, alemand right for a right and left grand, do-si-do, do-si-do, chicken in the breadpan pickin' up dough."

When it came time to do the Virginia Reel, there was no question who would be the head couple. Doc and Ben saluted each other, bowed, linked arms, then swished down the lane between couples and back again with a stylish flourish, Doc holding up her skirt so the moire gray petticoat ruffles were on view for all to see.

As the evening wore on, what constituted a couple became more loosely defined. Twosomes formed up consisting of two women, two children, grandmas and grandsons, any combination imaginable. As always, there were many more men than women in attendance. "Remember, I'm supposed to be a girl!" a cowboy would yell out in the midst of a square dance when a confused dancer tried to turn in the wrong direction.

Most of the men stepped outside for a smoke now and then, but Ben was never among them. He didn't smoke, nor was he present when Axel and his friends reached into a wagon and passed around a jug. To Doc, Ben's attitude toward booze was a plus; but many men didn't trust a fellow who wouldn't take a snort now and then.

From time to time, someone cut in on Ben. Doc was shapely, a superb dancer, slim; her body, unlike those of many Fraser wives, had never expanded to accommodate a pregnancy. But rather than being flattered by these intrusions, she resented them; Doc Susie knew that her attitude went against good manners, but she wished she could keep Ben to herself. When Karl Just claimed a dance with Doc, and Ben waltzed off with Christine Benson, Doc watched them closely, jealously. She hated to see his arms around someone else and she hated it more when she saw him smile and glance at his partner out of the corner of his eye, a special way of looking that she thought of as hers alone.

Well, two could play. When a handsome young rancher asked her to dance, Doc pretended she was drinking in his every word, laughing and rolling her eyes. From across the room you might have thought the young man was the wittiest conversationalist in the room; actually, he was pumping Doc for some free tips on how to cure his horse's colic.

At midnight, a buffet board covered with a checked tablecloth was balanced between two mangers. The ladies set to work lifting food from baskets and boxes, spreading out a cold supper. The board sagged visibly from the weight of the chicken, sage hen, bread and butter sandwiches, potato salad. Adella had soaked venison in vinegar to make sauerbraten, Karl's favorite. There were pies aplenty, but cakes were scarce. Most women gave up trying to bake them after their first two or three attempts came out of the oven with large craters in the center, soggy victims of high altitude thin air.

Doc and Ben sat together on a bench, appetites fueled by their dancing exertions. They tore greedily into their fried chicken.

"I'm going to head up a crew at Tipperary next winter," said Ben. Doc was familiar with the camp. "Looks as though I can make a lot of money there, maybe retire from the logging business by summer."

"Then what will you do?" she asked, lowering her eyes.

"I think I'll settle down, buy me a little spread and set up housekeeping. A man can't stay up in the woods all his life." That seemed to Susie a broad hint. "You know," he went on, "there's something I've been meaning to ask you."

"Yes?" Doc didn't really expect Ben to ask anything *important* right out in the open at a barn dance.

"How much do you make a year?"

"You need some lemonade," she said and retreated hastily to the big stone crock to ladle some into his cup. Was Ben being nosy or asking an appropriate question— appropriate to someone figuring plans for the future? She had the uneasy feeling that Ben was prying into something that was really none of his business. Unless it was really important, she would hate to reveal how little money she made. Not for the first time, she mentally chastised herself for being too timid about collecting bills. Still, a man had a right to ask that question if. . . .

No doubt the sideliners were making hay of her tête-à-tête with Ben. She had caught a snatch of conversation about "Doc Susie fetchin' and carryin'."

Doc's policy, difficult to implement but sound over the long run, was to ignore gossip with her chin up. She knew that most of the people she liked respected her and were wise enough to realize she was human like anybody else. The others—well, if they needed to have some drama to fill up their dull existences she might as well occupy center stage.

Dancing resumed after supper—slower, dreamier now. The invalids had long since wheezed off to the ranch house, the Justs' younger boys had fallen asleep on a bench. Della Just, whose pregnancy was just beginning to show, performed a stately waltz with her Viennese husband. Karl had trimmed the kerosene lanterns a little; the dimmer lights seemed to blend with moonlight through the big, wide-open barn doors—very romantically, Doc thought.

Ben's smooth-shaven cheek brushed against Susie's; his moustache tickled provocatively, and he held her close. She turned, swayed, bent, obeyed his lead in every move, her eyes closed—as was duly noted. Then one by one the musicians began to fall by the wayside; finally a succession of yawns made it clear that everyone was exhausted. The evening had gone so well that Doc Susie was sure Ben would ask to see her home in the moonlight or at least set a time to come calling another evening. Thirsty, Susie said, "I think I'll have another lemonade."

Ben said, "Will you excuse me?" Doc nodded, thinking he was answering a call of nature.

It was a few minutes before she realized he had disappeared. Someone said that he had never unsaddled his horse, just loosened the cinch. They saw him ride off toward Tabernash.

Doc was visibly upset. It wasn't the first time he had taken a powder. He would dance and flirt, raise her expectations, then pull his disappearing act. She was so mad she could spit . . .

In an attempt to calm herself, she turned her attention to helping with the bedding-down process. Families spread quilts brought from home in dimly lit corners of the barn or up in the hay loft, wherever space was available. Everyone stretched out to snooze for a few hours.

Except for Doc Susie. She kept listening, hoping to hear Ben Jones return for her, all through a restless night.

That autumn, Doc didn't see much of Ben. She hoped he wasn't trying to avoid her. One day when she was at the depot, collecting a parcel of pharmaceuticals, Ben walked in. She decided nothing ventured, nothing gained, so she asked him straight out: "Long time no see, stranger. Have you been keeping yourself scarce on my account?"

"No, Susie, I wouldn't ever try to avoid you." He took her two hands in his and squeezed them, pulling her fingers to his lips, running her fingernails back and forth along his teeth and tongue, sending shivers down her back. "We've been so busy in the woods. The mill pays me extra if I exceed my quota of logs, and I'm saving up for something special." He winked. "When spring comes . . ." It was enough to whet her anticipation.

In February her mood soared when she was called on a case to Tipperary where Ben's crew of fallers and skidders had been producing logs at a record rate.

The lad who summoned her was one she didn't know. He told her he had specific orders to get Doc Albers, but Albers was off on confinement, so would she come? Although Doc now saw some patients at her house, most days still found her on the road making house calls. The new patient, she learned, was a recently arrived child with measles. Measles—she hated the very word. This child had probably brought an epidemic with him. How she hoped this case wouldn't result in an early epidemic; usually the scourge held off until spring. Some children almost shrugged off the disease, but not many. Most ran high fevers that led to lung congestion. She reported more deaths among children from measles, complicated by pneumonia, than from any other cause. Doc presumed the child must belong to a "new hire" since he was in Ben Jones' camp.

As usual, at the thought of Ben her scalp tightened and she got goose bumps on her arms. Normally, she would don her coat and be out the door. This time she took a few minutes to fix her hair, sprinkle a little attar of roses behind her ears, to locate a red woolen muffler. This case might need some extra visits. Things were looking up.

Whispering George Smith—so dubbed for his high-decibel conversational style—drove her and the messenger out. Susie's feet were tucked atop a hot rock, a blanket snugged around her legs. In winter, George let his white whiskers grow because they kept his face warm; by Christmas he looked just like Santa Claus. Evidently he liked the comparison because he had fastened a string of sleigh bells to his team's harness; as they rode out their clang was low and musical against the clean, sharp smell of the woods. Or Susie enjoyed their music in the rare moments when

George wasn't talking. Whispering, George Smith's voice was so loud it could drown out church bells.

"Hope this won't keep you long. I've got to get back to meet the afternoon train," said George. "I can fetch you later if need be."

"I suspect I can get a ride back into town," she said, thinking she wouldn't mind being stranded with Ben in the woods. "Go on back to town. If you haven't heard from me in a day or two, come check up on me."

Arriving at the camp, the young messenger leapt hurriedly away after pointing out where Susie would find her patient. As she was collecting her bag from behind the seat of the sleigh, she heard a familiar voice—that of Ben Jones—raised in a stream of profanity. "God damn it," Ben concluded, "I told you to get· Doc Albers—only Albers!" How much like Pa in one of his angry moods Ben sounded! She was miffed to think Ben had so little faith in her professional skills.

The cabin she entered was one tiny room, barely more than a lean-to. The dark interior was totally dominated by a large woman who immediately set up a howl, "I told you I wanted a doctor, not a nurse. Can't you see this child is dying?"

Doc Susie, accustomed to this protest from new patients, simply said, "I am Doc Susie, Susan Anderson, M.D. If you would prefer a man you can wait for two days and if your child is still alive Doc Albers will be glad to come."

Momentarily cowed, the woman backed off a little. "Sorry. My boy is awful sick." Doc could see that before a recent weight gain, the woman had been pretty in a florid sort of way. Her full breasts threatened the buttons on her sweater and she had fastened her skirt together with a large safety pin. Her clothing was of a superior fabric, but disheveled and dirty. Unlike the hands of most hard working lumberjacks' wives, hers were soft and uncalloused, but her fingernails were ragged.

The sick child had just turned four, the mother said.

"Let's have a look at him." Doc grimaced a little at the familiar, gaseous measle smell that came from the boy's lungs. His fever was very high, the room was sweltering like a Finnish sweat oven, and the child was wrapped in myriad quilts. Doc put her stethoscope to the child's chest and was pleased when she could detect no wheeze to indicate that his lungs had become congested.

"What's your name, sonny?" she asked.

"Homer Jones," he replied.

Blood rushed to Doc's ears, then drained from her face. "Jones?" she echoed.

Returning to work, she thumped the little boy's back hard, hoping to control the shaking of her own hands.

"How long has he been sick . . . Mrs. Jones, is it?"

The woman nodded affirmatively. "Three days. Practically ever since we got here. Musta caught it on the train last Thursday." The woman prattled on, a litany of complaints: "His Pa kept writing for us not to come, but when he quit sending us money my old man, he's the sheriff of Bent County don't you know, bought us one-way tickets and put us on the train. I never woulda believed Ben Jones would live in a dump like this."

"Ben is your . . . husband?"

"He's mine, all right. Wait'll my pa gets aholt of him. He'll skin Ben alive for treating me so bad."

Fighting to keep the hot room from spinning, Doc took a deep breath. So that was why Ben was so elusive!

Almost mechanically, Doc stripped blankets from the boy, introduced fresh air into the cabin and explained to the woman why they must cool the child off so the fever would break.

When Ben appeared at the hovel door, Doc said, "Mr. Jones, there isn't room in this cabin for another adult. I will send for you if I need you. Your son is quite ill." Ben no longer needed to wonder how much Doc knew.

Doc gave the woman a professional demonstration on how to apply cool compresses, speaking soothingly to the child as she did so. She was relieved when, in the middle of the afternoon, little Homer's temperature returned to near normal and the rash spread across his chest and abdomen. With care, the danger was past.

"Thank God, you're a wonderful doctor," said Homer's mother, blowing her nose as she reached into a bedroll, pulled out a bottle of Lydia Pinkham's Tonic, tipped it up, gulped and belched, "Calms my nerves," she said apologetically. "You wouldn't have a little somethin' for my nerves, Doc . . . ? I been through a lot, what with a sick boy, tryin' to find my man. . ."

"I don't believe in spirits and I never carry morphine or cocaine," said Doc. "Brew yourself a little tea. You'll be all right."

She left the shack to find Ben. "Your boy will recover. I'll thank you to take me back to town, now."

Ben said nothing, but fetched an already harnessed horse and handed Doc up into a small cutter, then climbed in beside her. She did not speak to him as he spread a woolen blanket across their legs. Snow was falling gently now, so cold and pure that Doc wondered how anything could dare to look so white when her insides felt so black. Ben cracked his whip and the horse trotted out of Tipperary.

The woods were quieter than they had ever been.

Finally Ben spoke. "She's a mess, ain't she?" A sidelong glance, but no response from Susie. "I was forced into it. Her old man put a gun to my head—the sheriff. I wanted to tell you, a hundred times I wanted to tell you."

"Well, you had a hundred chances and you didn't."

"You never asked me if I was married."

Her laughter had a hard edge, "Then it's all my fault?"

"You saw her. Can't you see what a fix I'm in? Susie, Sweet Sue." He squeezed her arm hard enough to bruise it through her layers of woolen clothing.

"What fix?"

"She's common, a fishwife, a slut, spoiled rotten by her pa. She drinks, too, bottles of that Pinkham's stuff, even whiskey if she can get her hands on it. Then she flies off into rages." He lowered his voice, "I can't even be certain Homer is my child."

"He has your ears," snapped Doc.

Ben acted as though he hadn't heard her. "Susie, this doesn't have to make any difference between us. I love you, you know. We can go away from here where nobody knows us . . ." Ben threw his arm around her shoulder, grabbed her closer to his side and attempted to kiss her.

Susie struggled free, latched a finger around her medical bag and leaped from the sleigh into the snow, feeling a sharp twinge in her ankle as she hit. She fished her black bag out of a snowbank and brushed it with her woolen sleeve. In spite of difficulty standing, she said with some dignity, "I'll walk home, thank you."

As she limped along, Ben reined his horse to follow. "Listen to me," he pleaded, "I've got it all figured out. . ."

Susan set her hat straight. Icy little tears smarted in her eyes. Snow, shoved up her coat sleeves when she fell, was numbing her arms. She was almost glad that her ankle hurt so badly; walking along the road without snowshoes in eight inches of new snow was a trial, but at least it kept her mind off the real pain—total humiliation.

"You can't walk home," Ben called after her. "Don't be childish."

A sledge loaded with logs emerged from a side road. She knew the driver, a taciturn Swede, as one of the area's growing legion of old Scandinavian bachelors. Doc waved and asked for a ride into Fraser. Not one of Jones's men, he looked Ben over, clucked his tongue to his cheek in disapproval, then reached down to give Susie a hand up. Ben reined his horse to turn around; his cutter disappeared back toward the lumber camp.

Although it seemed to take forever for the heavily laden sledge to reach the outskirts of Fraser, Doc's lame ankle forced her to remain at the side of the Swede, shivering and sniffing. "I've acted such a fool," she thought. Through her mind flashed memories of the barn dance, how she had fawned over Ben, how she fetched and carried. The old Swede said nothing; she was grateful that his innate good manners rendered him silent. It was a relief to get home to her cabin, where she could be by herself to rage and sulk and soak her ankle in a bucket of hot water and Epsom salts.

Her injuries amounted to a twisted ankle and badly sprained pride. Within a few days, when her pride was sufficiently mended, Doc hobbled over to Hulda Wilson's house for afternoon coffee.

"Susie, I know it's none of my business but an hour ago I was in Lemmon's Mercantile and I overheard a couple of women from up at Tipperary talking about you. Did you know Ben Jones had a wife?"

"Not until Tuesday, I didn't."

"Well, they were saying some pretty strange things about you."

"Maybe you'd better tell me."

"You won't like it. They said you and Ben was coming back from Tipperary and you tried to cuddle up to him. Ben said he told you he was a married man and he throwed you out of the sleigh to protect his honor, threw your medical bag after you." Hulda laughed self-consciously. "A silly story, eh? Comical."

"Silly—but not so comical. Some people will believe him." Doc's hand was so shaky with fury that she had to put down her coffee cup. When she finally calmed a bit she said, "He sure moved fast to get his story out in front of mine, didn't he? If you hadn't said anything, I wasn't going to tell anybody what happened with Mr. Ben Jones. I suppose now I have the reputation of going around attacking married men. . ." A pixieish grin spread over her face. "Hulda, what if I had hurt him?"

Hulda stood up, reaching for her coat on a hook. "Where are you going?" asked Doc.

"Back to Lemmon's to set those women straight."

"No, you're not. Hulda, I have to live with a lot of nonsense and this is just one more thing. Ignore it. It will be forgotten next week. . ." She was wrong about that.

Not long afterward, word went around that a Hard Times Party was to be thrown at Fraser's Pinewood, a building whose purpose changed as frequently as its owners. It was alternately a dance hall, a roller rink, a saloon, a restaurant. At this moment it was a dance hall, no liquor allowed—at least, not officially. Hard Times parties were all the rage just then, and although it might be argued that most people in Fraser were on perennially hard times, the idea of dressing down instead of up piqued their imagination. For the night, crockery was banished; instead, people ate hobo stew that had been ladled into empty tin cans bearing labels that said Monarch Beans or S&W Stewed Tomatoes. They drank from tin cans, too, and carried their gear bundled in bandanas hanging from the ends of sticks. Everybody scrambled to assemble the best costume, not a difficult task since most of their clothing was already full of holes.

Among Doc's accumulated stuff was a stack of old flour sacks, a popular leftover because they made soft nighties, children's dresses or dish towels. "Pride of the Rockies" was a brand of flour milled in Denver. Doc did not launder the bags to soak off the stiff advertising letters, but incorporated them into her costume.

As luck would have it, Doc was called out to an emergency in Tabernash that afternoon. Although she could never be accused of hurrying through the chore of stitching up a patient, by the time she got the sufferer bandaged up she was barely able to catch a freight headed back to Fraser. She hurried home to don her costume.

She made a grand, if rather late, entrance at the Pinewood. She knew what people had been talking about when she entered the room and all conversation abruptly ceased. She smiled, making eye contact with each person, greeting each by name. With a flourish, she took off her coat and handed it to Axel. Deliberately, she stepped into the middle of the dance floor, turned around, bent over and displayed the back of her skirt for all to see. A chorus of bums and hobos cheered when they read across her rear end the words "Pride of the Rockies."

CHAPTER 9

A Long Time Between Pillows

Doc Susie awoke with a start, bothered by the distinct feeling that she had been neglecting her patients while she dithered away her concentration on that worthless Ben Jones. How long had it been since she heard from Della Just? The baby must be due any time now, although nobody had sent for the doctor.

Doc was worried about Adella's confinement. The Just ranch, off the more traveled roads, was an isolated place in winter. Karl had delivered their other children himself and from his description, Susie sensed that Della's labors had been protracted and difficult. When Karl described how he had helped, Doc became uncomfortably aware that his methods were more suited to wrenching calves into the world than to coaxing an infant from a delicate woman.

"You'd send for the vet if you were in danger of losing a valuable cow," Doc chided.

"OK, I send for you," he agreed. She liked Karl. He was industrious, sober and prosperous; she wished more husbands took as good care of their families. But he had a certain Germanic cockiness about him; would he send for her at the onset of Della's labor, or wait until his wife was in real trouble?

Doc decided to go out to the Just place. But how? It had snowed for three days and showed no sign of letting up. She hated to borrow a pony from Whispering George. If her hunch were wrong, she might have to stay quite a while, maybe up to a week, and that might mean Smith would miss a chance to hire his horse out. Renting horses and teams was how George fed the numerous Smith children. Six miles . . . no more than a good stretch of the legs in summertime, but an all-day project on snowshoes.

Her dog began to whimper when she started packing her medical gear. "Sorry pooch. Not this time." Older now, he wouldn't be able to walk that far in deep snow; a neighbor would look after him.

Doc pulled on men's long underwear, then donned several petticoats; she layered cotton waists and woolen sweaters over the upper part of her body and tucked her hair into a knitted bonnet. Into a rucksack she packed her medical kit, including forceps, then added her nightgown and a few personal items. She buckled her snowshoes over her felt "Russian boots," and headed out of town. She had become expert at that splayfooted waddle snowshoers master in order to travel swiftly across unpacked snow. She never went on skis, said she couldn't get the hang of using them. The skis made by the Norwegians and Finns around Fraser were long, heavy and stiff. They usually landed her in a snowbank face first, flailing to get herself back atop the skis. Certainly a woman alone was safer on snowshoes.

Heading out of Fraser, she panted as she trekked up hills, pausing to take deep breaths when she ran out of oxygen in the thin air. Susie took pleasure in realizing that the sharp pain she felt in her lungs was perfectly normal. She loved the hearty thump of her own heartbeat in her ears—how marvelous the body was when it functioned properly! Her recovery from tuberculosis made her appreciate her own ordinary bodily functions.

"Beat the Stork" was a game, almost as exciting as saving someone's life in the game of "Beat the Reaper." She didn't always get there before the baby arrived, but it wasn't for lack of trying. Once she got a call from a cabin on the William's Fork River, forty miles away. The logistics were formidable: first, a helpful neighbor raced to Tabernash with his sleigh so she could catch a freight train that was held until she arrived. Then she rode in its caboose for 28 miles, was met in a little town named Parshall by the rancher's husband, who drove her eight more miles on his sled to their remote ranch house. She got there in time to deliver the couple's first son. In comparison, this present trip was a cinch.

With luck, she should arrive at the Just ranch in early afternoon with a stopover about two miles out at Pete Benson's place to warm up and have a cup of coffee.

The Bensons were not among Doc's patients or admirers. A few years earlier, Doc and Pete Benson had quarreled. One of Benson's best draft horses, otherwise healthy, had dozens of ugly warts protruding all over his body. When Doc saw them she threatened that if Pete didn't shoot the horse and bury him, she would report Benson to health authorities; she was convinced other horses could contract the warts. Unfortunately, her convictions ran far ahead of her tact that day. Benson was not about to sacrifice a perfectly good work animal on the whim of some woman doctor; he didn't mince words when he told her so, either. The upshot was a certain coolness afterward between Doc Susie and the Bensons, although they weren't exactly enemies. A remote valley is not a good place to have enemies; too often, like now, people might need each other.

When she started down the slope toward the Benson

place she was surprised to see no smoke issuing from the chimney. The Benson dogs heard her and set up a yapping chorus, so Doc called, "Hallo the house!"

A door flung open and a woman's voice called, "Oh! It's Doc Susie."

While Doc shook thick snow from her outer garments, Beda Benson explained that because of the storm, she had allowed the children to sleep late; in foul weather they did not bother to send the children into Fraser to school.

"Doc Susie. What are you doing out in this weather?" Beda demanded.

Susie rubbed her slender, graceful hands together for warmth, waved and called hello to sleepy little Fulke and Hazel, the Benson children, who sat on the velvet davenport looking puzzled.

"I'm headed for the Just place."

"Is the baby on the way?"

"I don't know, but I have this feeling."

"And you are walking? I never heard of such a thing."

Now that Beda had a guest, she wanted to fix a real breakfast, complete with bacon and hot cakes. No eggs though, it was winter. Pete Benson, who had heard the commotion, came in from the barn carrying buckets of milk.

A quiet man, when he heard where Doc Susie was headed he said, "Soon as we have breakfast and I finish my chores, I'll drive you out there."

There was an edge in Beda Benson's voice, "In this weather?" she objected.

Doc could see her point. Why risk a team of good horses? But Doc recognized the good Swede in Pete Benson. If he said he was taking her to the Just place, that's the way it was going to be.

After breakfast and plenty of coffee, Pete harnessed his team and off they pushed toward the west. It was an uneventful ride, except that the horses had to struggle mightily to break through two feet of new snow along four miles of road.

The Justs were surprised to see them. When Doc explained her hunch Della said, "Do you know something I don't know? Nothing is happening yet and I think it might be a week or two, the baby hasn't dropped."

"My, but you've gained a lot of weight," said Doc aloud. To herself, she wondered if Della's puffy cheeks and swollen fingers might indicate that her kidneys were not functioning properly.

Pete offered to take Doc Susie back to Fraser. "No, I'm here and I'm staying," said Susie. Pete ate lunch with the Justs, swapped a few yarns with Karl, gave him a little advice about a harness he was mending, then returned home—convinced that Doc was running a fool's errand.

Karl hadn't exactly homesteaded the place; he bought it from a squatter named Rowley for $50 but every log, every corral post, every bit of sage brush cleared from hay meadows, every irrigation ditch and most of the house had prospered under his own hand. An Austrian immigrant who came to this country when he was thirteen, he had married Adella May Lehman, or Della as everyone called her, in 1896. Everybody wished they could be like the Justs: young, strong and successful with five strapping young sons.

That evening, Susie played with six-year-old Alfred and four-year-old Rudy in front of the fireplace; the older boys boarded in Tabernash during the week so they could go to school. Doc Susie sat on the floor, helping the children build a castle from home-made blocks and telling stories about knights and dragons. "Doc Susie, where does the princess live?" asked little Rudy.

"Now you must call her Dr. Anderson," said Karl.

"Please. Let them call me Doc Susie. It makes me feel special, like an auntie."

Although engrossed in the castle, Rudy occasionally grabbed his right side and frowned. After the children were put to bed Doc said, "Della, what's wrong with Rudy?"

"Oh, he complains that his side hurts sometimes. I think it's just a stitch in the side. You know how kids are."

"Do you mind if I take a look at him tomorrow?"

"Help yourself."

Susie was shown a little cot high in the loft where heat, rising from the fireplace and cook stove, made a warm, cosy nook. She undressed slowly, luxuriating in the unaccustomed warmth. Tired, relaxed after her strenuous day, Doc blew out her candle and slept instantly.

In the middle of the night she was awakened by a hand on her shoulder, shaking her gently. "It's Della. I think you were right; it's time." Awakening instantly was a trick Doc had learned in medical school and never forgot. She stood up, dressed in the dark, and climbed down a ladder to the big room which served as kitchen, parlor and play room. Karl was stoking the fire, filling kettles to augment the hot water in the reservoir on the back of the cook stove. It takes a very long time to heat water from nearly freezing to boiling.

Susie went into the Just's bedroom where a candle provided the only light. She sat on the edge of the bed and took Della's pulse. "I woke up when my water broke," she said. Then she chuckled. "I dreamed I was wetting my pants." Della clenched her fist and curled her body into a ball.

"Have you had many pains?"

"Three or four. Oh, Doc Susie, I'm so happy you are here. I was so afraid but I didn't want to tell Karl." Della squeezed Susie's arm. "I promise I won't be a pest."

Della had prepared well for her confinement. Karl helped Doc spread clean sheets on the bed; boiled receiving blankets and wrappers for the new baby were at the ready.

"Relax for a little while. I must scrub up."

Karl watched with fascination as Doc washed her hands, arms, cleaned her fingernails, then donned a fresh white apron and tied her hair into a turban.

"All this trouble for a baby?" he asked.

"Yes. All this trouble. Karl, do you know what puerperal fever is?"

"You mean mother's sickness?"

"Yes, that's what I mean. Do you remember how so many mothers used to die?"

A faraway look came into Karl's eye. "*Meine mutti . . .* died when my little sister was born. I grew up with no *mutti.*" Karl looked anxiously toward the bedroom.

Doc Susie distracted Karl's worry by throwing in a little lesson with her doctoring, "It's too bad your sister didn't wait a few years to be born because interestingly enough, the condition was first described in Vienna by a man named Ignaz Semmelweis. He discovered the fever was usually caused by dirty hands, bed linens or other items that came into contact with the mother. He proved that doctors and nurses caused the deaths." Karl was interested to learn that a fellow Austrian had been so clever.

"A little later, I want you to scrub yourself just the same way you saw me do. And I'll wash again if we must wait a long time. Tell me something, Karl. When you delivered Adella's other babies, which part came out first?"

"Da head, natcherly." He seemed surprised that she should ask.

"I'm going to need a lot more light, Karl. Your barn lanterns are the brightest." Karl pulled on his coat while Doc disappeared into the bedroom to examine Della in more detail. Doc suspected that the baby was in a breech position, its head up instead of down. Certainly the head wasn't engaged in the birth canal.

Doc could only hope that the baby was unusually tiny because she feared it could not pass through Della's small pelvis. She had delivered breech babies on other occasions, but did not think Della could deliver in that manner. Her trained fingers felt across Della's belly, confirming the baby's awkward position. She explained the problem to Della, said she was going to have to try to turn the baby. She told Karl the same thing, apologizing in advance for making Della so uncomfortable, then asked Karl to support Della's back or belly as instructed and ordered Della to brace her legs against the foot of the big pine bedstead, just so. Doc said, "Try not to bear down unless I tell you to."

Working with a sensible woman like Della was a pleasure for Doc, who remembered many times she had had to interrupt other patients' screams by saying, "If you keep up this howling business, I'm going home and you can do this by yourself." The women always saw it Doc's way and calmed down.

A woman physician had a real advantage in dealing with a breech position because her hands were small. As Doc probed, Della perspired, grunted and bit her lip but did not complain. Karl proved to be a capable assistant, following Doc's orders, fascinated to watch the process because he had frequently encountered the same problem with his precious calves and wanted to learn all he could.

Doc Susie reached carefully up into the uterus and very slowly, very deliberately, in tiny increments, turned the little body until she felt the head. With infinite care, she put her fingers around the cranium and felt it follow her hand into Della's birth canal. Now Doc asked Karl to sit on the side of the bed and take Della's hand. She explained to both of them that she was certain the baby would come easily. "It's a good thing I had that premonition and came on out, Della. Otherwise you would probably have been in labor for days before Karl sent for me. With your small pelvis, I don't think you could have delivered a breech baby. We probably would have lost the child." And, she added to herself, Della, too. But she didn't want to say that just now.

Doc told them that she had a little ether in her kit, but would prefer not to use it because the baby had been through so much already. Adella said, "I can make it. After all, Karl never gave me anything with the boys."

The relief Doc felt over repositioning the baby far exceeded what she would experience half an hour later when the crown of the baby's head presented itself. Della pinched her fingernails into Karl's wrist when she underwent a last, mighty contraction. "Push, push hard," Doc urged. She pulled gently, firmly, the baby slipped into her hands.

Doc Susie could never take the process of birth for granted, even in the most normal of deliveries—which this wasn't. As the slimy blue creature slid into her hands, it looked dead and lifeless for just a moment until the first convulsive breath instantly turned the little form from blue to pink. Usually, a quick finger through the throat would clear any mucus and make way for a rattling little gasp, followed by a gurgling scream. Only then did Doc check on the sex, "This is your girl, Della!"

Della's eyes streamed with tears; Doc couldn't help shedding a few of her own, though she tried to turn sideways so Karl wouldn't see. She wondered if a man could ever understand what the moment of birth meant to a woman; after pain—triumph. She wondered if the emotion of going into battle might compare to childbirth, but she didn't think anything as destructive as war could be as exciting as the miracle of new life.

After assuring herself that the baby was breathing normally, Doc wrapped her in soft flannel and handed her to Karl. "I'll wash her up later. Now I must see to Della."

"She's awful bloody," said Karl, alarmed when he saw the baby's head.

"That's not from the baby, it's from Della," I had to make a small incision to ease the birth. Now I must put in a few stitches. Why don't you show the baby to her brothers?"

Doc peeked around the corner of the bedroom door to watch Karl present the new baby. Two little boys in their pajamas clung to each other on the couch in front of the fireplace. They had awakened to a house in which no mother was rattling pans, no father was splitting kindling. Doc and Karl had been so busy that they hadn't had time to notice that Alfred and Rudy had come down from their loft. Karl explained that their mother would be all right, and held up their new sister.

Della winced as the stitches were completed. Not for the

first time, Doc wished she had something to give a patient for pain. Her "no drugs" policy sometimes hurt her as much as it did the patient.

After seeing that Adella was comfortable, Doc washed the baby as Rudy and Alfred watched. She dabbed the waxy substance from the skin, cleaned the ears, checked the throat for more mucus, showed the boys why a girl was different, then dried the baby and swaddled her in another clean blanket. She tucked the baby gently at Della's side, then busied herself with cleaning herself up and donning a fresh apron. As she watched Della and her new baby sleeping comfortably, Doc sighed to herself, "I've had more babies than anybody, but no family to show for it."

"What?" said Karl.

"Nothing, I was talking to myself."

Now came the tricky part—breakfast. Doc still hadn't learned the mysteries of the kitchen, and Karl wasn't any better. Together they managed to scorch oatmeal and burn toast. It didn't help when Alfred said, "That's not the way mama does it." Several times.

Doc laughed and told Karl about other disasters she had tasted at the mercy of new fathers. "When one of the Leonard babies was born, Pat decided to cook rice for the kids. He put in too much rice, and had to keep adding water until they had a whole washtub of the stuff. It just kept boiling over the top of the stove. That was back when Pat had a notion that rice was the best food for you. He insisted that Clara keep on cooking it, every day, every meal. Well, Clara told me that he finally got so sick of rice that one day he went over to the stove and threw all of that rice out the back door. And they never had to eat rice again!"

She sat down finally to rest, to sip a mug of coffee. The sun was up now, streaming in a south window, shining on a threadbare rug where a dog and a cat snoozed comfortably in the warmth. Doc thought she could be happy at the ranch forever, if the Justs had been her family. Which they weren't.

After she rinsed the dishes, Doc told Rudy to stretch out on the couch. She reached under his pajamas and probed his abdomen. When she worked her way around his little tummy the boy recoiled in pain and drew up his knee. He tensed, even though she tried to be gentle, "Does that hurt? That?"

Susie frowned. She had confirmed her suspicion that Rudy had an infected appendix—not yet at the acute stage—but the problem was serious. Knowing the terror that the word appendicitis held for parents, she hesitated to say it out loud. But she had to.

As soon as the boys got out their blocks again she said to Karl, "We've got a problem."

"Della?"

"No, Della is doing well. Her kidneys are not doing their work, but I don't think there will be any complications from this birth. However, if you have another baby she will have to wait out the birth in Fraser. I must have her where I can check on her frequently during the latter stages of pregnancy. With proper medical care she should do fine. The real problem is Rudy. Karl, we've got to get him to Denver and have his appendix taken out."

"Appendix?" Karl looked stunned. Only recently had the simple surgery necessary to remove an infected appendix come into general use. Until then, a burst appendix resulted in death. Period.

"Can it wait until spring?"

"No. The child is running a low fever, I wouldn't give him more than a few days until it bursts."

"But Della can't take him. Who will look after Alfred? . . . My cattle."

"Would you trust me to take him, Karl?"

"You would do that?"

"When I left Fraser yesterday the trains were still going over Corona. If Corona is open, I think we should get him into Colorado General Hospital."

Karl had another idea, "Can't you do the operation?"

"No, Karl. I'm not a surgeon. Unless there were no

other choice, I am ethically bound to see that a proper surgeon does the work. As things stand I have to recommend that he be operated on in a hospital where everything is clean and sterile. Many more people die from infections after operations than during the surgery itself."

Doc Susie and Karl broke the bad news to Della. "Oh, he might just need some castor oil," she protested.

"Della, a laxative could kill him."

Della looked sad, deflated. She wanted to go with Rudy, but resigned herself to the situation.

Doc Susie promised to send for Christine Benson, Pete's spinster sister who often worked as a nursemaid, to help until Della was on her feet. Doc ordered Della to stay in bed for at least a week, two if possible.

In emergencies, it was not unusual for a rural physician to accompany a patient to the hospital; too much could go wrong en route. If the patient should take a turn for the worse, or the travel process should be interrupted, it was risky to be without medical care. Besides, patients were admitted to Colorado General Hospital only upon being referred by a physician. Taking a small child to the hospital without his parents *was* unusual. Della explained as best she could to little Rudy that Doc Susie would take him on the train over the big mountain to the hospital. When her throat constricted, Doc Susie took over:

"We will see the big locomotives, and you can drink water in a little paper cup from the big jar. At the hospital they have ice cream!"

Late that afternoon, Karl, Doc and Rudy drove through the snow to Tabernash. Now that the railroad operated clear to Craig, day trains were reserved for summer tourist traffic. Local residents preferred to travel at night so they could arrive at their destination, whether Denver or home, in time to conduct an entire day's business.

Would the train be operating at all? So much snow had fallen the last few days, chances were no better than fifty-fifty.

The dispatcher at Tabernash was encouraging, "Looks

good." Behind him, a telegraph key clattered away. Although Doc knew Morse code, the railroader lingo was a mystery. "Rotary plow just reached the Ranch Creek Wye. They'll hold it there and couple you in behind."

Karl carried his son around and around the waiting room, "*Mein kind, kindschen, er hat kein gluck*, no luck my little one." With contrition in his voice, he said to Doc, "We had money put aside for the baby—to pay you—now with Rudy's operation, the nurse, I just don't know . . ."

Doc looked Karl in the eye. "First we get Della and this boy well, then we'll worry about it." She figured Karl was good for the delivery fee, although she probably wouldn't see her $10 until after haying season—longer if there was not enough rain or too much rain.

When the train pulled into the platform, Doc was heartened to see her old friend George Barnes leaning from the vestibule. Since that first desperate day when he had presided over her trip into the Fraser Valley, the conductor had officiated over many of her excursions to the city— usually in the company of a patient. "Karl," she said assuringly, "If anybody can get our train over the mountain, it's George."

Karl carried his son into the car; although he had slept on the sleigh coming into Tabernash, now Rudy was wide awake. George Barnes showed him how to run the window shade up and down, warned him not to pull the little cord above it and asked, "Can you whistle?" Rudy tried to purse his little lips. "Very good," said Barnes. "If you need anything, whistle."

Karl had feared his child might cry and raise a fuss when they parted, but he found it was his own emotions that were in danger of bursting. He patted Doc Susie on the shoulder, smiled with his eyes swimming in tears and got off the train as fast as he could.

Doc snuggled little Rudy to her side. She was glad he wasn't raising a fuss. In her mind, children who had the best upbringing were the least afraid; they trusted people.

Karl waved from the platform, fading into the night as the train pulled out.

The train chugged up the straight-a-way toward Fraser. Doc wished she could stop for just a few minutes, run to her house, console her dog and grab a few city clothes. That was out of the question, of course. She wouldn't have even raised the possibility with Barnes; she had as much respect for his timetable as he did.

The conductor lost no time in informing his crew that Doc Susie was aboard with a child whose appendix was in danger of bursting. The dispatcher had already telegraphed the news along the wire. Railroad men had a special feeling for emergencies, were glad they were in a position to help. And they all knew Doc Susie and respected her. Many times she had flagged a train to get to a patient's bedside, or to return home. Depending on the kind of train it was, and how far she was going, she rode in the caboose or locomotive cab; a couple of times she just hopped up onto the "cowcatcher" at the front of the train for a couple of miles. If no train were due or the roadbed had been washed out, a section crew occasionally took her down the line, pumping a hand car. Although she had never been appointed railroad doctor, she had never bought a ticket, either. It wasn't exactly policy, it was just understood that the railroad took her wherever she needed to go—and cleared the tracks ahead to get her there fast.

The child stretched out, his head on her lap, and slept. What a sweet little fellow he was! Curly blonde hair, high forehead, red lips. And how heavy . . . his head felt like a cannonball in her lap. She loosened his clothing, noting that his fever had increased. The next time Barnes came by, she asked him to bring a carton or paper bag in case the child vomited—a distinct possibility.

As usual, she was the only woman on the train. Fellow-passengers were ranchers going to do business in Denver, tired lumberjacks heading for riotous times on Larimer Street or worn-out miners fleeing from the coal fields over by Phippsburg in search of better jobs. Many of them knew Karl Just, were as concerned about little Rudy as if he were their own child. And most knew Doc Susie, too.

When the train stopped in Arrow, Barnes checked with the agent, then came back to report to Doc. They had orders to couple in behind a rotary snowplow at the Ranch Creek Wye, about six miles up the mountain—beyond that point, deep snow frequently drifted.

Since her last trip, the condition of the roadbed had deteriorated noticeably. The train lurched, practically rattling Susie's teeth over many stretches of track; in places, the engineer had to slow to a crawl. Matter-of-factly, Barnes told her that since Bill Freeman had become president of the railroad less money had been spent on "unnecessary" maintenance of the roadbed. As Barnes saw it, Freeman was so intent on finagling financing for a tunnel that he preferred to react to emergencies rather than prevent them.

She remembered Freeman, all right—the pompous ass who told her she had to move.

"According to Freeman," Barnes went on, "all those coal trains are costing money. The more freight we haul, the more money we lose."

"That doesn't make sense to me," said Doc.

"Freeman's in a bind. He has to keep his freight charges low enough so West Slope coal can compete with coal from Pueblo and Wyoming. Forty percent of the entire cost on this line is snow removal. Railroads along the front range don't have to put out money for snow removal; Freeman's got to keep the coal coming to attract potential tunnel investors, but the railroad is losing a lot of money hauling it."

"What's he going to do about it?"

"Reduce our salaries. What else?" So the rumor was true. Even though times were good, Freeman was going to reduce his men's salaries—men who merely risked their lives daily to keep his railroad operating over the Continental Divide.

"George, you could work for any railroad in the United

States or Canada. They'd be glad to have a man of your experience. Why do you go on working for Freeman?"

George Barnes looked down at little Rudy. "If we don't keep the road open over the hill, how would you get sick children to the hospital?"

"Fiddlesticks," she said. "Freeman would find someone else." Doc Susie had seen too much of living conditions among loggers and railroad men to have much sympathy for their big-city employers. She knew from her time in Cripple Creek that when miners banded together and stood up to their bosses, wages and working conditions improved. She would have liked to tell him about the Western Federation of Miners, but Barnes was busy coupling his train behind the snow plow and its Mallet.

She knew that from here to Corona danger lurked at every tie in the road. Nobody had to point out where Tom Conway and Sid Cane had been swept to the valley floor in an avalanche; their adventure had been written up in the *Denver Post*. The two men were trying to shovel snow into the water intake of a Mallet that was stalled in a snow drift and running out of water. To work the snow down into the boiler, they crawled down through a manhole and were shoveling mightily when an avalanche hit the locomotive, tumbling it over and over. Inside the boiler, the men were pitched into the icy water, out again to be dashed against its steel sides, then sloshed back into the water, over and over; in the total darkness they had no idea where they had come to rest when the terrible tumbling finally ceased. Only by sheer *luck* did the locomotive stop bouncing with the manhole boiler facing up. Otherwise, the men would probably have smothered before they could be dug out. Several other trainmen caught in the same avalanche were less fortunate. It took days of probing into the snow to locate their bodies.

Doc almost literally held her breath as the train entered "the Loop," in her opinion the most dangerous section of all. Here, the roadbed hugged one exposed side of the mountain until it went through a tunnel, looped around a hill and then crossed over the same tunnel via a spectacular trestle. It was here that avalanches often occurred; some of them hurtled over the upper level of tracks, gathered speed and snow, then bombarded the tracks below. In summertime you could look down the hill and see rolling stock— gondolas and boxcars—that had been lifted from the tracks and tumbled to the valley floor in the maw of an avalanche. Rolling stock was abandoned; only when expensive locomotives went over was any effort made at salvage.

Slowly, the train crept along, its speed reduced because it was pushing the rotary plow. Doc, keeping a mental inventory of the trouble spots, was relieved as they passed the Loop Trestle, Sunnyside Water Tank, Ptarmigan Point. They were nearly to the safety of the snow sheds when the train ground to a halt. There was a great deal of bustling in the vestibule forward; Doc gathered that a thick snowdrift had blown across the roadbed. Unlike fresh snow, a snowdrift could be as hard as concrete. The train backed up and the rotary plow attacked it again, with no discernible progress. It was so dark she couldn't see.

Little Rudy was stirring. His fever was definitely rising and he didn't know where he was. "*Mutti, mutti,*" he said over and over. "I want my *mutti.*"

Ahead, Doc could hear swearing. Outside the coach, men carrying lanterns hurried up and down the roadbed. A blast of cold air whooshed through the car as George Barnes appeared. He was wearing a McIntosh and shouted, "I need diggers!"

He didn't have to underline that a sick child would otherwise be marooned. Every man in the car rose and followed him. From time to time one of the volunteers, sweating although icicles clung to his beard, would burst into the car, help himself to a drink of water and jump out the door again. Later, they told Doc that the supply of shovels was limited so one man would work until he was out of breath, then hand the shovel to the man behind him and go to the end of the line—a frenetic relay devised to save Rudy.

Doc gave Rudy sips of water, but turned down offers of candy and food made by generous passengers. She had forbidden any food since before his lunch.

After an hour, the drift had been substantially loosened up. Men trooped back into the railroad car, stomping their feet, trying to restore circulation after the cruelties of the timberline wind. The train backed up and slammed into a snowdrift. As it ground to a halt, a sigh of disappointment, mingled with soft curses, spread through the car. But Barnes hadn't given up. He signaled the engineer to try again; this time the locomotive broke through the drift. As the train surged forward, everybody cheered.

Barnes apologized to his passengers, "I'm not going to stop at the Corona lunchroom. There are three other trains under the sheds. Word is that we're clear for down the other side, and I don't want to take any chances with bad air in the sheds." Hungry and thirsty though they were from their exertions, the men saw the wisdom of Barnes' decision; smoke and gasses that built up beneath the snow shed were notorious. More than a few members of train crews had died in those sheds when they passed out and were crushed against the side of the shed or under the wheels of the gigantic locomotives. There were places where a fuzee, or flare, would not even stay lit because there was no oxygen. It would be better for all of them, but especially for the child, to go where the air was pure.

They paused only as long as it took to uncouple the rotary plow and its locomotive, shunting them onto a side track. Doc looked out to see the lunchroom slip past—she wouldn't have minded a cup of coffee herself—but felt grateful to feel the wheels turning faster.

At every switch down the line, gandy dancers knew that Doc Susie was aboard with a sick child. Normally a local passenger train such as this one was not allowed to interrupt the momentum of an uphill freight; on this run switch blocks turned from red to green, shunting the uphill freights onto sidings.

It was about six in the morning when the train arrived

at the Moffat Station in Denver. Barnes helped Doc Susie into the depot, saying he wished he could accompany them to the hospital. Doc told him not to worry, the passengers on the train had passed the hat for their cab fare.

As they were driven toward the hospital, Doc Susie got a good taste of what it was like to be an anxious parent. She was surprised to discover that little Rudy was suddenly wide awake. He was as bright as a new button, looking out the window, saying, "Truck, car, trolley, honk-honk, clang-clang." It was the first trip to the city that the lad could remember, and he was wide-eyed at everything. He was even a little bit naughty, banging his heels on the car seat, rolling the windows up and down.

"Beautiful weather the last few days," the cab driver said. "Trees are starting to leaf out and everybody's been out in the parks." When they arrived at the hospital, Rudy hopped out of the cab on his own, waved bye-bye to the driver and skipped up the steps to the great lobby door.

An intern seated at a desk looked up to see a pajama-clad little boy trailed by a woman wearing voluminous skirts over God knew how many woollen petticoats. She was bundled to the ears, despite Denver's spring-like weather.

"I am here to admit this child," Doc said, as though giving orders to the young, white-clad doctor. She watched him carefully, gauging his reaction. He bristled as she had expected, quite unaware that he was being expertly baited.

"Your son?" asked the intern.

"No, his name is Rudolph Just."

"I can't admit a child on your say-so, lady. What's the matter with him?"

"He will need an appendectomy, an emergency appendectomy."

Just then an older man appeared behind the intern; Susie saw him, but the intern didn't. It was Dean Meador, the head of the hospital; he eavesdropped on the conversation with some interest.

"Lady—we are very busy here. You can't bring a patient

to Colorado General without the recommendation of a physician. You said the child is not yours and besides, he looks perfectly healthy."

That was true. Rudy's fever had dropped. He was pulling cushions from chairs in the waiting room, watching them fall to the floor and singing a song, "London Bridge is falling down . . ."

"Notify surgery," said Doc with no-nonsense sharpness. "His appendix must come out—immediately!"

"That's enough, I'm calling a guard." The intern rose importantly and reached for a bell. At that moment, his superior grabbed his wrist.

"Don't you think you should examine the patient?" asked Dr. Meador.

The intern was caught off guard. "But sir, the procedure in this case . . ."

"I don't see that any procedures have been violated. Examine the child."

The two doctors followed as Doc Susie took Rudy by the hand and led him into an examining room. She pulled off his clothes and cushioned his head as the child stretched out stiffly on the table, fearful and wide-eyed in the presence of strangers. "Doc Susie, what's he going to do?"

Hearing the word "Doc," the intern glanced quickly at Dean Meador who said, "Meet Doctor Susan Anderson, the finest rural physician in Western Colorado. Perhaps that fancy Eastern school you went to didn't teach you to respect your betters. Now by God, boy, what's wrong with this child?"

The intern's big hand passed up and down the boy's abdomen as he concentrated on his diagnosis. "I think she's right, sir."

" 'Think she's right! Think she's right!' Doctor Anderson is the best diagnostician west of the divide. She doesn't have an X-ray or a lab. She has to find out what's wrong with a patient by putting her ear up to his chest in the dark in the midst of a blizzard, and still gets it right. In the future, please don't assume that because a *woman*, dressed sensibly for the winter conditions she left behind, has the courtesy to save you the trouble of diagnosing a difficult case, she is wrong! Now go scrub up. You're going to follow this patient through.''

As the young man hurried down the corridor, the doctor slapped his knee and roared, ''By God, Susie, you teach these arrogant young pups more about humility in ten minutes than I can in six weeks. How are you? Would you care to scrub?''

Often before, Doc Susie had played a game at Colorado General that she secretly called: ''Get the Intern.'' These young men, educated from textbooks, trained in well-equipped examining rooms, had no idea what was involved with treating people outside of a hospital. Senior physicians at the University of Colorado, which operated the hospital, treasured their trove of ''Doc Susie'' stories. The past butts of her ambush somehow neglected to warn incoming junior interns about a quaint little woman physician who might wander into the emergency facility with a very sick patient in tow. Having once been goats themselves, they wanted to see rawer recruits taste Doc Susie's humble pie.

Susie loved her excursions to Colorado General; they reminded her of her own days in medical school in Ann Arbor. Nurses opened doors for her, doctors asked her opinion; the professional respect she was rarely accorded in Fraser caressed her shoulders. Everyone from deans to matrons on wards spoke with awe as the little woman, dressed as though winter were a permanent fixture, swept down the corridor.

Dr. Anderson usually donned mask and gown to accompany her patient into surgery. In the operating theater she brushed up her knowledge, learned new techniques, the latest theory. Of course it helped her patients, too; the last thing they saw before ether took them to the land of rotating gold balls was their trusted Doc Susie.

Doc was not apprehensive as a senior surgeon cut into

Rudy; she was absolutely certain of her diagnosis. When the physician located the appendix and exposed it she saw for herself that it was raw and bloated, an ominous bubble twisted at one end. The intern, also observing, told her, "You got him here just in time, doctor. He owes his life to you."

Back in Rudy's room, Doc Susie stayed with her little patient until he started to come out from under the effects of the ether. The child vomited a few times as she held his little head. By then, a friendly nurse with a big bosom had heard about the sick little boy who was a temporary orphan. She took over, speaking to Rudy in a comforting mixture of German and English, just like home, and gave him a small ceramic figurine of three little Dutch girls, dancing in a circle.

When the surgeon popped into the room he was quickly satisfied with Rudy's recovery. He turned to Susan, "Doctor, some of us are headed for the Brown Palace to have lunch. We would be pleased if you would join us."

She looked down at her clothes, serviceable for winter in the mountains, but hardly in fashion for Denver's best hotel.

"Don't worry about how you are dressed. It is of no importance."

The surgeon, his assistant, Dr. Meador and Susie rode to the hub of the city in Dr. Meador's new Buick automobile. The seamstress in Doc told her that the physicians' suits were hand-tailored and cut from superior cloth. Their kid gloves, tie pins and blocked hats all spoke of city doctors' prosperity. Being on the staff of a teaching hospital must pay very well. Although she no longer thought of practicing medicine any place but Fraser, she could not help but dwell briefly on the disparity between her own poverty and the economic ascendancy of her hosts. Although she had saved every penny she could garner, her meager savings would not cover the price of a second-hand Ford.

For just a moment she felt a little like a country bump-

kin when the uniformed doorman of the venerable Brown
Palace Hotel flung open the door and the little party swept
into the foyer. She looked up to see tiers upon tiers of iron
balconies, reaching up toward a massive skylight. Expen-
sively dressed people posed behind the balustrades, looking
across the concourse to size up still more stylish people on
the opposite side. Didn't they have anything better to do
with their time, she wondered, than to stand around looking at each other?

When they entered the elegant Casanova Room, draped
with silk from the ceiling and walls, the maitre d'—honing
in on the rather motley-looking Doc Susie—began to ele-
vate his nose and flare his nostrils. In mid-sniff, Dr.
Meador shot him a scalpel-swift warning. Taking his cue
from the doctor, a frequent patron, the head waiter's chill
melted to unctuous subservience; with great courtesy he
seated the four at a good table. Fashionably dressed people
at nearby tables, alert to notice just who was dining today,
looked surprised when they saw the small, inappropriately
attired woman. They shot each other inquiring glances.

Perhaps they expected a rustic show of manners; Doc
Susie, aware of the stir she was making—a little proud of it
even—accepted a cup of coffee. She extended her little finger, in a manner to assure everyone of the excellence of her
breeding, and sipped it.

A waiter took their order. To the astonishment of her
hosts, she ordered a very large meal: bisque, oysters, ome-
let, steak and dessert, explaining, "I haven't had a bite to
eat since yesterday morning. I suddenly find myself very
hungry."

But it wasn't going to be easy to enjoy her lunch. Her
companions were so interested to hear details of her practice that she was frequently forced to lob the conversational ball back into their court so she could have a chance
to chew her food. What luxury! Into her mouth went ex-
quisite, tasty morsels, and out came delicious, latinate
words. She had not realized how tired she was of explaining medical problems "in plain English" to lumberjacks

who barely understood it. She lingered lovingly over every multisyllable, speaking peer language to her equals, laughing over little in-jokes that only a fellow physician could appreciate.

Each time a waiter came by and offered more food, she took it. "How good the strawberry jam is at the Brown Palace," she said. The three doctors were beginning to doubt that such a small stomach could freight so much cargo. They were fascinated to hear how she had trussed up a lumberjack in a lady's corset to immobilize his broken ribs, cajoled pharmaceutical drummers out of sample medications so she could pass them on at no cost to destitute patients, sutured scalp lacerations by cleaning the wound then tying the patient's own hairs together to close it, saving the pain of stitches. She winked at the men condescendingly, "But of course your fingers are too large, and you never learned to tat." They hung on her description of how just yesterday she had turned Adella's baby in the womb. Over chocolate ice cream she described her inspection tours of lumbercamp sanitation facilities.

They wanted to know how she thought the railroad was faring. When she told them Bill Freeman was gouging the workers, the surgeon said, "Well, if he hasn't any faith in his railroad, he certainly doesn't act like it. My banker told me Freeman buys up every bit of D&SL stock that comes on the market. Do you suppose he knows something that we don't about the proposed tunnel?"

By the time the meal was finished, she could no longer suppress her yawns. "It's been a long time between pillows; I have a few hours before my train leaves. I've had only small snatches of sleep in the past two-and-a-half days. I'd like to catch a nap in the nurses' quarters."

As the comfortable big Buick headed back to the hospital, the combination of its soothing motion and the warm afternoon took their toll. She fell asleep.

But she was not sleeping too soundly to hear Dr. Meador say, "Rural doctors like her make me a little ashamed of myself. All she cares about is whether or not her patients get well. I'll bet she's as poor as a church-mouse. Something is wrong with the way we hand out money for medical treatment in this country."

CHAPTER 10

Working on the Railroad

When Doc Susie held her stethoscope to the chest of a patient she paid no attention to the thump of normal heart beats, nor to the standard rush of air into and out of the lungs. No, it was that extra thump or reedy wheeze that alerted her to trouble. Similarly, she gave little heed to the bassoon voice of Mallet locomotives as they echoed up and down the valley or to the scores of smaller engines that paused at the depot. But should she hear an unaccustomed hiss or clank, she stopped what she was doing, even if it was sleeping.

One night she knew something was wrong at the Fraser depot. She awakened to the certainty that there was a short, downhill freight train halted on the main line where it had no business being. She could not see through her frosted bedroom window, but was already lighting a kerosene lamp when she heard pounding on her door. She threw open the frosted upstairs window that faced the street.

"Doc Susie, Doc Susie! Tom Kowalski is in bad trouble. He's havin' a heart attack!"

She did not bother to dress but threw a wrapper over her nightgown. Lamp in hand, she carefully descended her narrow, steep stairway. When she opened the front door she saw two men—the fireman and a gandy dancer from the train halted at the depot—steadying a third man, their engineer, between them.

"Doc, you've got to help Tom," said the fireman. "Something is wrenching his gut terrible." Through multiple layers of woolen clothing a rotund, middle-aged Pole with a bulbous nose clutched his hand to his chest. He was breathing heavily, his face ashen.

Doc Susie motioned them to assist the engineer to a stool, told them to unfasten his striped overalls and unbutton his shirts. She stirred up the fire in the potbelly stove in the examining room, stuck her stethoscope into her ears, pressed it to Kowalski's muscular chest and listened. His breath was coming quickly, but she could detect no abnormal heart rhythms. "How long since you last ate? What did you eat?"

"I've got a bad ticker, Doc. I can't tell the railroad doc or they'll fire me. I've got a family, Doc Susie."

"Answer me, what did you eat?"

His wiry young fireman spoke up. "His wife sent along some sausages, big stinky Polish sausages. Couple of hours ago he heated up a chunk of boiler plate in the fire box and fried them sausages on it. Washed 'em down with a bottle of beer he had hid in his jacket. I told him I didn't think they smelled too good. I wouldn't have none of them." The beer accounted for the faint odor of alcohol that mingled with garlic on the man's breath.

The worried fireman continued, "Doc, we're halted on the main. If we don't get to Tabernash in twenty minutes, we'll be on the law. If Freeman finds out, we'll all be fired. Ever one of us has got spots on our work records. Besides, it's against the law to have any suds along, and I drank one, too. If we're accused of violating Rule G, we've had it."

Nobody had to tell Susie that "on the law," meant violating the railroad's book of work rules; in this case being behind schedule because of an unauthorized stop. And the dreaded "Rule G" forbade drinking or intoxication on the job. Everybody knew that Bill Freeman, the much feared boss of the railroad, had a muted telegraph key in his office in Denver and another in his home. They clattered away incessantly in the background; he eavesdropped night and day, knew where every unit was on the Moffat line, knew what kind of locomotives were powering them, who was at the helm. Freeman had been known to stop right in the middle of a conversation, cock his ear toward the key; if he didn't like what he heard he would pick up a phone and launch into a profane tirade aimed at straightening out the perceived problem. He had fired "rails," as men who worked on the railroad were often called, for much less than being "on the law."

Doc knew that the train crew had already violated work rules by halting "on the main." Those tracks were normally reserved as a right-of-way for through traffic. Nevertheless, if Doc had to choose between a printed timetable and the health of her patient, she would have sent the gandy dancer to the depot to phone up the dispatcher in Tabernash, requesting more time.

She turned, stirred some bicarbonate in a glass and gave it to the man to drink. He gulped it down. Almost immediately she was rewarded with a hearty, window-shaking belch. "Doc, I feel better already."

"Not so fast. You say you have a bad heart?"

"Ever since I had the fever when I was a kid, it hasn't worked quite right. I never told the railroad doc."

"Sometimes indigestion and a heart attack have the same symptoms. I've got to keep an eye on you for an hour or so."

"Doc, we can't do that," injected the fireman. "If we

leave him here, there'll be questions. You'll just have to come with us."

Susie knew Tom Kowalski, knew him to be the sole support of his wife, five children, mother and father who spoke no English, all living together in a run-down neighborhood in Denver. "Get him back into the cab, I'll get dressed."

She charged up the staircase, threw on petticoats and all the other warm clothing that was within easy reach; cold as it was in Fraser, it would be much colder in Tabernash. Doc grabbed her black bag, dashed out the door and ran the half block to the depot. The train consisted of one locomotive, its tender, a couple of freight cars and a caboose.

The service ladder to the cab had not been designed to accommodate a female person wearing several petticoats and a skirt, but Doc scrambled up as she had done many times before.

Space inside the hot cab was very limited; the engineer was suffering from the exertion of the short climb. The fireman looked back out the engineer's window for the gandy dancer to signal with his lantern from the caboose; he prepared to drive the train. Doc Susie braced herself against the cab wall, supporting the sick man who sat on the fireman's stool. Just as the fireman notched out the throttle, Doc looked out of her cab window to see a white blur racing along, trying to chase the wheels of the huge locomotive.

"Stop, stop," she screamed. "It's my dog! He'll freeze to death if I leave him."

The men could scarcely believe their ears. Hold up a train on the main to pick up a pet dog? On the other hand, they were in the habit of obeying Doc Susie's orders. She climbed down, scooped up the frantic spitz, handed him up to the fireman, then hitched her skirts again to climb into the cab.

The freight hurried down the four-mile straight-a-way to Tabernash, stopping only long enough for the fireman to jump out, throw a switch, climb back in, pull the locomotive onto a siding, then scramble out and secure the switch again. They made it through the bloc signal just "under the law," thus avoiding questions from Denver.

With great care the fireman, gandy dancer and some other recruits helped Kowalski down from the cab, then steadied him to a room in the hotel near the depot. Doc stayed at the sick man's side for two hours, checking and rechecking his heart and pulse. "You're not gonna tell the rail doc?" Tom pleaded.

"I won't if you'll promise me never to try another stunt like this. Your problem was a bellyache—this time. You ate that greasy meat, drank a foamy beer. Have you ever seen what happens to an inflated balloon that is brought up here from Denver? Air expanding within it makes it much larger. At high altitude, gas in your stomach can swell you up, too. If I were you, I'd move to a lower altitude. Sooner or later, your weak heart is going to give out under the strain of going over the hill so often."

She was only too glad to assure Tom that she would not report the episode. She was miffed at the incumbent railroad doctor because he had told Della Just, "Doc Susie would have made a good nurse, but a doctor . . ."

When she walked out of the hotel into the cold night air, she suddenly remembered that she had left her dog behind in the locomotive cab. She hurried to the depot; if someone other than herself tried to handle the dog, he would bite.

The locomotive, she was told, had been pulled over to the roundhouse. So, she headed along the siding in search of her dog.

Tabernash was a thriving town, a division point where trains changed crews. At the shops, shifts worked night and day to keep the hill supplied with power. The shops were located in a half-round house, a busy place because most of the wear and tear—and damage—to machinery occurred on the brutal West Slope.

She wrinkled her nose at the usual foul Tabernash air, a

disagreeable mixture of freezing fog, smoke and steam from the locomotives. Doc's shoulders hunched against the cold. She depended on the even spacing of railroad ties beneath her feet to guide her through the dark. Ahead, she could hear clanging noises of men beating on metal, hissing sounds of steam being tested through pistons and valves. Through the huge doors and across the barn, electric lights shone onto work areas where men stood on tall ladders, servicing the big Mallet locomotives. But most of the cavernous expanse was black.

As she tiptoed along the ties, trying to peer through the gloom, she could see a small clutch of men looking down into one of the pits and pointing. She moved toward them. Too late, she realized there was a gap between the ties beneath her feet. She plummeted into an engine pit, grabbing frantically at a steam pipe on her way down. Her body slammed into the pipe, burning and scraping her hand; she caromed forward, thudding abruptly, face first, on the floor of the pit. The breath was knocked out of her; she could barely get it back as she fought through a thick layer of fine ash. She didn't need a doctor to tell her that the piercing pain she felt in her side meant broken ribs.

Nobody saw her fall because men at the opposite end of the same pit were intent on trying to rescue the spitz, who had leaped from the engine cab when they pulled it into the roundhouse, falling into the pit.

Spitting gritty ashes from her mouth, Susie tried to figure out what to do. She could barely see, and didn't know whether or not there were hot ashes in the pit. She couldn't call out because the agony of her ribs prevented her from taking a deep breath; besides, she probably wouldn't be heard over the idling locomotives. Nobody had seen her enter the roundhouse.

She looked up. What if—well, she just wouldn't think about the possibility that the locomotive at the other end of the pit would be pushed into position directly over her head. She knew that the first item of routine maintenance was to dump fire from the locomotive's fire box. In that case ashes—still white hot—never mind, she just wouldn't think of it.

By closing her eyes and opening them repeatedly to help her pupils adjust to the dark, she finally spied what she thought was a safe route toward the men at the other end of the long engine pit. Slowly, using bricks protruding from the pit wall as hand holds, she picked her way. Her breath came in shallow pants because her ribs hurt so badly.

The men were closer now, but still unaware of her. When she finally managed to locate a protruding pipe to use as a foothold and to reach her fingers up onto the pit rim, she saw three men staring down at her, wide-eyed, immobilized. Finally, one yelled, "Oh my God, it's not a ghost! It's Doc Susie!"

She tried to warn the men about her ribs but, eager to effect a rescue, they grabbed her under each arm and hauled her up—only to be rewarded by screams of pain as her ribs separated. "My ribs . . ." she moaned, and fainted. If one of the mechanics hadn't grabbed her, she would have fallen back into the pit. A workman ran to the first aid station and returned with a stretcher and smelling salts.

After what seemed a long time, internal fog began to clear from before her eyes. The first thing Doc was aware of was a black dog, formerly white, licking her face. For the first time in anyone's memory, she said, "You stupid mutt! This is all *your* fault."

The rails carried Doc's stretcher into the heated office. "Get Grace Schryer," she pleaded. In her filthy state, she wanted to get out of the roundhouse as quickly as possible, certainly before the incident was reported to the railroad doctor.

The Schryers' home was two blocks away. George Schryer's immense nose was the loveliest sight she had ever seen as it preceded him through the glass door of the roundhouse office. He took total charge, saw to it that a blanket was tucked around her, lifted one pole of the stretcher himself. He alerted the other three men to take it easy over rough spots in the road.

Dawn was breaking over the divide as the litter bearers, a small black dog nipping at their heels, carried Doc to the safe haven of her friends' home. Now that Susie was transported, George pulled a red bandana from his pocket and blew his mighty nose with a flourish. "Sorry bout dat. Gotta bad colt."

Plump little Grace, Canadian like George but of English rather than French heritage, assisted Doc onto the day bed in the kitchen, shooed the rails out, secured the dog in the coal bin and brewed a pot of tea. Grace was well named: warm, hospitable, a comfortable woman to be with. Her halo of curly hair was normally coiled around her head; but this morning she hadn't had time to wind it up so it spilled cheerfully down her back. Even in the rough, dry Rockies, her cheeks spoke of English gardens blooming with roses. George always said she was a "real darb," meaning he liked his women full-figured and pretty.

"First thing, Susan Anderson, look at yourself in this mirror. We will laugh when you feel better."

Doc looked into the glass to see an old woman with stringy gray hair, gray eyebrows and a smudged face caked with white ashes and grease. "Oh!" she gasped.

George stoked the stove, drew water from a hand pump in the kitchen, dragged in a big copper bath tub and put it in front of the kitchen range. Soon water was steaming on the stove and the kitchen was hot as summer. "Yer sure you don't need no help scrubbin' her back?" said George with a wink.

"George Schryer! What will we ever do about that French blood of yours?" Grace shooed her white apron at him. "Just you wait outside the door. I'm going to hand out Susie's clothes and you take them to the laundry."

She helped to unbutton Susie's skirts, sweaters, shirtwaists, peeling them one by one to avoid jostling the injured ribs. "Just as I suspected, you're a sensible woman," ·

said Grace as she pulled off the final layer—men's long johns concealed beneath Doc's petticoats.

Grace steadied Doc to the tub, helped her lower her naked body into the soothing warm water. "Uhmm," said Doc, "I can't tell you how wonderful this feels."

"Tell me when you want more hot water."

"When was the last time my body was warm all over? Maybe my idea of heaven would be someplace where it is forever warm."

Doc accepted Grace's gentle scrubbing without protest. "I'll swan," said Grace. "Underneath all those clothes you have a beautiful figure, although you're as muscular as a young boy. It's all that running around you do. And never eating regular meals, either."

Grace washed Doc's hair, scrubbed splotches of grease from her face, arms and legs. She took a small brush to Doc's fingernails, carefully cleaned the burned hand—cooing as though to a small child when Doc grimaced with pain. Then she helped Susie to stand up, not minding that her own clothes were getting wet. Grace poured clean water over Susie's head and down her shoulders, rinsing her gleaming body until every trace of soot had vanished. Susie stepped out of the tub into a fluffy flannel blanket that Grace wrapped around her, then sank back onto the day bed. Susie instructed Grace where to find some iodine in her black bag. Grace dabbed skin abrasions on Doc's face, arms and legs, which were turning an angry scarlet. "Ouch, that hurts!" said Doc, as the iodine stung her burned hand.

"You can dish it out, Susan Anderson, but you can't take it. Now you know how iodine feels!" chided Grace.

"I have one more chore." Grace opened the coal bin door, scooped up the dog and plopped the squirming animal into the same wash water. Shaking and whimpering, the dog stood quietly, looking ashamed. Grace scoured his hide with a rough scrub brush, saying, "I have a score or two to settle with you!" Finally, she snatched him out of the water and bound him tightly into an old woolen blan-

ket. She proceeded to rub him dry with such furious
strokes that when she finally released him to run around
the kitchen and shake, there was barely any moisture left
for his obligatory attempt to shower the two women.

The dog raced to the day bed and crawled under it, not
daring to venture out from under Susie's protection. Grace
laughed, Susie smiled. It hurt too much to laugh.

"Grace, I need to borrow something . . . personal."

"Anything, don't be embarrassed to ask," said Grace.

"Could you let me use a corset so I can immobilize my
ribs? It's the only way to treat them."

Grace laughed heartily. "I should have known that you
don't wear one." She disappeared into the bedroom, returning quickly with a clean corset, picking at its laces to
take it in. She laced Susie into it, imprisoning the ribs. "I
wish that thing did as much for *my* figure," laughed
Grace. Then she handed Doc a silk wrapper, ordering her
to put it on. "But this is too nice," objected Doc.

"This is my house, and I say who does what around
here. After what you've been through, you deserve a touch
of nice." Doc slipped into the beautiful black robe, luxuriating in its silky softness.

Doc was no stranger to the Schryers' hospitality. Their
home had long been her private retreat when she needed to
get away for a night or two in friendly company. George
was gallant and told funny stories; Grace read all the newspapers and subscribed to magazines. The women loved to
talk, and occasionally argue, politics.

By Grand County standards, the childless Schryers were
well off. An engineer was well paid and Grace was thrifty.
Their white frame house was located along the street called
Sunnyside, above the smoky air. Although her home
boasted no architectural distinction, Grace Schryer had
something other women could only envy: a real parlor.
Visitors were shown a horsehair couch covered with ma-
roon plush; stern ancestors framed with gilt glowered from
above it. In a walnut china cabinet gleamed genuine cut
glass, silver and porcelain figurines; there was the family

Bible and a stereopticon set. Doc had never seen a grain of dust on any of Grace's precious possessions. Guests were guided through the parlor, encouraged to admire its wonders; then Grace would say, "But it's cold in here, let's go sit in the kitchen." If anyone had ever actually sat in Grace's parlor, Doc had never heard of it.

The big kitchen table was shoved up to a window. While they ate, the Schryers liked to watch horses pastured in the foreground. Beyond the meadow trains passed along the right-of-way. Across the valley the magnificent Indian Peaks, stretching along the Continental Divide, formed a backdrop. The table was covered with blue checkered oil cloth, across which Grace constantly smoothed her fingers searching for errant crumbs. George was so tall, and so skinny, that her principal delight was feeding him tarts and pastries.

On his return, George was welcomed by the sizzle and smell of frying bacon, "You sure scart them guys down at the shop. Thought you was a spook!"

"How's Tom Kowalski?" asked Doc.

"Doin' OK. Train they come down on was the last one through. Snow's driftin' bad between Ptarmigan Point and the sheds at Corona. I was down talkin' to the maintenance foreman. Told him up at the Loop thar's a terrible cone-shaped drift overhanging the track. Told him as long as the line is closed anyhow, he should get him a howitzer and shoot it down."

The earth-shaking rumble of huge locomotives could call down tons of snow, trees, and rocks onto passing trains. Safe practice dictated that if an avalanche was imminent it should be "shot" by firing a large cannon at it. But the line was sure to be tied up for a few hours while the snow and other debris were removed from the tracks.

"Maintenance foreman won't do it. Says Bill Freeman don't think it's bad enough. Roadmaster'd ruther take a chance than rile Freeman."

"Fine for him to say," objected Grace. "He's not the

one in the path of it. Then you won't be going tonight, with the pass closed?"

"Roadmaster thinks the drifts'll be cleared by then. I'm drivin' a helper, leavin' at eight o'clock." Grace turned her back. From its stiffness, Doc could see she was angry that her husband would be sent on a dangerous trip.

Yawning as the soothing morning sun streamed through the window, Doc whimpered with pain. "Let's just nap off for a while," said Grace. "You and George will be needing your sleep." Doc hobbled to the day bed and stretched out. George and Grace retired to their bedroom.

Doc heard the sound of George's big boots hitting the floor. She wondered if Grace ever thought about how beautiful the thump of a husband's boots sounded. Probably not . . . soon, the only noise was that of Doc's dog, snoring under her bed.

When she awakened in the middle of the afternoon, Susie felt better. She was surprised to see Grace quietly wiping grease and soot from the boots she wore in the roundhouse. Grace turned to the happy bustle of preparing a dinner fit for a patient and for a man who would spend the night battling the hill.

George padded out from the bedroom in his sock feet, stretching. Grace handed him a cup of tea and he pulled up a rocking chair opposite Doc's bed. Susie asked, "Have many men quit their jobs since the twenty percent wage cut was announced?"

"Naw. Don't know why they call Swedes dumb. We're *all* dumb. Nobody much quit. Take them firemen. . ." George set his mug of tea on the floor so he could use his hands; he was unable to punctuate his stories properly without them. "Don't know why a fireman'd shovel coal uphill to 12,000 feet. Hardest work in the world. Tough in summer when things go pretty good. But in winter, when the rotary is stuck and that old Malley, she is gulpin' down coal like a dragon . . . terrible work."

"I took Rudy Just to the hospital to get his appendix

taken out a couple of weeks ago," said Doc. "The roadbed has deteriorated, I think."

"Terrible. Don't know what holds down the tracks. Freeman, all he's doin' is tryin' to find money for a tunnel. Won't spend a dime he don't have to." George pinched his thumb and forefinger together, as though crushing a coin.

Doc frowned, "Well Freeman isn't sparing any expense to look after his locomotives! I saw a lot of that fancy new maintenance equipment at the roundhouse. Thousands of dollars for machinery, but the men who operate it have to work for less."

George nodded, "Section hands have it the worst. Shovel snow, crawl under derailed cars, pick out ice so they can put in a new rail, freeze to death in the wind. They make a little fire out of kerosene and kindlin' to warm the hands." George held his hands before him, rubbing them vigorously together, "All that suffering, making less money than they used to.

"Different in old Dave Moffat's day. Once, when we was poor and needed more wages, bunch of us enginemen went down to Denver to see ol' Dave. We told him we needed more money because it was so hard to work the hill. He didn't even think about it. Told us to write our own contracts. Said he knew we would treat him right. And he said. 'When we make it to Salt Lake, I'll give you a hundert percent raise.' That's how Dave Moffat treated *his* men. Now, nobody talks about Salt Lake anymore, just the tunnel and a Dotsero Cutoff to join up to the Rio Grande line."

Doc Susie sighed. "If Moffat could have put a tunnel through, things would be different for all of us. George, why do you stay on, working for Freeman?"

"Grace 'n me moved here when I was about to die of consumption. Hard as life is, she's better than dyin'. Lak, if I was to leave I'd be lettin' the other men down. That hill. She's so mean and ornery but if she win, it's lak we ain't men a'tall." George made a fist and gestured toward the mountain. "War, some fellas call it. War. Only the enemy is snow, ice, wind. Meaner she get, tougher we get."

"Sometimes you really do remind me of Cyrano. Your white plume," said Doc.

At the mere mention of Cyrano's name, George turned his head so his profile was displayed in its full magnificence. But at that very moment his *white plume* fell victim to a fit of sneezing.

Doc didn't like the sound of it. She suggested he beg off this trip.

"Naw. They're gonna need me. Doc Susie, another reason I lak workin' on the hill. Malley engines, the 200's. Except for lovin' a good woman, drivin' a Malley is sweetest thing is in the world. Course they're useless on a straightaway, lak we had on de Great Northern in Canada, 'cause she can't do no better than thirty. But when you put the steam to 'er and open 'er up she just burn 'er heart out climbin' up that hill. Susie, I love them Malleys; my big old engine pantin' steam is the purtiest noise in de world— 'cept for my fiddle, natchurly."

After a leisurely meal of pork chops and Yorkshire pudding smothered with gravy, the three lingered over their apple pie. "Have some more," George urged, turning the pie tin toward Doc. "Put on some weight, like Grace. Then you'll be a real darb, too."

As he got dressed, Grace handed layers of warm clothing to George; Doc rummaged in her black bag to concoct a vitamin tonic. She stirred it and urged George to drink it down.

"Tastes terrible! Like red peppers and sewing machine oil," he sputtered. He stuffed red bandanas into every available pocket, anticipating a night of battling his running nose at high altitude.

George gave Grace a big hug, and Doc a small pat on the shoulder, "Wouldn't want to hurt yer ribs." The doors banged behind him as he stepped out into the evening, heading toward the round house.

"I never can get used to him going up there," said Grace, finally.

"I'll watch with you tonight. The weather's clear, we should be able to see his train climb all the way up; we can go to bed after we see him safely through the worst of it," said Doc.

Grace's seat at the table gave her a clear view southeast to the Rollins Pass area. She had a powerful spyglass through which she often watched the progress of her husband's train up the side of the mountain, especially in winter when she was concerned about his safety.

When the women saw the train start its climb up the Tabernash straight-a-way they counted: a lead Mallet and tender followed by twenty cars of coal, George's Mallet, tender and another helper engine with tender, fifteen more cars of coal, a caboose and a fourth Mallet.

Grace knew how much time it would take for George's train to reach Arrow, climb to Spruce Wye, take on water, add the rotary plow at the Ranch Creek Wye. Railroad wives memorized timetables; she knew George's slow coal drag would be behind schedule that night.

Trimming the wick on a kerosene lamp, Doc flipped through the latest *Sears* catalogue. "The things people spend money on! Store-bought underwear for children!"

Grace, crocheting a doily, looked up. "It's times like this make me glad I have no children—the worry would be worse," said Grace.

"Did you and George want a family?"

"Of course, but it just didn't happen. George thinks it might be his fault, thought maybe the consumption did something to him. I don't know."

"I wanted children, too," said Doc. "Grace, sometimes I wonder which is worse, to be like you and George, married and not able to have children or to be a childless spinster like me."

"It's not so bad now," said Grace, pulling a length of thread from the ball, "but when I was younger George's sisters used to look at my stomach and cluck their tongues, make jokes, threaten to tell me 'how it's done.' George comes from a big Catholic family. I wanted to hide from them."

Grace sighed, "A married woman with no children has an awful lot of time on her hands. At least you can move among your patients and help people."

"You do a lot, Grace. I know that every time anyone has trouble, you're right there with a loaf of bread . . ."

"It's not the same." said Grace. "Not like saving their lives. Not like being *important*."

"Don't tell me that you envy *me*!"

"Sometimes I do."

Grace kept an eye on the mountain, watching places where she knew the train's headlamps could shine through openings in the forest. It took an experienced watcher to locate trains, especially after the rotary snowplow and a fifth locomotive had been coupled onto the lead. The rotary's single headlamp was frequently obscured by a plume of snow.

Finally, Grace saw a light appear along the treeless hillside of the lower Loop roadbed. She peered through her spyglass, squinting to see tiny lights nearly four miles away; Doc stood behind her.

Grace gasped, "That's strange, I just saw the headlamps on George's Malley light up." By the rule book, engineers operating helper locomotives were forbidden to turn on their headlamps. Grace flinched, "It's gone, no . . . there it is again. His Malley isn't moving, I'm sure of that. Wait a minute. I see the light again. No, it's gone. I don't like it, I don't like it at all. I think that cornice came down."

All thought of sleep was put aside. The women took turns staring through the spyglass in their attempt to see something, anything, in the dark.

Minutes passed, then half an hour, an hour; no light pierced the dark. Neither woman dared speculate aloud. Doc Susie made a determined effort to distract her friend. "Looks like we'll get into war in Europe after all. Youngsters in Fraser are drilling up and down the street. Now that I see mothers sending their boys off to slaughter, I wonder if it isn't better to be without children."

"Be without," Grace echoed absently.

Susie steered the conversation to the Kaiser, to President Wilson, to General Pershing pursuing Pancho Villa into Mexico (Grace thought that was silly). An avid reader of both the *Denver Post* and *Rocky Mountain News*, Grace had strong political opinions, generally in tune with Doc's inclinations toward the trust-busting conservationism of Teddy Roosevelt. But she refused even to consider becoming a U.S. citizen until women were granted the vote.

As for the Volstead Act—Doc favored "prohibition" because she believed many medical problems stemmed from drunkenness. Grace didn't think it would work. "People will get the stuff," she declared. "But they'll have to become thugs and scoundrels to do it."

Dawn was beginning to break behind the Divide. In the gray light Susie saw the deep lines of worry etched between her friend's brows. Grace tried the spyglass again, then dropped it on the table, "I think . . . I'll just pop down to the depot and see what I can find out."

In ten minutes she was back, her slow tread and heavy silence carrying the answer. Still, Doc had to ask, "Avalanche?"

Grace nodded.

"On the Loop?"

Another nod. "A lot of rolling stock went over."

"And the men?"

"Nobody knows."

Neither woman spoke. It was a time beyond words. Nor was there any thought of breakfast. Doc Susie returned to the day bed, acutely conscious of her friend's anguish. Musing on the human cost of "progress," she dozed off.

She was awakened by a great stomping noise on the porch, followed by the furious barking of her spitz, and a cry of relief from Grace, "It's George!"

Struggling up from the day bed, Susie's eyes went to the door where a haggard, begrimed George was tugging at his clothes. Grace pulled him into the room, "Never mind taking your dirty clothes off outside. Come in and get warm."

Doc saw immediately that George was suffering from exposure after hours of wearing wet clothing while working in the frigid air. He was weak; uncontrollable shivers racked his rangy frame. "Get those filthy clothes off him and let's put his feet in warm water," said Doc.

The usually talkative George submitted himself to the two women. Grace peeled his pants legs from where they had frozen to his boots.

Doc Susie carefully examined George's toes, hunting for tell-tale gray patches that would indicate frostbite. She found a few. "Soak his feet, but don't make the water too hot. Just warm to your wrist," she said.

George sank forward in his chair, slipping his big feet into the pail of water. Around his shoulders Grace planted a warm blanket. She poured him a freshly brewed cup of tea. George sighed, blew his nose and sipped from his mug.

As he stared at steam coming from the teakettle on the stove, he began to chant, weaving forward and back on his chair, "That dirty sonofabitch, dirty sonofabitch," he said, over and over. "Dirty sonofabitch." George wasn't normally given to swearing at a level much above "By gar."

Finally the shivering stopped. George looked around the room, focusing on Grace, then Doc. "You is beautiful ladies, I nefer thought to see such beautiful ladies ever again. Doc Susie, you is a real darb, just like Grace."

"Did the cornice come down the way you thought it would?" asked Grace.

"Chure did. Right thar on the Loop." George pulled his bare white arms from the blanket, finally ready to tell the story. "We stop at Ranch Creek, couple up behind the rotary and take on water, all five units. Takes a while. Charlie O'Neill is stokin' fer me. New man, gota lota kids. We head into the Loop, tradin' slack back and forth between

Malleys." George moved his big hands back and forth in tandem to indicate the motion of "tradin' slack."

"I switch on my headlight, not supposed to, but I had a hunch that cone was agonna let loose." Grace and Doc nodded to each other, but didn't interrupt.

"Fireman say, 'Now why'd you do that?' I tell my fireman 'cause I think she's a gonna slip. Course, all we see is the back of the coal car ahead of us. But 'twasn't five seconds. I say 'Thar she be!' and she hit us. Oh, they is huge boulders, tree limbs, snow everywhere. Rocks is ahittin' the bell and steam domes. Shoulda heard the bell. Windows is all stove in, and the snow comes a pilin' in through the gangway. We was climbin' up and up on it, stompin' our feet, gettin' closer and closer to the ceiling of the cab.

"We is still on the tracks, but we can hear coal cars goin' over the side—sounds like dynamite blowin' up 'cause they is fallin' end over end, seven hundert feet down. Snow, she's over the stacks . . . smoke and fire is a belchin' back outa the fire box. Wall, Charlie, he ain't been in nothin' lak that before.

"Another wall of snow come down, hits us again. Locomotive raises up," George extended his arms, tipping his entire body in explanation, "then settle back on the tracks.

"We is stompin' as hard as can be, tryin' to keep above snow that is comin' in. Oh, you can't imagine the smoke, and gas, and steam. We is chokin', somethin' terrible." George had his hand beneath his chin, squeezing hard against his throat.

"Charlie, he's crazy. Starts screamin' about 'is wife and kids, clawin' at me. Chokin', snot flyin' outa his nose. So, I pull bandanas outa my pocket, and hold 'em over his face, tell 'im to breathe through 'em. I tie another one around my nose, I'm lookin' like a train robber.

"Third time, snow lifts up the locomotive. I thought that was it, fer chure. Seven hundert feet down, top o' that locomotive cab would crack in like an egg. We'd be scrambled fer sure. Charlie, he's cryin' and tryin' to punch me. Finally, I get aholt of 'im and slug 'is head up aginst the

roof o' the cab, 'cause he's crazy. Knock 'im plumb out.
Oh my Malley, she's buried alive. First I dig with the fireman's scoop, then with ma fingernails. Charlie, he's unconscious. I'm glad 'cause he ain't fightin' me, but I gotta get
'im outa thar. Finally, I break out. Fire musta melted some
of the snow around the stacks 'cause we was gettin' fresh
air by then.

"I pull Charlie outa thar, drag him to the back of the
Malley. Other guys is diggin' out, callin' to each other. I
drag Charlie along clear to the back of the second unit,
'fore he come to. All the Malleys was still on the tracks,
thanks be God." George paused to cross himself and blow
his nose.

"Them firemen, all of 'em refuse to shovel any more,
not even snow, scared it would come down again. Can't
blame 'em, but somebody had to dig those Malleys out.
The conductor, Blaine Markle, and all them gandy dancers
and engineers, we set to shovelin'. Ahead of me, eight coal
cars had went over, seven behind, but my engine stayed on
the tracks." George still couldn't get over the miracle of it.

"Nothin' else to do, gotta back them Malleys offa the
roadbed, down to the shops here in Tabernash. Firemen,
neither man would dig. That's what took us so long. You
oughta go down to the roundhouse and see my Malley.
Snow, she's packed six feet deep on top of the roof of the
cab. It's somethin'."

George pulled his long arms down from his last gesture;
his shoulders shook, as though he were reliving the horror.

"So, it's your fireman you are calling a 'dirty sonofabitch'?" asked Doc, imitating his French accent.

"Hellsabells no, sonofabitch is Freeman!"

"Freeman," asked Grace. "Was he there?"

"Naw, when Blaine Markle telegraph him to report the
damages, Bill Freeman ask 'im, 'Did any of the Malleys go
over?' Blaine, he was so mad I never seen a human so red.
He told Freeman: 'No, and neither did any of the men!' "

CHAPTER 11

The Big Bore

"Bang, bang, bang." The knock conveyed such authority that when she opened her door Doc Susie was not surprised to see Grand County Sheriff Mark Fletcher. Rawboned, bespectacled, Fletcher had spent most of his forty years trying to scrape out a living as a rancher. Although he had held office less than a year since winning election in 1924, he already presented the perfect picture of a seasoned, respected lawman. Doc Susie liked the new sheriff of Grand County, even if he was a Democrat.

Usually, the presence of an officer wearing a badge and a holstered six-shooter at Doc's door meant her services would be needed to stitch up some drunken Denver motorist who had driven his flivver through a mountain curve with more enthusiasm than skill. Now that the road over Berthoud Pass had been improved and graveled, hordes of tender-footed tourists motored to the mountains. Doc *al-*

most longed for winter, when snow would close the highway until spring.

Over Fletcher's shoulder, Doc spotted two strangers sitting in the back seat of the lawman's Ford. By their neckties, pin-striped suits and city hats she knew at once what the sheriff had come for. Whisking off her white apron, she grabbed a hat, her medical bag—and her ax—and sprang out the door.

"Where is it?" she asked as she hopped into the car, not bothering to conceal her excitement.

"Up St. Louis Creek." Fletcher spun his car around in the middle of the street, shooting up a fine spray of gravel. "Some crook from Nebraska is trying to set up business. Consider yourself deputized."

With mock seriousness, Doc Susie put her hand on her heart, then snapped a salute at the sheriff.

As the Model T bounced past new shacks that had sprung up since the beginning of construction on the Moffat Tunnel, Fletcher said, "Dr. Anderson, tell the boys about Miz Carch."

"Oh, they aren't interested in that . . ."

"No, tell 'em."

The little woman swung her whole body around so she could see the two men riding behind her, "Summer before last, the former sheriff, name of West, came to get me one day. He suspected a man named George Carch was bootlegging right in Fraser. Sheriff West, Sam Wilson, Charles Jenne and myself went to his house.

"This Carch fellow came out and closed the front door behind him. Said he didn't know anything about bootlegging, and he was sorry but he couldn't let us come into the house because the missus was sick." Doc brushed away an errant lock that had blown loose from her bun and grinned at the fellows in the back seat as they bounced along the country road.

"Sheriff West said 'Ain't you just in luck! We've got Doc Anderson with us and she'd be glad to have a look at Miz Carch.' So Sheriff West pushed him aside and we elbowed our way into their shack. Sure enough, Mrs. Carch was in bed with the covers pulled up around her neck. In August, mind you! I thought to myself that her hair was combed quite nicely for someone who wasn't feeling well.

"When I asked her what was wrong, she just shook her head, wouldn't say anything. So I reached down to feel her forehead, and she was clinging to those covers for dear life. Sheriff West, he just reached over and pulled the covers off her—whoosh! And there beside Mrs. Carch were six pints of whiskey! Of course, she was fully clothed—even had her shoes on—and there wasn't a thing wrong with her."

The deputies howled with laughter. "George Carch was fined $300 and spent thirty days in jail for those pints and the other hooch we found," Susie reported proudly.

"Doc Susie's the perfect deputy," commented Sheriff Fletcher. "Show 'em your gun." Susie reached into her bag and pulled out her Iver/Johnson, the bigger one.

"She can use it, too. If we find any ladies out there— and I use the term loosely—nobody can accuse us of anything improper with Dr. Anderson as witness. What's more, Doc keeps her mouth shut both before and after we skirmish. And there's another reason . . ."

One of the men leaned forward. "What's that?"

"You'll see."

Sheriff Fletcher pulled his car off the road to hide it in a grove of golden aspen trees, frosted from the first cold nights of September. He waved to six other men who were waiting, shotguns at ready. At his signal, some of them moved toward a narrow trail leading into a clump of spruce trees. Others took off on a path along an irrigation ditch that would lead them in a circle to behind the trees.

Fletcher motioned to Susie to follow closely. They plunged into the woods, Doc carrying her gun in one hand, her ax in the other.

The Sheriff gestured to Doc to stand behind a tree. Peeking around it, she saw a large cleared area in the woods, sheltered from the elements by a tautly drawn canvas tarpaulin. Four men dressed like lumberjacks bent over an apparatus, tinkering with it. Around them was a collection of make-shift tents along with a jumble of crocks, jugs, jars, barrels, tubs, hoses and firewood. A fifth man, delegated as lookout, stood with his back against a tree whittling a toothpick; his shotgun rested on a nearby stump. Doc could see they hadn't the least idea anyone else was nearby.

Fletcher pressed his finger to his lips, then pulled out his pocket watch. Susie was sure the sound of her heartbeat and breathing could be heard as far away as Tabernash. A pine cone fell from a tree and thumped onto the tarp, sounding to her as loud as a rifle shot, but the men remained absorbed in their task.

Finally, Sheriff Fletcher cupped his hands to his mouth, bugling an excellent imitation of a rutting bull elk, then stepped into the moonshiners' hide-out—his shotgun aimed straight at the quartet. They snapped erect, literally dropping what they were doing as four pairs of hands shot up into the air. At the same time, another agent rested his pistol barrel between the shoulders of the hapless lookout, causing him to jab his expensive toothpick into his tongue. He howled with pain, but held out his hands to be cuffed. "In the name of the U.S. Government," bellowed Fletcher, "you are under arrest!" No shots were fired. Muttering oaths to themselves, the men looked a little sheepish as they offered their wrists to be manacled; lashed to a tree, they were guarded by one of the city agents.

The revenuers poked their heads into tents, lifted lids from barrels, stirred sticks into crocks. "They have all the latest equipment," said one of the Treasury men. "This outfit could produce at least fifty gallons a day. Looks like they were just finishing up the last batch of the season."

Agents made notes, stowed evidence in their cars, asked some questions which the moonshiners refused to answer. When he had accumulated enough proof to satisfy the judge, Sheriff Fletcher turned to Doc, "Ready?"

"Ready!" shouted Doc.

Cradling her ax in both hands she advanced toward a

barrel, aimed its head at her stave of choice, wound up her swing and laid into the side of it with the assurance of Casey at bat. She watched with great satisfaction as colorless liquid gushed onto the ground. Then she whacked it again, lower this time, to make certain every bit of its contents would soak into the earth. After that she smashed jugs and crocks, then turned her attention to the apparatus itself. By now, her hair had sprung free from her bun and her forehead was beaded with perspiration. Apart from the copper boiler, which Susie said some poor woman could use to boil her wash, she made smithereens of all of the expensive gear.

Behind her, several of the federal men were laughing so hard they had to pull handkerchiefs from their pockets to wipe their eyes. "Carry Nation!" one shouted. "Carry Nation lives!"

"Wonderful woman," responded Doc. "I knew all about her in Wichita."

When the site had been thoroughly wrecked and the offending brewers had been herded into the back of a truck for transportation to jail at Hot Sulphur Springs, Doc rode back to Fraser with Mark Fletcher.

"That was mighty satisfying," said Doc. "But I notice that you never seem to bother the local boys who are doing the exact same thing."

"Now Doc, we all know how hard it is to make a living up here. What with the thirsty tunnel workers and all, somebody's going to make the stuff. I'd just as soon keep tabs on who's doing what. I don't want anybody dropping dead from a bad batch, and I want to keep hooligans and gangsters out of my territory."

"A man gets just as drunk and makes just as much trouble, no matter who does the brewing."

Fletcher frowned. "I know, but I guess I have to go along with those as say 'You can't legislate morals.'"

Susie was tired of hearing that phrase, so tired she didn't bother to argue about the merits of home-grown rotgut versus imported hooch.

As they came to the bluff overlooking Fraser, Fletcher braked his car and pulled to the shoulder of the road, "Susie, I have something important to ask you."

"Ask away. I think I've been asked nearly everything."

"Would you consider becoming Coroner of Grand County?"

"Coroner? Mark, I specialize in *live* people."

"I know, I know. But hear me out. You remember when Doc Albers lost the election?"

She knew, all right. Doc Albers was one of the few incumbents in the history of Colorado to lose re-election to the uncoveted office of coroner. Just a couple of weeks before the last election he had been arrested in Denver, accused of violating federal narcotics laws. Everybody in Fraser knew that Albers was a "whiskey doctor" who would prescribe alcohol for those wretched souls who claimed to be suffering life-threatening withdrawal symptoms caused by prohibition. Gossips circulated the rumor that Doc Albers was on "dope" himself.

When Albers' legal embarrassment had surfaced, there were dark whispers that Doc Susie had reported him to one of her revenuer friends. She knew the futility of denying the tongue-wags, but felt comfortable discussing the matter with the sheriff. "Mark, let's set this straight. I don't approve of the way Doc Albers prescribes whiskey, but I don't want to be the only doctor in this town, either. It's hard enough to get around to all of the people who need me. I'm glad he's back, even if he is on some sort of probation. What with the tunnel construction, we could use even more doctors if they'd consider coming up here."

"I know, Susie. People don't understand how hard you work. But this fellow B. J. Moon who was appointed coroner by the county commissioners, he don't want the job anymore."

"I shouldn't wonder. He had to handle that terrible thing at the tunnel last June when that twenty-year-old student from the School of Mines, that George Biegle, was killed. According to the *Post*, the boy had been on the job only a week when he picked into that bad shot of unexploded dynamite and it blew his face off. I don't know how Moon's panel came up with that 'unavoidable accident' judgment. If the previous shift had done a proper checkout on that dynamite string it wouldn't have happened. And what about the three others who were hurt? Are they all right? I never heard."

The sheriff sighed, "The Moffat Tunnel Commission and the contractors, Hitchcock and Tinkler, they don't much want to talk about those things. As construction jobs go, I think this one is pretty safe. Biegle was only the third man to die. They say that when the Simplon Tunnel was built in Switzerland twenty years ago, over 2,000 men died."

A sharp edge came into Susie's voice, "When they say only three died, they don't count the fellows who die of pneumonia from sweating in the tunnel and then coming out into temperatures 20-below zero. I know for a fact that fifteen men died at the West Portal Hospital during the first year of construction. Remember the collection we took up for that fellow who died from pneumonia? His wife was all broken up, said she didn't have money to bury him? I even contributed a dollar myself."

Fletcher nodded, a grin creasing his face. "The widow looked at that $250 we collected and said, 'Don't expect me to spend all this on a funeral, boys,' and cheered up smartly. By the way, have you heard that she came back—with another, er, uh, 'husband?' She told him to go get a good job in the tunnel."

"Hekaroon!" Doc laughed. "What'll those tunnel stiffs be up to next? But seriously, Mark. From what I hear, things in the hole are going to get a lot worse. Rock on our West Portal side is so crumbly they can't bore through it cleanly. And over on the other side, all that water is pouring into the tunnel—they can't pump fast enough to keep up with it. I heard a couple of workers climbed up to Crater Lake, even though it was middle of winter, looking for its source. That's 1,400 feet above the tunnel. They chopped a hole in the ice and poured chloride of lime into the lake. Within twenty minutes, there were signs of it pouring into the tunnel. I'm afraid the crews are going to run into even worse conditions."

Mark nodded, "What I can't understand is why they decided to dig two tunnels instead of just one. It seems to me to be making twice as much trouble."

Doc Susie was also unconvinced that the engineering scheme being employed—that of first digging a "pioneer bore," from which to excavate laterally into the main tunnel—was a good idea. From what she knew of mining, it only added expense and complication.

"My doctor friends at Colorado General warn me that this is one of Bill Freeman's schemes. They say he's in cahoots with the Denver Water Board. People in Denver weren't about to vote bonds to pay for a water tunnel so the Moffat Tunnel Commissioners are drilling them one, only they're calling it a pioneer bore. Later, Denver can cement the walls so it can carry water. But I don't see why we should pay for Denver's water tunnel. It would have been faster and cheaper if they dug the three-mile tunnel up at 10,000 feet, where we always thought it should be. The only reason I can see to drill a six-mile tunnel at the 9,000-foot level is so they can catch more water when the snow melts.

"All this fuss about having the longest tunnel in America . . . I want the tunnel as much as the next person, but it didn't have to cost so much."

The sheriff polished his wire-rimmed glasses with a bandana, replaced them on his nose and looked at her squarely, "All this tunnel business leads me to believe we need someone like you to be coroner. You know that in most counties the owner of the furniture store doubles as a mortician and county coroner. I don't think a casket salesman is good enough for Grand County. I want our coroner to be a real doctor. Besides, I want somebody who can stand up to the Tunnel Commission and the contractors when there is an accident. You would tell the truth."

Doc gazed across the valley toward the Continental Divide, noting the smoke from the mail train as it traversed the Loop. It would take about an hour for the train to arrive and the postmaster to sort the mail.

"It pays cash, by the body, plus expenses. All you have to do is file the death certificate and a voucher."

Although both of them knew Doc could use the money, she was too proud to admit it. "Well, I'll think about it. If you don't mind, I'll walk home from here. I want to gather some asters, probably the last flowers I'll get this year."

The sheriff chugged away leaving Doc looking down on her village, which was mushrooming with shacks thrown up to house those who flocked to the area in hopes of profit. She didn't share the faith of some of those neighbors who fervently believed the new railroad tunnel would cure the county's financial woes. Some dreamers even speculated that businessmen would build fine homes in Grand County and commute through the tunnel to work in Denver! Doc chuckled at the idea that anyone would leave a liveable climate like Denver's for the privilege of freezing to death all winter.

Ambling unhurriedly toward Fraser, to time her arrival with that of the mail, she reflected on the sheriff's offer.

She was fifty-four years old, and didn't have much in the bank to show for it. Along with most people in Colorado, she had been on hard times ever since the war. The gold boom at Cripple Creek, Colorado's last, had busted ten years earlier when the richest of the gold ore gave out at the same time the price of gold fell. Most of the billions of dollars made in Cripple Creek and other mining towns had been spent out of the state, leaving Colorado so poor it couldn't even finance a railroad tunnel to open up its West Slope to development. Yet newspapers were full of stories of how prosperous most Americans were in the "Roaring Twenties."

Times were especially bad in Grand County; prices for cattle on the hoof were so low that many local ranchers had sold their breeding stock and resorted to the unheard of humiliation of raising sheep. Around Fraser only a few of the biggest lumber mills were still in operation; most had shut down because lumberjacks had flocked to take jobs in the tunnel where a man could double his wages. The mill in Fraser had been paying workers nineteen cents an hour; a tunnel mucker could earn fifty shoveling rock and mud. Doc was doubtful the lumber industry would ever rebound; she didn't have to be a forester to note that virgin growths of the best trees, formerly cloaking the hillsides, had almost vanished.

Much as she regretted seeing a rowdy element flock into the area for jobs, she certainly looked forward to a new train route, safer than climbing over "The Hill." The D&SL bragged that it had "never lost a passenger," but workmen still died up there on a fairly regular basis. Despite improvements in snow-removal machinery, the line was drifted shut for days at a time during the winter, and almost certainly would be closed for most of April and May. She remembered one long spring blockade when ranchers ran out of hay; their stock nearly starved. When the drifts were finally conquered, the first train was loaded with hay. And the second? They said it brought snuff for the Swedes.

The tunnel, touted as the longest in the United States, would alleviate all that. But she knew enough about politics to suspect Bill Freeman's motives. He had contrived to have a Moffat Tunnel Commission formed, independent of the railroad. The commission persuaded taxpayers in the counties along the railroad to vote to finance the debt for the tunnel so that they, not the D&SL railroad, would pay for it. Already, the digging was running over its $6 million estimated budget.

It wasn't just a second sense that warned her the whole story hadn't been told. She hadn't forgotten how Freeman had treated his men during the World War. Locomotives hauled more and more coal over the Divide to help fuel war industries on the East Slope. It still made her angry when she remembered how Bill Freeman ordered men to work ninety hours at a stretch, but refused them extra pay. Beset by the rising cost of beans and flour plus demands for unpaid overtime, train workers finally got fed up and went on strike for the $180,000 owed them in back wages. They celebrated when the U.S. government granted Freeman $1,300,000 to keep "The Hill" open. The war did all right by Bill Freeman. Extra freight dollars and the government's gift enabled him to substantially reduce his railroad's debts.

Just after the war, Freeman slashed the men's salaries again. But nobody paid much attention because at the same time the great influenza epidemic of 1918 slammed into Grand County. Karl Just had been the county's first victim. He developed pneumonia and went so quickly that Della didn't even have a chance to send for Doc; he died at the hands of the railroad doctor in Tabernash. Poor Della. Once the envy of her neighbors, now people didn't know how she coped—what with raising seven children and running a large ranch, all by herself.

During the epidemic Doc Susie had rarely slept as people rushed her from one deathbed to the next. Her reputation for saving pneumonia patients put her in much demand, but more often than not the Grim Reaper beat her to the patient. Entire families died. Victims were found dead beside country roads; bodies stripped of identification were abandoned at the Fraser graveyard, left to the taxpayers to bury. Doc Susie had never felt so helpless.

Now, seven years later, most of her patients were still the ones who couldn't afford to pay and there were more of them than ever. A woman in her fifties ought to be thinking about the future. After all, she couldn't go on practicing medicine forever. She finally accepted the fact that she would spend the rest of her life alone. True, she did have a friend; Hugh Harrison, the former Fraser postmaster, had been re-elected County Clerk. He often dropped by to visit when he was in the east end of the county. But she couldn't really think of their friendship as a passion—just two aging loners who enjoyed a good talk.

As Doc walked into Fraser a matted cur dashed across the road, nearly knocking her over; he was chased by a ragged boy about eight years old. Boy and dog were so motley as to arouse Doc's suspicion that both were lousy. From one of the shacks a woman squalled to the child, "Get your stupid butt back in here." Doc sniffed her disapproval of these riffraff and wondered, idly, how many of these transients died under mysterious circumstances—becoming clients for a coroner. They didn't work at the tunnel; rather, they hustled hard-earned dollars from the pockets of workers who came down to Fraser seeking a little fun.

Most tunnel workers lived four miles away, near West Portal. The Tunnel Commissioners—along with the contractors, Mr. F. C. Hitchcock and Mr. C. C. Tinkler—were absolutely dedicated to keeping the atmosphere around the tunnel wholesome. Single men slept in barracks and ate in the company mess hall. Families lived in houses called the "Lost Twenties" because twenty little houses were hidden in the woods. Although workers were provided with movies and pool tables, no dance halls, gambling parlors or other "debilitating amusements" were allowed.

Fraser was the nearest place where a fellow could blow off a little steam and seek out some pleasant corruption. Doc Susie knew just which corruptions were the most popular; after all, she had grown up in Wichita and Cripple Creek.

Some of the very same faces she had seen staggering across Myers Avenue in Cripple Creek appeared on the Fraser scene. Ironically, lumberjacks made steadier tunnel diggers than miners who had a hard time showing up for work every day when there was no gold to be discovered. Average pay was $5.15 per day; Doc joshed that she was considering applying for a job. But conditions in the tunnel were so disagreeable and dangerous that hordes of new faces were in constant demand, some from as far away as Arkansas and West Virginia. Company recruiters travelled throughout the United States, seeking strong backs wherever mining had fallen on hard times. A recent clampdown by U.S. immigration officials on the importation of workers meant that the Moffat Tunnel was the first major railroad project in America to be built without cheap labor from China or Mexico.

Doc wasn't really surprised when Hitchcock and Tinkler appointed young Roderick J. McDonald as company doctor for the specially built West Portal Hospital. He was charged with looking after the five hundred men, and their families, who worked there. Tall, thin, Dr. McDonald was a good emergency physician; she liked him. Her own patient load, nevertheless, kept growing. Tunnel stiffs suffering from chronic lung and back conditions, the sort of illnesses a fellow would hate to talk to the company doctor about for fear of being fired, sought her out.

Just then, a "taxi" honked and its driver, a likeable young Swede from a good Fraser family, waved happily. The fellow had bought himself a car and was paying for it by shuttling men over the bridge to the other side of St. Louis Creek where a flourishing row of cribs had just been established. It was far enough from town to allow its hostesses to entertain, unmolested by people who were offended by the nature of their services. Individual hens from the covey of soiled doves were rarely seen in town, except when women who looked suspiciously like flappers arrived or departed at the depot. Doc was aware that one of the home-grown stills that Mark Fletcher ignored was thriving near the cribs. The cheerful young Swede would haul one carload of clients, drop them off, then come back for another. Many days he kept his car busy in both directions, dropping off eager customers and hauling satisfied men back to town.

Doc's stroll to the Post Office took her past a dance hall where, it was rumored, liquor could be bought—if you uttered the right combination of words. Indeed, the term *blind pig* was bandied about in connection with the hastily built place. As she walked past, trying not to glance in the direction of a group of louts gathered in front, one she didn't know broke away and sidled up to her. Youngish, his blond hair slicked back, he spoke out of the side of his mouth and wore his hat at a cocky angle. "You a doctor?" he asked.

She wrinkled her nose at the smell of whiskey on his breath. "Yes, I am a physician."

"Well, you see doc, I got this problem. It's kind of . . . well, kind of personal." He pointed to the fly in his trousers, hunching his shoulders sideways as though to hide his hand gesture from his friends.

"You will want to see Doc Albers," said Doc.

"Wall . . . I seen him, and he didn't do me no good. Please, you gotta help me."

"I would prefer that you contact a male physician."

"Now I heared you was as good a doctor as any man." The fellow obviously knew how to pull Doc's string.

"I refuse to see people who have been drinking," Doc said severely. It was a convenient lie; she had sewn up victims of many a barroom brawl. "Besides, I examine patients at my office."

The man tipped his hat and limped away. That was curious; Doc hadn't noticed any limp when he approached her. The fellow rejoined his fellow loafers who seemed interested to hear what he had to say. "Neversweats," muttered Doc to herself.

She picked up her mail and returned home. No yapping clatter greeted her arrival. She had received word two years earlier, while in Denver admitting a patient to the hospital, that her spitz had died. She hastened home, performed an autopsy to confirm her suspicion of cancer, then took the corpse to a rancher who excelled at taxidermy—and owed her money. The presence of her stuffed pet provided some solace and she talked to him, just as she always had, when something was on her mind.

"Pooch. They want me to be the coroner. You know I've done autopsies, like yours, out of curiosity. Seems they want me to do a few for profit. God knows we need the money but it doesn't seem right, somehow. I just don't know."

She had forgotten about her encounter with the loafer in the street when, about sundown the next evening, the fellow appeared at her office door. She was surprised to hear anyone knock so late.

"Remember me, Doc? I have this, uh, problem."

"Yes, I remember you." She looked him over to decide if he was sober then admitted him to her examining area. "Well, tell me about your symptoms."

The fellow squirmed a bit. "It's kind of hard to explain. I think you'd better have a look."

She sighed in resignation, "Very well. Undo your trousers."

The man unhitched his suspenders, arched his back a little, unbuttoned his fly and with some flourish dropped his trousers around his ankles, holding his arms out from his sides, palms of his hands open as though in triumph.

Doc put her hands on her hips, studied the exposed region in a professional manner and asked, "Well, what's wrong with it?"

Grinning, the man said very slowly and very loud, "Nothin'. But ain't it a dandy?"

Doc put her tongue to the side of her cheek for just a second, then stepped toward him, lowered her voice and ordered, "Pull up your pants." She leaned over him in a menacing manner and cocked her fist as though pretending she were holding something. "Now you get out of here and don't ever come back. If you do, I'll slit you up your belly with a butcher knife."

The surprised needler, who had been so sure the woman doctor would collapse in embarrassment, reached awkwardly to his ankles, unable to pull his pants up as he hobbled toward the door. Doc circled around and stood between him and a clean exit. "My fee is ten dollars. Payable *now!*" She held out her hand.

A chorus of guffaws sounded outside the door. Thoroughly chagrined, pants still unfastened, suspenders trailing, the man dug into his pocket and proffered a bill. As he stumbled out over the threshhold Doc heard a sarcastic male voice, "Congratulations, Sandy! Thought you'd make a monkey outa the lady doc, did you?"

Another derisive fellow, "Paid her good. Now you can pay me!"

Furious, Doc closed the door and leaned her back against it. Only then did her face flush and blood pound through her temples. When her breath came regularly again, she resisted the temptation to call Mark Fletcher. Word would get around. The rowdy newcomers in town wouldn't be so anxious to give the lady doctor a hard time again.

One point was settled in her mind. If somebody was going to realize income off these ruffians, handling their corporeal remains, it might as well be Doc Susie. A few days later she authorized Sheriff Fletcher to submit her name to the county commissioners for the post of coroner.

CHAPTER 12

Susan Anderson, Coroner

On the day after Dr. Susan Anderson was sworn in as Coroner of Grand County, January 1, 1926, two men named Pete Giaconelli and Dan Metroff were overcome by gas in the East Portal when an unsecured protective curtain was whipped aside by the power of an explosion. They inhaled exhaust fumes from the dynamite charge. Although taken to the mouth of the tunnel alive, both died almost immediately. A third man was also near death. In a valiant effort to save his life the company physician at the East Portal Hospital, Dr. Ray Sunderland, hooked the man to a welder's oxygen tank and kept him breathing, emptying six tanks in a period of seventy-two hours. The novel technique worked. Doc Susie admired her colleague's cleverness, but wondered whether the victim's lungs would ever allow him to do manual labor again. However, she was relieved that the case was not hers, belonging rather to the Gilpin County Coroner in Central City.

Her respite was brief.

On January 5 she was summoned to her first case. A body, believed to be a suicide, had been discovered near Kremmling in the west end of the county. Sheriff Fletcher met her train and escorted her to a disagreeable location where she had occasion to inspect at close range the damage that a Colt could wreak on a human head. Having satisfied herself that the unhappy man had inflicted the damage on himself, she stopped at the court house on her way back through Hot Sulphur Springs, chatted for a while with her friend Hugh Harrison, filled out a death certificate and was promptly reimbursed $26 for her ordeal.

For the rest of January there were no incidents in the tunnel noteworthy enough to be reported in the newspapers. Work was going better than she had anticipated despite a marked disparity between progress from east and west. Two months previously workmen from East Portal had reached the apex, which had been engineered to occur at the center of the tunnel to facilitate drainage. The original plan called for crews from east and west to approach the apex at about the same rate of speed. Except for the draining of Crater Lake, crews from the east had found excavation relatively easy because the rock was solid granite. They encountered no great problem in drilling at a slight downgrade toward workers on the west where progress was much slower.

Considerable grumbling reached Doc's ears. Workers on the west were unhappy about the Tunnel Commission's geological surveys, hastily completed before the tunnel was started, which had failed to predict the presence of a nasty mixture of fractured stone and glacial till beneath the west slope of James Peak. The vast glacial moraine, with its fragmented, crumbly rock, sometimes oozed into the tunnel from below and above. Along many stretches it was not necessary to blast because there was no way to stop rocks from coming down. Great caverns were emptied of thousands of yards of loose material.

In the worst areas, 12" x 12" timbers of resilient wood from Oregon were being twisted and splintered into toothpicks by the pressure of the mountain. At one time the rumor spread through the work force that the expense of removing the crumbly mass and shoring up walls against such strong pressure would prove too high; there was talk of abandoning the tunnel effort. The project was saved when a bright engineer named George Lewis went to sleep one night and dreamed about a huge cantilevered bar device that would actually dig into the till ahead of the workers, holding it up long enough for them to shore up pilings with more conventional materials. He convinced the dubious Moffat Tunnel Commissioners to build it. It worked. After that, digging was faster and a little safer.

On February 24 a man named F. W. Snow was killed, again on the east side. The official cause of death was listed as poison gas, but rumor had it the man was crazed on dope and had walked into the tunnel in a crazy suicide scheme. Again, it wasn't Doc Susie's problem.

But she became apprehensive when, four days later, progress in the tunnel took a disastrous turn. Crews working on the east, after firing off a routine round of explosives, suddenly found the walls of the tunnel transformed into streams of water, cascading from all directions. Workmen fled for their lives. Until then, the presence nearby of an entire underground lake had not been suspected. Engineers reported 3,000 gallons of water per minute flooding into the heading, a torrent that soon filled the bore, backing up to the apex. Pumps had to be located, purchased and installed to keep the tunnel clear. It took seven weeks for two huge pumps to clean out the water and for workers to remove the compacted silt left behind. By April 21, the clean-up chore was accomplished. Almost immediately a vicious storm on the East Slope brought down electric lines feeding the tunnel project; while the pumps were down, the tunnel once again filled, flooding the pumps along with everything else.

Nevertheless, the "official" count of six men killed so

far, kept by the Denver newspapers, lulled the public into thinking that construction on the project was relatively safe. Only when accidents were spectacular did they excite the interest of the press. Doc Susie knew that the tunnel death toll was, in fact, much higher. No running count was kept of men who were blinded or who lost limbs when they picked into "bad shot." Some who were injured left the area and died elsewhere, their fates not recorded. Reading in the *Denver Post* or *Rocky Mountain News* about serious accidents to workers—accidents almost invariably attributed to "their own carelessness" or "unpredictable circumstances"—Susie could not repress a bitter smile.

She was thankful that through the spring and into summer her calls to duty as coroner were confined to the task of "fumigation," a ritual often performed after someone died of a communicable illness.

All of that changed on July 22.

Doc was summoned to the tunnel after a man named Ralph McClellan was crushed by an ore train. Although she had visited the tunnel project several times, it was her first trip into the tunnel itself. Climbing aboard a tiny electric tram to be pulled through the pioneer bore to the site of the accident she was surrounded by sullen faces. The workmen resented her presence; not because she was coroner, but because they shared the miners' superstition that the presence of a woman underground was bound to cause accidents and cave-ins. She mused to herself that they were right; a coroner in pursuit of a corpse could never mean good luck.

The little electric train bucked along its narrow two-foot roadbed, lurching from side to side. Light bulbs strung along the ceiling illuminated the rough tunnel walls. As Doc looked up, a muddy drip hit her forehead. The burly crew boss accompanying her handed her a slicker to drape around her shoulders. Before long, she saw water oozing from around struts and between forms, running down a ditch beside the track.

Doc Susie had attended a lot of deaths in her time, occasions usually observed by hushed silence. But here work did not cease while she carried out her grisly errand. When she glimpsed to her left through cross-cuts into the main bore, it seemed that hundreds of men were at work clawing rock from the bowels of James Peak. She had not been prepared for the noise of the tunnel, reverberating thunderously between the walls of the twin bores. There was no escape route for the clamorous din of drills, mechanical shovels and earth-moving equipment.

Here before her eyes were the sources of the chronic health problems suffered by men who drove slag trains. The drivers alternated constantly between the steady, sheltered 60 degrees inside the tunnel and the weather outside where winds drove temperatures that dipped to 20 degrees below zero, or soared to 80. Here too were the muckers, shoveling whatever came loose from the inside of the mountain in badly ventilated air, wading in freezing water. Sweating inside their nonporous slickers and rubber boots, working for hours with a pick and shovel, they would come off their long shifts wringing wet and exhausted. A slight cold could endanger a man's life. The hot showers provided by the company were of some help; even so, Doc Susie knew that far more men died of pneumonia than from injuries. But the newspapers weren't interested in anything so common as death from pneumonia.

A workman ahead signalled the train to stop. "We're going to have to wait here," her guide explained, "while they explode a charge in this next cross-cut. Want to watch?" She nodded yes, although no one had warned her about this aspect of being coroner. They joined a crew of men who emerged from one of the cross-cuts and stood chatting and smoking. They watched as one of them, obviously an expert, put one wire in his mouth, then another.

"He has to taste them, know if they're 'salty,'" her companion explained. The man then twisted the two wires together; abruptly the lights went out. From not far off Doc heard a low "boom." She was about to ask if that was the explosion when the ground started reverberating beneath and around her. "Boom, boom, boom," a string of charges exploded. It seemed the earth would not stop heaving and shaking as she counted off twelve explosions in relay. The lights came back on, swinging crazily, and the little ore cars on the tram swayed dramatically from side to side. Doc Susie felt her body whipsaw back and forth.

The crew chief grinned down at her, "You did fine."

When the ground quit moving, a greenish pall of smoke drifted along the tunnel, stinging Susie's nostrils with an acrid smell that made her eyes water and her throat constrict. It seemed a long time before smoke drifted back toward the portal and she could breathe without difficulty. After a few minutes the crewmen helped themselves to newly sharpened drills from a car behind the one she rode in; they stepped back into the main bore, to set about mucking out debris from the explosion.

Only then did the electric train proceed, passing numerous cross-cuts where crews were at work in the railroad tunnel. When it stopped again, Susie did not at first see why. The crew chief pointed toward a tarpaulin covering an object, then pulled it back. The gray, dilated eyes of a man of about forty stared into hers with a look of surprise that seemed to say, "So this is death." Dried blood matted the man's whiskers, where it had been squeezed out of his mouth. It wasn't difficult to see that the dead worker, in a moment of inattention, had stepped between the wall of the pioneer bore and an ore car, just as it was being filled with slag by a noisy mechanical shovel. His chest was crushed instantly.

Now that the coroner had been shown the scene of the fatality, shift workers pulled the slag car away. With the crew chief's help Doc Susie went through the man's pockets: a little cash, a pouch of tobacco, a cheap watch. She slipped them into an envelope brought along for the purpose. She did a thorough search of his clothing; after the "accident" involving F.N. Snow, the contractors had warned her to be on the outlook for evidence that workers were using dope on the job. The corpse was loaded onto an ore car with little more ceremony than was accorded to a rock.

When the man-train emerged from the tunnel, carrying Susan and the tarpaulin-covered corpse, bright mountain sunshine had never looked so good to her. As with so many of the workers, nobody knew where Ralph McClellan came from or where to send his body. So Doc Susie released his body to the "company," which detailed a work crew to bury the corpse in the Fraser graveyard.

A few days later, July 31, Doc Susie was in her office removing a fish hook from the buttocks of an elaborately outfitted Easterner. As he squirmed, more in embarrassment than pain, she consoled him, "Don't feel bad. Happens all the time. Fish hooks catch more fishermen than trout—especially city people."

"You mean a lot of your practice is stuff like this?"

"It was—until they started the tunnel."

"Did you know that Selak fellow, the one the Denver papers say is missing over by Grand Lake?"

"Everybody knows him. As they say, he's a bit of a hermit. I can't think of any good reason why he would disappear, though . . . hold still now." Doc snipped the barb from the hook with a pair of pliers, then slipped the hook back through the soft flesh of the man's bottom.

"Now why didn't I think of doing that?" said the man, as he winced from Doc's obligatory splash of iodine. "Do you believe that talk about the hermit having a fortune stashed away in his cabin?"

"I doubt it. Even country people have sense enough to use banks."

The door suddenly swung open. Bursting in without so much as a preliminary knock was the ticket agent from the Fraser depot. The patient grabbed for his trousers. Susie began to protest the intrusion, then stopped in alarm at the realization that she had never seen the agent leave his post at the telegraph key; his messages to her had always been delivered by someone else.

"Cave-in at the West Portal Doc," the agent blurted

breathlessly. "Lots of men trapped in there, maybe twenty or thirty. Dr. McDonald wants you up there right away! Iver Florquist is coming to take you in his car!"

Susie wasn't certain whether she was being summoned as a physician or coroner, but it didn't really matter. "That'll be a quarter," she told the fisherman. "You'll have to excuse me." She left him standing alone in her office, buttoning up his pants.

Young Iver Florquist, a local mechanic, was glad of a chance to see how many horses Henry Ford had put into his engine. For once Doc Susie didn't pester the handsome young Swede to drive more carefully as the car sped past the Cozens Ranch and through the tiny settlement called Hideaway Park.

When they arrived at West Portal a cluster of women immediately swarmed around Iver's car. Many were the wives of lumberjacks working in the tunnel. "Doc Susie! Doc Susie! Help us find out about our husbands! They won't tell us nothin' Doc."

Doc looked toward the mouth of the tunnel. Unlike the occasion when she brought out poor McClellan, business was not going on as usual. All digging had been suspended at news of the cave-in, in accordance with an unwritten law governing mines and excavation projects. Scores of men, maybe hundreds, were milling around atop tunnel tailings, running here and there like ants on an ant hill. If there was a pattern to their wild dashing she couldn't discern it; there was no use going there for information. She told Iver to take her to the hospital, a temporary but well-equipped facility that boasted a half-dozen beds, an X-ray machine and a room where antiseptic surgery could be performed.

Inside the hospital, a small group of workers stood in hushed silence, hats in hands. She recognized Martin Green, a stolid assistant superintendent who had worked his way up from mucker. Begrimed, his right arm bleeding from a deep scrape, Green stood with another shifter whose streaked face showed signs of intense exertion. "We brought out a young fellow named Thompson, Doc. He's bad, real bad. We couldn't get to the others."

Susie headed for Dr. McDonald's surgery. From beneath a shock of straight, dark hair, the doctor looked up at Susie from across the bed of his young patient who didn't look to be older than twenty. "I'm glad you came," McDonald said. "I'm afraid young Thompson here was the only one to get out. More men are buried."

McDonald motioned her to a window, behind a screen that shielded them from the patient, "No hope, I'm afraid. His chest is crushed, I think the ribs on the right side have pierced his lungs; his right arm is broken in several places and the bone of his left leg at the knee is mashed. There's not much I can do but keep him comfortable."

"Mind if I ask him a few questions before the morphia?"

"Go ahead."

Doc went to the bed, took the young man's left hand in hers and gave it a motherly squeeze, "My name is Doc Susie. I'm a physician. I help Dr. McDonald out sometimes. Would you mind to tell us what happened?"

It was very difficult for Thompson to speak, but his head seemed clear enough, "We was shoring up a heading, working in a section of . . . blocky rock. It seemed like on the north wall the mountain was . . . trying to cave in. But it was the other side that come down. I heard someone yell 'look out' and I jumped. A big rock come down . . . right where I was standing. Then everything went black." He paused, trying to get some breath.

"There's no hurry, son. Take your time," she said.

"After that, can't remember much . . . except seeing my leg twisted at a right angle to my body. I wondered what happened. I think I hollered out. And—yes—I saw one of the other men . . . knocked flat . . . at my feet."

Susie glanced sharply at McDonald. Word that another worker might be close by where Thompson was found could be important to the search. McDonald stepped out of the room and spoke to Green. Troy Branigan, the other shifter who had brought Thompson out, took off running toward the mouth of the tunnel.

"How many of you were there, son?" asked Doc.

"Five, besides me. One of them, Pierson . . . it was his first shift."

Doc was relieved to hear there weren't more men trapped. But the news was bad enough.

"Could you call my father?" the boy went on. "He'll be worried."

"Where are you from?"

"Walsenburg."

"Walsenburg?" That was a little coal mining town in the southwest part of the state. Doc knew it well.

"I think . . . I'll go back to it." The boy's voice trailed off. In Walsenburg, a family would be grieving tonight.

Leaving Thompson to Dr. McDonald, Doc Susie stepped outside to go to the company offices. She found a knot of anxious women waiting for her. "I don't think any of the men trapped in the tunnel are from around here," she assured them. "I'm going over to the office to see what I can find out."

She was immediately ushered into the office of F. C. Hitchcock who, with several of his engineers, had just come from assessing the disaster scene. Hitchcock, a big man whose jowls, extended earlobes and large nose accentuated his authority, nodded to Doc Susie, "Well, Coroner, you're the person we need, all right. There's not a chance in a million that those men are alive. We believe there are five of them in there."

"Do you have their names?"

He handed Doc Susie a sheet of paper. Glancing down the list she was relieved to see no familiar names.

"Are you suspending operations?" she asked.

"Of course, of course," There was a hint of annoyance at the question.

A tall, blond young man stumbled into the office. He was filthy and his cheeks were streaked with tears.

"Oh, young Adams, I'm sorry, son." said Hitchcock. He turned to Doc Susie, "His father was the shift boss."

"My pa, my pa! I saw the rock come down on pa," the young man said, dazedly, several times. Doc was told that John Adams, Jr. had been driving an electric tram, had pulled it up to the place where his father was working and arrived just in time to see his father disappear beneath a crashing block of granite. The son immediately set to work trying to move, by himself, boulders the size of pianos—and had to be forcibly removed from the tunnel when he succumbed to exhaustion.

Hitchcock put his arm firmly on the man's shoulder. "I want you to stay out of the tunnel. That's an order." Doc Susie took young Adams out into the corridor where she turned him over to a couple of workmen, "Get this man to the hospital." She knew Dr. McDonald would sedate him so the grieving youth could retreat temporarily into the oblivion of sleep.

Then she gathered the waiting women around her. The missing men, she told them, were Adams, Gasoway, Pierson, Prosek and Ferguson. The women were visibly relieved. "But you know there's probably no way you can talk your men out of going in there to try to rescue their friends. The best thing you can do," she advised, "is get back to the Lost Twenties and bake a pie for your husband."

A few minutes after she had returned to the company office, Susie heard a commotion at the door. "Let me in there, I'm Joe M'Meel from the *Denver Post*. How many men are dead? I want a picture of Thompson before he dies." Hitchcock looked at Susie and shook his head. She could see how he dreaded dealing with the man.

Hitchcock poked his head into the corridor. "We will be speaking to reporters," he said gruffly, "after the rescue effort has been thoroughly organized."

M'Meel, topped by a gray fedora, had a pencil stuck behind his ear between his head and his horn-rimmed glasses. He pushed very close to Hitchcock and in a whiskey rasp shouted up in his face, "I'm entitled to my scoop, Hitchcock. First man on the scene gets the first interview."

Another male voice broke in, "I'm John P. Lewis from the *Rocky Mountain News*. I've got a deadline to make. How soon you gonna let me in the tunnel?"

The two men were left cooling their heels, growling their complaints and elbowing each other aside to pester anyone who came into the building. At one point M'Meel from the *Post* buttonholed Doc Susie, "Who are you, anyway?"

"I am Susan Anderson, M.D., Coroner for Grand County."

"Coroner, huh? Heh, heh. Then you get paid by the body. You could get rich in this job, eh?" She turned her back angrily and walked away.

Through the next hours successive shifts of volunteers were hauled into the tunnel on the man-train to take turns digging. Although most of them knew better than to hope they would find anyone alive, they knew also if they were the ones pinned beneath tons of rock their fellow workers would risk the shifting walls of the tunnel for them.

Doc Susie volunteered to go in with them, but Sheriff Fletcher vetoed the idea, "Wait till there's something you can do." She did not argue.

Late that evening Thompson died. In his final delirium his only request was that someone take the time card from his pocket and turn it in, so he could draw his pay. Doc Susie heard the frustrated *Denver Post* reporter, unable to get past the tunnel diggers who guarded Thompson, ad lib his own version, "I sat with the dying man," he rasped into the phone. "Thompson's last words were, 'Don't give up, boys. There may be a chance all of them are alive.'" Doc Susie and Dr. McDonald exchanged disgusted glances.

Now there was nothing to do but wait. Wait, wait. Doc Susie accepted Dr. McDonald's invitation to bed down in the hospital for some sleep.

The next morning she went back to the tunnel office. Hundreds of volunteers were lined up to serve shifts, heedless of the danger caused when they set off small charges of dynamite to facilitate moving the collapsed rocks. Working in short shifts because they were quickly exhausted they dug carefully, set off more small shots; still there was no sign of the missing men. Undaunted, the men doubled their efforts.

Bystanders outside the tunnel told the reporters how Bud Lall, a bridegroom of a few weeks, had been lucky. As a member of the fatal crew his job was to report their progress. He had been speaking on the phone 100 feet away when the cave-in occurred and was the first to relay news of the tragedy to the mouth of the tunnel.

Another "lucky" fellow was Luther Barton of Hollywood, Kansas. Earlier in the shift he had fallen through a second tier of timbering and broken his arm, but not badly. Far less fortunate was the man who took his place. W. E. Pierson had been hired only the day before the cave-in and was in the midst of his second shift. He wasn't supposed to be working with that crew at all, having been hired on to work with a buddy. But as a new man he was ordered, over his protests, to fill in for the injured Barton.

Susie was talking with Hitchcock at the mouth of the tunnel when they were joined by Hitchcock's partner, C. C. Tinker. His bulby little nose shining over his moustache, he seemed dissatisfied with the progress of the rescue. "This delay is costing us thousands, F. C. Worse, we've had over a hundred men quit so far."

At 12:30 p.m., two pencils and a garter were found at the site, the first signs of the men. But Mark Fletcher once again forbade Doc Susie from entering the tunnel.

As she sat on a bench outside the hospital she watched a bird, one of the big gray jays called "Camp Robbers," pick bread crumbs from someone's discarded sandwich. How oblivious he was to the tragedy around him!

She felt a hand on her shoulder and looked up to see Mark Fletcher, "Susie, they'll be needing you now. They've reached the site and . . . nobody alive. Do you think you are up to this?"

"Nothing much ever happens in Grand County, eh Sheriff? Don't worry. I'm up to it."

The *Denver Post* reporter was already on the man-train at the mouth of the tunnel. Clambering up behind him, Susie noted five coffins lined up on a flat car. Young Adams stood next to one of them, a vigil he had kept ever since he awoke the morning after the cave-in.

Inside, Susie heard no rumble of machinery or dynamite. When the tram reached the cross-cut to heading Number Nine it stopped. Assistant Foreman Charles Miller, who had discovered the bodies a short time before, led Doc into the main bore. "I saw two pairs of legs and one arm," he told her.

"If you should feel anything peculiar," he went on, "such as a slight movement of rock or debris falling from the ceiling, get back into the pioneer bore as fast as you can."

"From the looks of things here," she replied, "that could never be fast enough." She had to crawl over and beneath fallen and crushed timbers that criss-crossed in crazy fashion—as if some giant child had been careless with his toy Chinese pick-up sticks.

Pat Gasoway's body was the first they uncovered. How quickly he had died could be seen by his hammer, still clutched in his hand. Next, John Prosek's terribly torn and mangled body was uncovered. It had been shoved forward to the head wall, so a tunnel had to be bored around it to remove it. The only way Doc Susie could identify him was on the word of a fellow worker who said he knew those were his boots. As she went through Prosek's clothing, she found several hundred dollars in currency and his last month's paycheck. He must have mistrusted banks.

She looked up to see Joe M'Meel, the *Denver Post* man, watching her handle the remains. Suddenly, he bolted to the side of the tunnel and vomited—a detail that, as she anticipated, never appeared in his news story.

Henry Ferguson was beneath two great timbers which had wedged his body with their weight, augmented by thousands of tons of rock above. To remove the remains men had to cover the torn corpse with blankets and lie prone across it to dislodge the timbers. Doc Susie found a tobacco sack filled with money in his pocket and took charge of it.

One by one the bodies were removed until the only corpse missing was that of the shift boss, John Adams. Doc Susie was unable to face his son until she could bring out the remains of his father, so she sent the other four bodies out on the man-train and sat near the workers as they labored, turning stone after stone, for the hours it took to locate the elder Adams beneath the rubble. Perhaps his was the body young Thompson had seen just before blacking out.

Once the final body had been hauled out the only thing left for Doc Susie to do was to impanel her coroner's jury—purely a formality improvised on the spot—to certify that the men had died instantly of a cave-in.

That done she gave Mark Fletcher a bill to carry back to Hot Sulphur Springs. It totalled $27.20.

Surprised, Fletcher looked up at her. "Susie," he said gently, "there were six bodies."

"Yea," she said. "But I only had to make one trip."

CHAPTER 13

We Built This Tunnel

Doc Susie's footsteps were sure and measured as she hurried down the Moffat Station platform to board the train heading over Corona into Grand County. She never raced to catch her train without remembering herself as a pathetic invalid who had to be trundled on a baggage tram, vain even when she was too weak to walk. She was well aware that these days people thought her woolen petticoats and padded coat a bit eccentric. So be it. She had no interest in passing herself off as a flapper. She was confident that her fifty-eight-year-old self looked and felt better than that thirty-seven-year-old rag of a thing riding the luggage cart.

In February, 1928, all Colorado was a-buzz over the impending opening ceremonies for the great Moffat Tunnel, hailed by *Popular Mechanics* as the "engineering feat of the decade," locally trumpeted as the greatest thing to happen to transportation since the Panama Canal.

As ever, Susie's old friend George Barnes was on the platform checking his watch. Barnes had to tug a little harder these days to fasten the brass buttons of his coat across his conductor's vest. When he doffed his official hat to a lady, his thinning hair was the color of buffalo nickels. Swinging aboard, Susie asked Barnes if this would be her last ride over the top.

"Yep. Unless you have to come to Denver again before next Sunday. That's the big day, February 26. Can't come soon enough for me."

Not many fellow passengers shared the single car as the night train pulled out of the station. Doc Susie looked them over . . . just a few Oak Creek coal miners returning from days off in Denver and sheep ranchers headed west to Craig. All men, as usual. She turned to Barnes, "Next year, the tunnel. That's what we kept telling ourselves. Do you realize that was over twenty years ago?"

"Twenty-four years operating this *temporary roadbed* over the top." He shook his head. "Sometimes I don't know how we did it. So many good men come and gone. When Bill Freeman cut our salaries again—after the war— the only workers who stayed were hard-headed stiffs like me and George Schryer. If we'd of had any sense, we'd of gone off to jobs where the work was easier and the pay was better—and you got some appreciation."

"Still, you're here to see Moffat's dream come true. That's what you've been hoping for all this time, isn't it?"

"Yeah. I guess so."

"I was at the West Portal last week," she said, "That concrete entrance is massive; a beautiful thing. When I stood in the entrance and looked up and around I felt so small, like a teeny little ant. Are you going to be the conductor on the first train through the tunnel? You should be. They tell me you were conductor on the very first passenger train the Moffat Road ever ran, back in ought-five."

"I don't know," he sniffed. "The *Denver Post* hasn't decided."

"What do you mean?"

"Well, Bill Freeman and Fred Bonfils, feller who owns the *Post*, have got the opening ceremonies all sewed up."

"Bonfils? What's he got to do with it?"

Barnes warmed up to her dismay. "Remember when the tunnel was first holed through the pioneer bore? How within five minutes the *Rocky Mountain News* was celebrating by exploding bombs on its roof, while the *Post* was waiting for President Coolidge to launch the official opening from the White House? The *News* was crowing about their scoop for days."

"But that was over a year ago. There have been a lot of stories since. Six men have died blasting through the main bore and laying down track."

"Don't make no difference to Bonfils. All he cares about is getting back at the *News*. That man's the stingiest Italian in Denver, kind of believes in vendettas from what I hear. Guess he figures if he runs the show, he can keep the other guys out of it."

"How'd he get Freeman to go along with him?"

"Way I heard it, Bonfils promised to donate a golden spike to pound into place at the opening ceremony, like they did with the Union Pacific in Utah. Man like Freeman ain't about to look a gift spike in the mouth. Afterwards, it's supposed to go to the Colorado Historical Society. Besides, who knows how much stock Bonfils owns in this railroad . . . or anything else?"

"Are they holding the ceremonies at West Portal?" asked Susie.

"Nah, the big excursion trains are going as far as East Portal, then they'll unload all the passengers. The bigshots are gonna make speeches, drive the spike, bury a time capsule, make lots of hoopla, all for the benefit of the *Post*. Then they'll haul 'em through the tunnel." Barnes moved on down the aisle.

Doc Susie was heartily sick of this Denver newspaper war. Competition had been fierce ever since the recent purchase of the sleepy *Rocky Mountain News* by the Scripps-

Howard chain. Bonfils, after the death of his partner
Harry Tammen in 1924, was totally in charge of the *Post*.
He rivaled the *News* for want ads, outrageous promotions,
and sensational coverage. Doc Susie had been furious over
their lurid stories on the cave-in, and was still smarting
over her treatment by *Post* reporter Joe M'Meel, who got
her name and title wrong, then crowned the insult by inti-
mating she was getting rich on the disaster.

After that came the hullabaloo in the papers when Fred
Selak's body was found, and was reportedly examined by
"Grand County Coroner H. B. Moon" who had been replaced by Susie eight months earlier. Even before the dis-
covery of the body, the papers had played up Selak's
disappearance, characterizing him as "a wealthy miser,"
although Doc Susie had never thought of him as being
more than prudent where money was concerned.

Her mind went back to that morning, a couple of weeks
after the tunnel cave-in. She had been sitting at home reading about Rudolph Valentino's critical condition after an
appendectomy. Between the lines, she knew the actor
would probably die of peritonitis and she felt sad. Even a
mature country physician from time to time dreams about
running away with a handsome desert sheik. At that moment a message came from Sheriff Fletcher summoning
her to the site of the murder, not far from the summer re-
sort village of Grand Lake.

It was bad enough that she, as coroner, had to cut Fred
Selak's body from the tree where it had been hanging for
three weeks. She was outraged when the *Post* story started
out: "The decomposed and blackened corpse of Fred N.
Selak, the 'Hermit of Grand Lake'. . ."

Not to be outdone, the *News* told how: "The body, so
badly decomposed that identification was almost impossible, was suspended from a limb of the tree by an eight-
foot rope which was noosed around the neck. It was plain
that at the time of the hanging the body had been two feet
off the ground but the stretching of the body and rope now
allowed the toes to touch the earth."

"Why," she asked herself, "did anybody other than the coroner need to know those terrible things?"

The murder had soon been laid at the feet of a pair of cousins from Missouri, Arthur Osborne and Ray Noakes. At their trial, the newspapers had tried to generate some suspense about the verdict; impossible, since the two had already admitted the crime. Twelve male ranchers—as property owners ranchers were generally considered to be the solidest citizens available for jury duty—took less than three hours to review the young men's confessions of how they killed Selak after quarreling with him about hauling wood across the old man's right-of-way.

Susie sighed as the train lurched along. Awful as the offense against Selak was, she hated to have any part in sending two young men to the gallows. It went against everything she believed in. "It was the worst thing I ever had to do," Susie told her friends, referring as much to her testimony at the trial as to the disagreeable postmortem examination. She did not feel the least bit guilty about submitting a bill for $33.90 for her services as coroner on that case. Nor did anybody ever question the size of the bill.

After the train started up the Giant's Ladder out of Tolland, Susie sensed that something was different about the trip tonight, and it wasn't just the rotten shape of the roadbed. Suddenly it occurred to her: "George, where are the freight trains?" she called to the conductor.

Barnes looked disgusted. "Going through the tunnel. Been going since Valentine's Day."

"Before the official inaugural train?

"That's right. When you read the papers, notice that Bill Freeman is being real careful to talk about 'the first official passenger train.'

"You've got to really be *somebody* to get a seat on that train. Now I can't blame Freeman for not shipping any rolling stock over this miserable roadbed when he doesn't have to. I can't even blame him for slipping it by the Tunnel Commission and the taxpayers to the tune of $13,000 because he won't have to pay any rent for the tunnel until he officially accepts it on opening day. But it does seem wrong to me to risk the lives of passengers by sending them over the top, when freight trains are rolling safely through the tunnel."

"Why doesn't somebody say something?" asked Doc.

"Freeman's got the newspapers in his pocket, both of them. Nobody is going to ruin this big splash for Colorado. The whole country is watching us."

"Is there going to be another ceremony at the West Portal when the train comes through?"

"Not that I know of. Freeman said he doesn't want to unload everybody again, said it would get the big shots back to Denver too late."

"It's not fair, George. The tunnel stiffs do all the work and the bigshots get the glory." Barnes was silent. Susie settled back to catch up on some sleep but between the violent bucking of the train and her anger at Freeman she didn't have much luck. Getting off at Fraser she called out to Barnes: "I still hope you're on the first train."

The next day, Doc was summoned by Grace Schryer to Tabernash to set the broken arm of a child, the son of a roundhouse mechanic; the last company doctor, who left months before, had never been replaced. The workman's family shack in the Smoke Town area was neatly kept, the sheen on the oil cloth bespoke pride of ownership. Several women had seized on the boy's mishap as an excuse to sip coffee together.

The arm was a simple matter, handled by a small tug and a splint. Grace Schryer assisted Doc. Usually ebullient, Grace was solemn, a signal that something was wrong. After a dish-towel sling was tied in place around the child's neck, Doc took her friend aside: "What's the matter, Grace?"

"Haven't you heard? After Sunday, all of the men in the Tabernash shops will be fired. Oh, some of them might get transferred to Oak Creek, but most of them will be out of a job. The foreman says there's no reason for a roundhouse in Tabernash now that Denver will be less than two hours away. They're going to tear it down."

"George? Will George be fired?"

"No," Grace hastened to explain. "They'll keep shifts of engineers because some of the trains will still need helper engines to push them up the grade to the tunnel."

Doc turned to the other women. "Mass firings, eh? I guess that's Freeman's idea of how the tunnel is going to help Grand County."

The child's mother, her hands chapped scarlet from scrubbing clothes and floors in cold weather, crossed her arms: "You might as well burn Tabernash down. It will become a ghost town overnight."

A plump neighbor added, sadly: "My husband has worked in the shops, fired trains over Corona, got gassed in the snowsheds. My son, he got his back ruined mucking in the tunnel. Now what are we going to do?"

Another woman—judging from the length of her skirt much younger—tried to lighten the gloom: "The *Denver Post* says the opening of the tunnel is going to be the biggest celebration anybody in Colorado has ever seen. I sure would like to go to East Portal and see that gold spike. Just imagine, real gold!"

"Wouldn't that be wonderful," echoed the mother wistfully.

Doc's glance moved from woman to woman—honest, hard working, bad-luck Bessies—they certainly deserved better than they were getting. The least this railroad owed them was to haul them to a ceremony featuring boring speeches by a lot of stuffed shirts they had never heard of.

"Let's do it!" said Doc. "Let's go to the dispatcher's office and ask for a train! If anybody deserves to be at that ceremony, it's the workers' families from the west side!"

"Oh, I don't know," objected the child's mother. "My man gets riled if I criticize the railroad. Might get him in dutch."

"In dutch?" asked Doc. "What more trouble can he have than losing his job?"

The woman grabbed her frayed jacket, wrapped a blanket around the shoulders of her splinted child and said: "Let's go."

As they set out down the sooty streets of Tabernash, other women called out to ask where they were heading. "We're going to get a train," they shouted. Hurriedly pulling on boots and coats the neighbors joined the parade. The procession grew steadily as, full of purpose, it neared the station. The women's breaths rising into the cold air made them look like a five-Malley coal drag steaming up the hill.

With an air of authority, Doc Susie stepped up to the iron cage separating the waiting room from the dispatcher's office. A few feet away, a man in a green eyeshade leaned back in his chair. His thumbs stretched his braces forward; his chair hit the floor and he smiled in recognition: "Look who's here! Doc Susie, what brings you to Tabernash today?"

"We want to go to the opening ceremonies at East Portal," The dispatcher did not answer her immediately, but glanced toward the large chalkboard on which blocks were plotted showing where each of the trains was at any given moment.

"Then you'd be wanting tickets on the last eastbound over the top. I'm glad you ladies dropped by because we weren't sure they were even going to run that train, but if you want to go . . ."

"The train that leaves at midnight?" asked Susie.

"Same one we always had," replied the dispatcher, suddenly wary at her tone.

"The one that arrives in Tolland at three in the morning?"

"The same."

"And where would we go to keep warm between three in the morning and noon when they hold the ceremonies?" she demanded.

"I don't know. There isn't a real station at Tolland."

"You're telling me that we should take the chance of

riding the last train over the top, even though the roadbed is crumbling and we've had a foot of snow already this week. If we don't get caught in an avalanche or aren't stranded on top, then we would have to walk or find our own way from Tolland to East Portal where there is no place for us to stay warm, either. We would be out in the cold for nine hours. Is that what you're telling us?"

"Now Susie, I don't make the rules . . ."

"That's not good enough," said Doc Susie, stamping her foot resoundingly on the old depot floor. She exploded: "These are the wives of workers who kept this railroad operating for 24 years, men who were maimed and injured digging the Moffat Tunnel. Some of these people knew and loved old Dave Moffat. They deserve to go to the tunnel opening. Why are the papers making a big fuss about how heroic the workers were and then keeping their families away from the ceremonies?

"Tell Bill Freeman he can do better. You call him on the phone or send a telegram, but you tell him we want to ride to the opening ceremonies through the tunnel. It doesn't have to be a regular passenger train or anything fancy, we can all pile into a box car. But we deserve to be there."

Doc Susie could see that the dispatcher was not happy with the hot potato she had thrown into his lap. Dealing with Bill Freeman on a fractious topic was nobody's idea of a pleasant way to spend a shift. On the other hand, Doc Susie was not to be dismissed lightly—especially with a contingent of his wife's friends behind her to back her up.

"Now, Susie. You know Bill Freeman is a very busy man." The dispatcher motioned Susie to lean closer so he could whisper a confidence in her ear: "What with moving the shops out of Tabernash, the dispatcher's office is agonna go, too. Doc, my job isn't safe . . ."

"Well, we're not moving until you get hold of Freeman. Call him up or wire him. It's up to you." The dispatcher chose the telegraph key, knowing that Freeman was likely to be eavesdropping in any case, that way he would get the message personally—better than trying to relay it by telephone though a clerk in the main office.

The women retreated into the waiting room, dusting themselves off a place to sit. Since work had started on the tunnel, the Tabernash depot had been allowed to deteriorate. Benches sagged, the chimney carrying smoke from the pot-bellied stove was twisted at a peculiar angle, filling the room with the gassy stench of coal smoke. Doc looked with distaste at a scuffed floor that had not suffered a broom for at least a month.

Waiting out a reply, the women exchanged rumors about the tunnel opening. One woman had heard that a film star was going to attend.

"I read that the first Chinese woman born in Colorado is going to be on the train," chirped another.

"What's that got to do with anything?" asked Doc.

"Don't know. Her husband must be a big-shot," came the answer.

"They say the *Denver Post* is going to fly an airplane over the ceremonies."

Doc Susie looked at the speaker: "You'll never get me up in one of those things. I might die of airplane poisoning."

"Airplane poisoning? What's that?"

"One drop will kill you," chuckled Doc.

The women tried not to think about their homes, soon to be worthless now that nobody in Tabernash could get a job. The constant klack of the telegraph key clattering senselessly in the next room was mesmerizing; heat from the stove made them feel sleepy. A couple dozed off, glancing up occasionally to see a train pull through the station. They all knew what it meant when the freights did not stop to couple on helper engines. A train going through the tunnel didn't need five Malley engines. The days when all that heroic steam had pushed coal trains over the top were over.

Finally, the dispatcher appeared at the window. "I'm sorry Doc Susie. Bill Freeman says that nobody, *nobody* rides through the tunnel before the dignitaries. You'll have to ride over the top to East Portal."

Doc Susie thought, but just for a moment: "Seems to me Mr. Freeman defines his verbs in a real precise way. He's been running freight trains through that tunnel for a week now, at no expense to his railroad because his lease hasn't officially started." She paused for just a moment as though trying to peer out the dirty depot window, then snapped at the dispatcher: "Since Mr. Freeman is so *precise*, ask him if we can *walk* through the tunnel. That way, the dignitaries could still be the first people to *ride* through. It's only six miles, on the flat, too. For working people, an easy stroll."

The women, now solidly behind her, nodded their heads, "No trouble at all. We can carry our babies."

The dispatcher opened his eyes wide and shook his head, but tapped out another message on his key. This time, the answer was not so long in coming. Again the dispatcher appeared at the window: "Freeman says repeat: nobody, *nobody* goes through the tunnel ahead of the dignitaries."

"You tell him something for me," shouted Doc. "A lot of nobodies went through that tunnel before those bigshots. Nineteen nobodies died in there, too. And a lot more got pneumonia and died because of *being* in there. Tell him that!" She stomped out into the cold.

The dispatcher ran after her: "Do you want reservations on the train over the top?"

"No." She stopped and looked him in the eye. "No passenger's life was ever lost going over Corona. But lots of working men were killed up there. The people who most deserve to be at that ceremony next Sunday aren't about to be the first passengers to die on Freeman's worn-out old roadbed."

Gloomily, the women disbanded. The Rockies could be cracked open, but not Bill Freeman.

Susie was still smoldering the next morning when she had an unexpected visitor. Axel Bergstrom had not crossed her threshold in months, not since he went to work at the tunnel. The man was a wonder. Even though he had been grubbing underground as a mucker, he looked as clean and neat as if he had just stepped out of the Denver Dry Goods store. Even his fingernails were pristine.

"Come in, come in. I'm so glad to see you. How are you feeling?"

"Oh fine, fine. I don't have no pains, I just come to visit."

She poured a cup of coffee. "Are you being laid off at the tunnel?"

"Ya, chure. I guess I go back to the woods now. Pay's not so good, but better to work outside, in daylight. Chust hope I get outa there without bein' last man kilt on the job."

"How are the men taking it, losing their jobs and all?"

Axel shrugged. "Dey never expect nothing better. Lots of 'em save a little money. Some didn't. But dey know the jobs is gone when the tunnel is over."

Silences between them had once been a large problem. Now, when the lumberjack and the doctor chatted, long pauses were just comfortable respites allowing old friends to reflect.

"Are they going to celebrate when the tunnel opens tomorrow?" asked Doc.

"I don't hear nothing like that. Lots of the men sure wish they could go see that gold spike. But, that's the way she goes, I spect. Work's done, they don't want to feed us no more than they have to. Lots of them has already went. Those of us left, I guess we'll just stand outsida West Portal and wave at the train when it comes out. Near everybody from town is plannin' to go up there, from what I hear."

Doc scratched her head. Suddenly she sprang to her feet: "Axel, up at the tunnel, can you find some boards that are going to be thrown away or burned? Maybe one-by-tens about twenty feet long?"

"Lots of 'em Doc Susie. No trouble atall." Axel had

long ago resigned himself to taking directions from Susie; she always had her reasons.

"And can you get me a bucket of tar, and would you heat it up tomorrow morning, so I can spread it?"

"I guess so, Chure."

"And find me an old mop?"

Axel eyed her curiously, but asked no questions. "Doc Susie. I don't know why you want dat stuff, but you got it."

Sunday, February 26, 1928, dawned severely clear in the Fraser Valley. On a day so cold, the sky arced blue as a robin's egg over the virginal white peaks. What a glorious day! History would be made today, the entire United States was going to know that the West Portal of the longest tunnel in the country opened right into Grand County!

Some people rode to the tunnel entrance in the "mantrip," an enclosed sleigh that had been rigged to take workers from Fraser to their jobs at the tunnel; its comforts included a pot-bellied stove to keep them warm. Ranchers harnessed up their teams to hay sledges and invited anybody who wanted a ride to nestle into sweet dry hay. Their passengers snuggled beneath thick blankets, sang songs and hollered to everybody they saw on the road. Cowboys, atop their ponies, wove in and out of the procession, trying to spot the pretty girls. Anybody who stayed home never dared admit it later. Everybody wanted to see that "first" train come out of the Moffat Tunnel—the longest, best, toughest, most beautiful tunnel in the United States—the one they built.

When Susie got to West Portal, she quickly found Axel who had, of course, scrounged around for everything Doc had ordered. Axel led her to one of the work sheds, where he steadied the boards across two saw horses. "I'm going to make a sign," she explained.

"Figgers," said Axel.

After testing the hot, sticky tar, she wound some string from a mop around a stick, and began to swab and drizzle tar onto the boards with the same steady hand she had used for so many years to set bones and stitch wounds.

Steady, steady; she wanted the lettering to be bold and firm, and big enough to be read from a long way off. Her excitement made it difficult to keep from smearing the letters.

By now, other tunnel stiffs had heard about Doc's audacious plan and hastened to help. After an hour she stood back, looked at her work and said: "There, I think that will do the job nicely." Husky volunteers dragged the boards to a spot opposite the great West Portal entrance, nailed them to two-by-four uprights and pounded them into a snowbank.

Everybody cheered and laughed when they read it: "Atta girl, Doc Susie. That's showin' those big-shots!"

"Let's take a picture!" One of the women held a box camera at her waist, sighted her friends standing in holiday finery beneath the sign and snapped the shutter.

Her project accomplished Doc Susie looked around, interested to see who had come to the celebration. Except for a few of the tunnel stiffs, she knew everybody. When she looked into younger faces, she was astounded to realize that she had brought at least half of them into the world! She chided herself when she realized that she was mentally sorting them into categories of "paid for," and "not paid for." Some of those who were almost grown would be mightily surprised to learn they were never paid for.

Rudy Just came over and extended his big paw. Rudy was a man now, towering above the little woman who had once taken him to the hospital in Denver. Every day he looked more like Karl. Della was right behind with some of her other children. "Don't know what I'd ever do without Rudy," she said proudly. "And if it wasn't for you, I wouldn't have him." The tough years of hard work since Karl died had turned Della from an attractive woman into a handsome one who commanded respect.

Hulda and Gustaf Wilson's three bright boys had been scrubbed to within an inch of their lives. Doc knew how clean they were, could practically see Glenn's ears shining through his woolen stocking cap.

"Get the number of the locomotive. I want to remember which one it is," said Bud Willhite. Doc still ribbed him about how he "blowed his nose up" that day in the lumber camp.

Susie saw Mark Fletcher hurrying in her direction. She suddenly feared the sheriff would take umbrage at her sign and ask her to remove it. But he smiled and said: "By God, Susie, you've got guts. Wait'll Freeman sees this!"

Bill Woods hobbled up. He was old now, tenacious and grizzled as lichens on a rock. "Won't be the same without sending provisions from my mill up to those stranded on the top. But it'll cost less to ship my lumber." He looked at the sign. "Susie, Susie, what ever would we do without our Doc Susie!"

Little by little, person by person, everybody made it a point to come visit with Doc Susie. Even the ones who owed her money or preferred Doc Albers extended hugs that were more than perfunctory; they were prolonged, affectionate mauls frequently accompanied by the words: "If it wasn't for you, I'd of been dead by now . . ."

Grace Schryer came alone that day because George was driving one of the trains that would steam through later: "George says they're going to couple the first two sections together so all of the dignitaries can brag they were on the first train through the tunnel."

Watching all the people greet her friend, Grace said: "Susie . . . look around. How many of these people wouldn't be alive if it hadn't been for you?"

"Oh, come on," Susie protested.

"I'm serious. Look around and tell me."

Doc scanned the faces, counting the broken arms, stitches, babies, heart attacks, belly aches, pulled teeth, gall bladders. In some cases, she could remember the malady but had trouble placing the name. The scores of people in pain she had taken over the top to the hospital seemed to all have the last name of Ectomy, preceded by Append, Hyster or Tonsil.

"Maybe ten percent," admitted Doc.

"Maybe a lot more," said Grace. "You do realize, don't you, that these people who love you so much are your family?"

"Guess I never thought of it that way."

"It's time you did."

Watches were being yanked out of a dozen pockets. "It's noon!" someone shouted joyously. The *Denver Post* had printed a schedule of the East Portal ceremonies, detailed to the very last minute. The invocation was to be given at exactly 12:15 p.m., followed by the driving of the gold spike and addresses by dignitaries ranging from Colorado Governor W. H. Adams to Denver Mayor Benjamin Stapleton to Bill Freeman. Each would speak exactly three minutes. Then, invited guests were allowed 45 minutes to walk to the East Portal entrance. They could even go into the tunnel a little way to inspect its walls if they chose.

"It's all gonna be on the radio," squealed little Lucille Peterson. "Over KOA."

"Too bad the reception is so lousy up here in the day time," grumbled Tom Arkell, the local radio bug. "I'd love to hear them bombs go off from the roof of the *Post*." Six blasts were to be exploded when the train entered the tunnel, and six more when it came out.

"We'll have to supply our own fireworks," said Doc Susie wryly. She looked over at her sign.

One of the Hitchcock-Tinker foremen, following her glance, frowned. "I don't think Bill Freeman is going to like that. Or the tunnel commissioners, either."

Doc Susie moved in front of the sign, her expression stonily stubborn. Axel and another sturdy lumberjack planted themselves at her side. "We say it stays. Feel free to stand as far away as you like."

"It's 1:20," called Jim Leonard. "The train should be going into the tunnel now!"

"With Freeman and Bonfils probably riding happily

along," said Grace Schryer, "expecting that when they come out the West Portal everybody will be cheering them as the greatest heroes on earth."

"I wish I knew what Fred Bonfils looked like, because I sure want to see how he takes it," said Doc Susie.

"You'll know him," said Grace. "I hear he's tall and thin, but he'll be the one with the purple face!"

The scheduled arrival time came and went. The newspapers had calculated that a passenger train could speed through the tunnel in only eleven minutes, a considerable improvement over the three hours it took to go over the top in summertime. But the machinery that had been installed at the East Portal to ventilate the tunnel did not perform as well as it should. The two locomotives put out a great deal of smoke and took a long time, over twenty minutes, to get through. Doc learned later that passengers were not very comfortable in the tunnel. Everyone suffered from irritated eyes and coughed a great deal.

Smoke issued from the tunnel's mouth well before the locomotive did. Small excited boys ran onto the tracks and stared intently into the gloom, trying to spot a headlamp. Their mothers frantically summoned them back, only to have them slip loose again and run onto the tracks. Doc Susie told one fretting mother: "Let him be. No smart boy is ever run over by a train he sees coming."

Finally Locomotive Number 205, a splendid Mallet of the Denver and Salt Lake Railway, chugged out from the gloom and smoke of the tunnel into the brash sunlight of a glorious Western Slope day.

A great cheer went up from the waiting crowd.

Doc Susie watched the faces peering out of the cars, eyes blinking from the combined irritants of smoke and sudden sunshine. But she could see that when passengers spotted her sign, their lips spelled out its message. Out a vestibule window leaned the conductor; sure enough, Freeman had denied George Barnes the honor.

When the lengthy slow-moving train dragged to a halt, she saw two men stepping onto the rear observation platform of the final car. She recognized the portly, pompous figure of Bill Freeman; beside him stood a taller, thinner man.

Freeman waved his fedora aloft in a victory salute, his look that of conquering Caesar acknowledging an assembly of grateful slaves greeting his triumphant arrival. Beneath his dome, shining brightly in the mountain sunshine, he was posturing a big smile—an expression not many people had ever seen gracing the lips of Bill Freeman.

Then his eyes lighted on Doc Susie's sign. Freeman's hat hand fell suddenly to his side, his grin collapsed into the familiar frown. Too late he turned to divert Fred Bonfils' attention; already his Corsican features were suffused with a purple glow. The two "heroes" stood frozen before a jeering, whistling, laughing mob hopping up and down beneath the boldly-lettered proclamation:

WE BUILT THIS TUNNEL
THE POST DIDN'T

Postscript

"Hot diggity-dog" shouted the sailors as they dropped happily from their troop train onto the platform of the Fraser depot. It was autumn of 1941, two months before Pearl Harbor—where the sailors were headed.

One of the swabbies, a tourniquet bound tightly around his arm, was helped off the train and steered into the depot toward an older woman whose authoritative manner was all the more remarkable because she was so tiny. Her hair was tied in a tight white turban, a white apron covered her dress. Roger Richards of Brooklyn, New York, had been scuffling with a fellow tar in the vestibule of the westbound train when he injured himself seriously by plunging his fist through a glass window. The volume of blood that spurted from his lacerated arm caused his alarmed C.O. to request that the train be stopped at the first town that had a physician.

"Cuss, if you like," said Doc Susie as she explained her no painkiller policy. Using her well-honed skills she stitched up the young man's arm. By the time she finished, Fraser had been emptied of every bottle of beer, soda pop and candy bar stocked in its stores. More fortunate sailors enjoyed their first taste of liberty in several days. Finally, the engineer blew his whistle and pulled his passengers toward war. Later, Doc Susie received a beautiful thank-you blanket from the sailor's mother.

By then, Susie was Fraser's only physician; indeed, hers was the only care available for miles around. The opening of the Moffat Tunnel brought no prosperity to Grand County. Although nobody except scenery-hungry summer tourists regretted the loss of the dangerous route over Rollins Pass, Doc Susie's suspicion that the Moffat Tunnel would do very little to improve the lives of local people proved all too true.

Grand County taxpayers, who had voted to oblige themselves for a hefty portion of the $18 million in bonds needed to pay for the tunnel, found that instead of adding to their income the Moffat Tunnel took it away. A few years after the railroad tunnel was opened, its pioneer bore was lined with concrete so that the Fraser Valley's most valuable commodity—water—could be transferred into Denver. Ranchers' water rights were quickly bought up; once-verdant hay fields withered and were struck from the county's tax rolls. For Denver's citizens the tunnel's benefits were virtually free—thanks to the machinations of Bill Freeman and his cronies.

At the same time the great depression forced the desperate citizens of Fraser to scavenge the former rail route for anything of value: bricks, coal, ties, telegraph insulators— anything that could be moved. When Bill Freeman retired in 1934, the *Denver Post* printed a glowing tribute to the multi-millionaire's rescue of the railroad from financial oblivion.

Ironically, what came out of the Moffat Tunnel proved to be of more value than the hole itself—tailings mucked from the interior provided fill for the base of a ski area. In 1939, Denver's city parks department opened Winter Park to winter sports enthusiasts. Although advancing in age, Doc Susie was frequently called to the area to set the bones of people who hurtled down the mountain with more speed than control. Eventually, a town grew up to serve the ski area which eventually became one of the largest and most popular in the United States.

In the forties, with the virgin stands of great timber gone, most of the Swedish bachelor lumbermen left the Fraser Valley. One of the few who stayed behind was Axel Bergstrom—despite urgings from Doc Susie that he should move to someplace lower and warmer for the benefit of his heart condition.

As ever, Doc Susie collected little in cash for her services. But she never wanted for firewood, the commonest currency in which she was paid. She developed a unique way to sustain herself. At meal times she would appear, uninvited, at this house or that. Nobody minded; some people speculated that this was her own quaint way of collecting bills. She didn't eat much, seemed to be more interested in good conversation around the table than in the food on top of it.

As Susie grew older, her dream of Indiana remained as strong as ever. Soon after the end of World War II, tired of the long mountain winters, she decided to load all of her worldly goods—a formidable hoard—into a boxcar and to move to Indiana. Fraser people gathered at the depot, waving sadly as her train receded toward the tunnel. Less than a week later—before her boxcar had even made it to Indiana—she was back. "Property values are too high," she sniffed or "I didn't fit in." Fraser was her home; its people were her people. They were glad to have her back.

One day in 1947 my school-principal brother, Elwood Miller, was in the Fraser pharmacy at the same time Doc Susie was buying penicillin. A friendly fellow, "Woodie" wanted to pass the time of day pleasantly. "Doc Susie, what did you give your patients before you had antibiotics?"

Doc Susie peered up at him over her little black-rimmed spectacles, "I'll tell you what, Professor. They died!" she chirped, and swept past him out of the store.

People in Fraser were very disappointed when Doc Susie turned down Ethel Barrymore's offer to make her life story into a movie. It was no secret that Doc could have used the money. She said, "Fiddlesticks!" And that was that. She enjoyed the publicity of an occasional feature story in a magazine or newspaper, but resisted any efforts to elaborate on her history.

Although everybody remembers Doc Susie as being religious—reading her Bible constantly, citing passages of scripture—nobody remembers seeing her at church services. As Glenn Wilson said, "I don't think she liked to go to church because that's where they had the funerals."

She lived to be 90, spending all but her last two years in Fraser. Finally, her physician friends at Colorado General Hospital took charge of her care. They amputated a blackened toe which many years earlier had been bitten by frost and saw to it that their fellow physician was treated respectfully in a rest home.

Her frequently stated wish was to be buried next to her brother John in Mt. Pisgah Graveyard in Cripple Creek. Indeed, one side of the family pylon had been left blank, awaiting inscription of her name. Unfortunately, by the time she died the graveyard had become so overgrown and derelict that the family plot could not be located. Consequently, she was laid to rest in a newer part of the cemetery. When residents of Grand County learned she had been buried in an unmarked grave they took up a collection and bought a handsome stone etched with the honorable symbol of her profession—entwined serpents curling around the staff called the *caduceus*. It says:

Susan Anderson, M.D.
Jan. 31, 1870–April 16, 1960
Doctor of Grand County
1909–1956

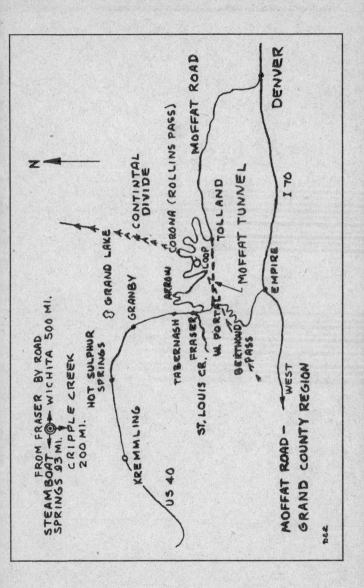

About the Author

Virginia Cornell is a free-lance writer and columnist. In 1946, when she was ten years old, her family established Miller's Idlewild Inn in the village of Hideaway Park, just two miles from Fraser. Although she attended public schools in Wichita, Kansas, she spent her summer and Christmas vacations in Colorado.

She received a B.A. from the University of Kansas. Just after she received a Ph.D. from Arizona State University in Renaissance English Literature, she returned to the Fraser Valley to manage the family ski lodge. Later she bought a fledgling newspaper, the *Winter Park Manifest*, which she operated for five years.

At present she writes a column called "VaCuum," which appears in three weekly newspapers in the Santa Barbara area. She is married to Donald Longmire; together they raise avocados and cherimoyas. She has three grown children.